INDICES: 1

General Editors

D. M. Gabbay
F. Guenthner
U. Mönnich

-

INDICES

Type-Theoretical Grammar

AARNE RANTA

University of Helsinki

CLARENDON PRESS • OXFORD

1994

Oxford University Press, Walton Street, Oxford OX2 6DP

Oxford New York
Athens Auckland Bangkok Bombay
Calcutta Cape Town Dar es Salaam Delhi
Florence Hong Kong Istanbul Karachi
Kuala Lumpur Madras Madrid Melbourne
Mexico City Nairobi Paris Singapore
Taipei Tokyo Toronto

and associated companies in
Berlin Ibadan

Oxford is a trade mark of Oxford University Press

Published in the United States by
Oxford University Press Inc., New York

© Aarne Ranta, 1994

A catalogue record for this book is available from the British Library

Library of Congress Cataloging in Publication Data

ISBN 0 19 853857 X

Typeset by the
author using LaTeX
Printed in Great Britain by
Bookcraft (Bath) Ltd
Midsomer Norton, Avon

PREFACE

The idea of studying natural language in constructive type theory occurred to me in spring 1986. It grew out of my parallel studies of logical semantics and type theory in a very natural way: type theory seemed to provide solutions to a series of diverse linguistic puzzles, there was a close relation between type theory and computer science, and in spite of the famous philosophical arguments by Dummett, hardly anyone had made a concrete effort to extend constructive semantics beyond the language of mathematics. Topics related to my project were discussed in a seminar led by Jan von Plato at the University of Helsinki. He encouraged me to continue my doctoral studies in Stockholm, where I started early in 1987. After a short intervening period in Amsterdam, I returned to Helsinki in summer 1990.

In Stockholm, when I first discussed the project with Per Martin-Löf, he said that he had designed type theory for mathematics, and that natural language is something else. I said that similar work had been done within predicate calculus, which is just a part of type theory, to which he replied that he found it equally problematic. But his general attitude was far from discouraging: it was more that he was so serious about natural language and saw the problems of my enterprise more clearly than I, who had already assumed the point of view of logical semantics. His criticism was penetrating but patient, and he was generous in telling me about his own ideas. So we gradually developed a view that satisfied both of us, that formal grammar begins with what is well understood formally, and then tries to see how this formal structure is manifested in natural language, instead of starting with natural language in all its unlimitedness and trying to force it into some given formalism.

This idea, to be called the sugaring point of view, later evolved into a kind of structuralistic view of language as a family of systems, whose rules can be spelt out with precision, without the assumption that language as a whole is such a system. In this perspective, a type-theoretical grammar cannot be a total account of language, but a study of its type-theoretical aspects—of judgements, contexts, propositions, proofs, etc. This is almost everything there is in the language of mathematics, but it is more mixed up with other factors in everyday discourse.

However, this book does not even give a full account of how type-theoretical aspects are manifested in natural language, but concentrates on a few of them, namely those that are relevant for the standard topics of logical semantics. The area covered will thus be a part of what is known as Montague grammar, categorial grammar, and the theory of discourse representation. To compensate for the narrow coverage, I hope that the treatment provided will be natural and unified, and that, moreover, some totally new perspectives are opened by the formal and conceptual resources of type theory.

I am deeply indebted to Per Martin-Löf for his devotion to my project during my three-year studies in Stockholm and his generous help even after that. In addition to what can be traced back to his published writings, there are many ideas that I have learnt from him in private communication. But even though a lot of the material is derived from discussions with him, he is not to be held responsible for the views I present here.

In Helsinki, the activities of Jan von Plato's seminar soon developed into a small research group of type theory, with Petri Mäenpää as the third member. Despite our different educational backgrounds and research topics, we have enjoyed a condition of perfect mutual understanding about matters of type theory and about intellectual life in general. As for this book, I am particularly grateful to Jan and Petri for reading and commenting on various versions of the manuscript.

During the process of writing, I have also enjoyed communication with Thierry Coquand, Jaakko Hintikka, Arto Mustajoki, Bengt Nordström, Gabriel Sandu, Peter Schroeder-Heister, Jan Smith, and Göran Sundholm. The participants of my courses at the universities of Helsinki and Tampere have given me important stimulation and criticism. At the penultimate stage of the manuscript, I benefitted greatly from the thorough reading by Urs Egli, Klaus von Heusinger, Uwe Mönnich, and Pekka Pirinen. And it was Franz Guenthner, the editor of the Indices series, who gave me the conviction needed for finishing the book, and a clear view about what exactly the book should be like.

The chapters of the book form a linear sequence, although a reader familiar with type theory can perhaps skip Chapter 2. The last two chapters and the Appendix present a formalization and implementation of some of the ideas developed in the first seven chapters. But some of the ideas are only discussed informally. Franz Guenthner's happy suggestion was to include applicative and comparative material at the ends of some sections, in the form of examples and notes only presented in outline. The reader is encouraged to work them out in detail himself. This material is not presupposed in the main text. It is undoubtedly with pencil and paper, or perhaps with a computer and proof editor, that type theory is learnt.

It remains to express my gratitude to Veronica Gaspes, Pauli Kuosmanen, Lena Magnusson, Kent Petersson, and Irene Saarinen, who have helped me in questions of programming both ALF and LaTeX, as well as to the vii

Academy of Finland for financing my research. Pihla, Eemu, and Uula have created a marvellous family atmosphere.

Tampere
November 1993   *Aarne Ranta*

CONTENTS

1

PRELIMINARY REMARKS

The aim of this book is to show how constructive type theory, in the form developed by Per Martin-Löf, helps us to understand the structure of natural language. The study of similar questions within simple (= classical) type theory was inaugurated by Frege and given a standard of technical detail by Montague. The point of shifting to constructive type theory is not in the constructivist criticism against classical reasoning, but in the positive observation that constructive type theory has new things to say. Some of the problems to which grammars based on classical type theory have not found satisfactory solutions will be shown to require precisely these new things. These problems appear in a simple form in what is known, since Geach, as donkey sentences. But they are repeated in other guises, for example, in the functioning of tenses, and in a larger scale, such as in the progressive structure of texts, and in the significance of context in communication.

At the same time, we shall make some effort to achieve a better understanding of grammatical research. This includes finding the proper place of semantics in grammar, as well as developing type-theoretical data structures for other levels of linguistic description. These questions are, however, posed explicitly in the last two chapters only. Until then, the discussion follows themes familiar from logical semantics.

1.1 Types and propositions

There are several points at which the additional richness of constructive type theory, as compared with classical type theory, can be located. One is the type hierarchy, which in simple type theory is generated by the formation of function types

$$(\alpha)\beta,$$

where α is a type and β is a type, the type of functions taking objects of α into objects of β. Constructive type theory allows dependent function types

$$(x : \alpha)\beta,$$

where α is a type and β is a type depending on the variable x of type α, the type of functions taking any object $a : \alpha$ into an object of $\beta(a/x)$ (see Section 8.2). This generalization is, so to say, the prototype of all of the dependent structures constructive type theory offers. There is, for example, a generalization of the classical conjunction

$$A\&B,$$

where A is a proposition and B is a proposition, into the progressive conjunction

$$(\Sigma x\,:\,A)B(x),$$

where A is a proposition and $B(x)$ is a proposition depending on the proof x of A (see Section 3.5).

Another source of richness, already presupposed by the progressive conjunction, is the view that propositions are sets, not truth values. In classical logic, all propositional expressions are interpreted as either True or False, and there are thus only two propositions. But in intuitionistic logic, there are as many propositions as there are sets. This results in a high degree of 'intensionality', that is, fine distinctions among propositions.

The word proposition is used, throughout this book, in the sense of Russell (see e.g. *Principia*), for what logical operators like & and $\sim$ operate on, and not in the sense of Montague (1974), for functions from the type of possible worlds to the type of truth values. In simple type theory, propositions in Russell's sense are objects of type t, whereas propositions in Montague's sense are objects of type $(s)t$.

1.2   Judgements and contexts

An enrichment on a larger scale is the use of judgements, rather than propositions, as basic units of expression. Propositions do occur in judgements, but their position is relativized within a more general view of language. The interpretation that predicate calculus receives in this view is that it only comprises judgements of one special form: of the form

$$\vdash A,$$

stating the truth of the proposition A. This form is found explicitly in Frege and Russell, but in the contemporary notation the distinction between propositions and judgements is not made explicit. Type theory, as presented in Martin-Löf 1984, comprises four forms of judgement, but it is in the spirit of the theory that the number of forms of judgement is not limited to this, and that judgements are just one kind of linguistic act, and of act in general. As it is based on judgements, the type-theoretical view of language is fundamentally pragmatic, giving the central role to acts and not to propositions.

A structure that will be employed repeatedly is context, a sequence of judgements progressively depending on each other. The notion of context is essential in the functioning of type theory and, it can be argued, of any logical calculus, but it is seldom recognized in its own right. The closest in classical logic is Gentzen's notion of a sequence of assumptions, such as occurs as the antecedent of a sequent. But we shall see that contexts do what many different devices added to classical logic are intended to do, such as

discourse representations,
situations,
possible worlds,
belief contexts.

1.3 Constructive and classical logic

All of these type-theoretical structures are not peculiar to constructive logic. Even classical predicate calculus can be formulated as a theory in which the basic units of expression are judgements in context. Such a formulation will be developed in Chapter 2, to show where constructivism then comes in. It comes in when the view that propositions are truth values is rejected, and in the ensuing view that propositions are sets of proof objects. But as the constructivist view of propositions brings in so much more structure, we shall spend little time with the classical calculus of judgements and contexts.

A word could be said about the well-known weakness of constructive logic in comparison to classical logic. An axiomatization of intuitionistic predicate calculus, in the style of Hilbert or Gentzen, can be extended into classical predicate calculus by adding the law of the excluded middle, the scheme

$$A \vee \sim A.$$

This adds to the deductive power of the calculus, so that many theorems not provable in the intuitionistic calculus are provable in the classical calculus. In this sense, then, constructive logic is weaker than classical logic. (We sometimes say intuitionistic, instead of constructive, especially in locutions like intuitionistic predicate calculus, which are established by convention.)

But there is an interpretation of classical predicate calculus making all its theorems provable in intuitionistic predicate calculus. It is due to Kolmogorov (1925) and Gödel (1932a). One can, for example, interpret

$$A \vee B \text{ as } \sim (\sim A \& \sim B).$$

The law of the excluded middle then takes the form

$$\sim (\sim A \& \sim \sim A)$$

which is provable constructively. Given this interpretation, the difference between the two calculi is no longer one of deductive but of expressive power. The intuitionistic calculus makes a distinction between $A \vee B$ and

$\sim$ ($\sim$ *A&*$\sim$ *B*), but the classical calculus does not. So it is well known, since Gödel (1932b), that to interpret intuitionistic predicate calculus in classical logic, a modal operator has to be added.

1.4   Background in constructive semantics

The use of constructive logic outside mathematics was hardly considered before Dummett's argument about the theory of meaning (Dummett 1975). For Dummett, the constructivistic theory of meaning was a thought experiment rather than a research programme, and did not lead into work of technical detail. Sundholm (1986), starting from a discussion of Dummett's arguments, made a suggestion about proof-theoretic semantics, and gave an analysis of the famous problem sentence

every man who owns a donkey beats it

within Martin-Löf's type theory. Mönnich (1985) presented a type-theoretically interpreted fragment of English in the style of Montague. In the Automath project, aiming at formal representation and checking of correctness of mathematical proofs, lots of observations about informal mathematical language have been made (see e.g. de Bruijn 1970). It was largely within this project that Ahn and Kolb (1990) presented an interpretation of discourse referents in the theory of constructions of Coquand and Huet (1988).

My own work has been greatly inspired by the game-theoretical semantics of Hintikka (Hintikka and Carlson 1979, Hintikka and Kulas 1985), which turned out to admit of a systematic interpretation in type theory (Ranta 1988). Via this interpretation, the results from game-theoretical semantics can be implemented in a formal linguistic theory. This has not been systematically possible before, because there has been no adequate formalism for representing games and strategies.

1.5   Grammatical form in natural language

There is a difference between formal and natural languages with respect to grammatical research. Formal languages, in the sense of formal language theory, are inductively defined sets of expressions. The grammar of a formal language is the inductive definition of it. Consequently, any expression of a formal language has a grammatical structure essential to it, in the sense that it is an expression of that language precisely in virtue of having that structure, that is, in virtue of being generated by just those applications of rules that the structure reflects. Thus a formula of Peano arithmetic, say

$$0 = 0 \& s(0) > 0$$

has a grammatical structure that everybody must understand in order to understand it as a formula of Peano arithmetic (Figure 1.1). (Cf. Stenius

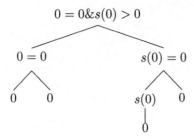

$$0 = 0 \& s(0) > 0$$

Figure 1.1

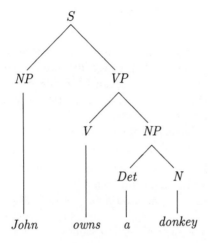

Figure 1.2

1973 for a careful exposition of this point.)

But natural languages exist independently of the grammarian's activity. They are not defined by grammars. A sentence of English, say

John owns a donkey

is used and understood without grammatical analysis. What is more, if an analysis is to be given, grammarians do not agree about it. The phrase structure grammarian sees here a sentence (*S*) consisting of a noun phrase (*NP*) and a verb phrase (*VP*) (Figure 1.2), whereas the classical categorial grammarian sees a quantifier applied to a propositional function (Figure 1.3). The grammarians use different formalisms to formalize an expression originally given by means other than formal rules. What they see depends on the formalism they use.

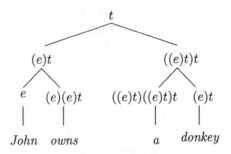

Figure 1.3

Here there is a double use of the words *formalism* and *formalization*. First, a formalism is a formal language, like predicate calculus, and formalization is translation into the formal language. Second, a formalism is a system of forms, or concepts, and formalization is seeing a form belonging to the system in natural language.

The use of formalisms prominent in linguistics is of the latter, 'informal' kind. Examples of formalisms used are

the traditional grammarian's repertory of notions like subject, predicate, verb, adjective, subordinated clause;

the phrase structure grammarian's rewrite rules for categories like S, NP, VP, Det;

the logician's machinery of truth values, entities, functions, and arguments.

The first of these formalisms does not have a mathematical backing in a formalism in the sense of a formal language, but the other two do.

1.6   Syntax and semantics

We shall treat on one and the same level what is often seen as two distinct levels, namely *syntactic* and *semantic* representation. Usually, only the first level is called grammatical, and there is a tradition stemming from Chomsky (1957) that holds that grammar, in the sense of syntax, is independent of semantics. Semantical notions are forbidden in syntax. An expression can be syntactically well formed without being meaningful.

But there is an older tradition according to which it is in the nature of an expression to be meaningful. Thus for Saussure, a sign (*signe*) has two *faces*, a *signifiant* and a *signifié*. Without *signifié*, no *signe*, no unit of the language (*langue*); cf. *Cours de linguistique générale*, pp. 97–100. A set of expression-like elements without a concomitant semantics is not yet a *langue*, and its elements are not *signes*.

Applied to generative grammar, Saussure's principle entails the principle of *compositionality*, to the effect that there must be a semantic rule corresponding to every syntactic rule, for the only way to give meaning to all expressions of an infinite set is by induction along the rules that define that infinity, that is, along the syntactic rules. Compositionality, in this general sense, is an unquestioned methodological principle in the tradition of formal languages conceived by Frege (1879). In the grammar of natural language, it was advocated by Montague, who wrote, 'I fail to see any great interest in syntax except as a preliminary for semantics' (1974, p. 223, note 2).

A closer study of Chomsky's arguments for the 'autonomy of syntax' in his 1957, chapter 9, reveals that what he really wanted to expel from grammar were 'vague semantic clues' (op. cit. p. 101), and replace them by 'formal structure' (ibid.). But if semantics is given as a formal structure, like Montague did, it is not just vague clues. On the contrary, the requirement of compositional semantics is a rigorous constraint on the grammatical formalism that can be used.

1.7   Generation, parsing, and sugaring

A *generative grammar* is the inductive definition of a *fragment*, a set of strings recognizable as English expressions (or expressions of whatever language in question). A procedure of formalization for the strings *generated* by the grammar, that is, belonging to the fragment, which tells how they are formed by the rules of the grammar, is a *parsing algorithm*. It is customary, for example, in Chomsky and Montague, that generation is studied without paying attention to parsing.

Generation and parsing are not quite exactly the reverses of each other. Parsing takes strings into *grammatical representations* (parse trees), but generation does not merely take grammatical representations into strings: it simultaneously defines those representations. It is useful to articulate this procedure into two components, one defining a set of unambiguous grammatical representations, another taking them into strings, which may be ambiguous, that is, obtained from several different grammatical representations. This latter procedure will be called *sugaring*, following the terminology of computer science. Sugaring there is transformation of formal notation into a more readable form. For example, the arithmetical term

$$*(+(2, *(3,5)), 4)$$

is sugared into the term

$$(2 + 3 * 5) * 4.$$

Figure 1.4 shows the relations of these notions.

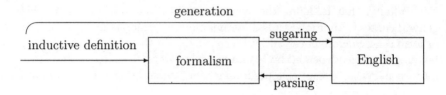

Figure 1.4

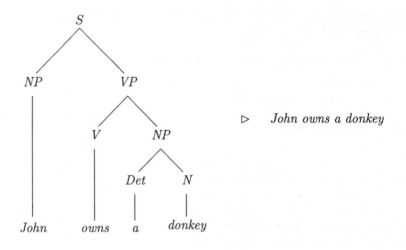

Figure 1.5

This division of generation into the definition of the formalism and the sugaring procedure was presented by Curry (1963) under the titles *tectogrammatics* and *phenogrammatics*, respectively.

In phrase structure grammar, the representation formalism consists of phrase structure trees. Sugaring at its simplest is the removal of everything but the leaves of the tree, like in Figure 1.5. (We shall use the sign ▷ for sugaring.) But in transformational grammar, it may happen that such a tree, although it is the grammatical representation of a sentence, does

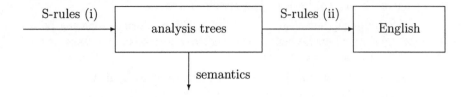

Figure 1.6

not contain that sentence as the sequence of its leaves. Then the sugaring requires a transformation.

In Montague's PTQ ('The proper treatment of quantification in ordinary English', Montague 1974, chapter 8), the sugaring procedure is scattered in individual generative rules. Each *S-rule* consists of two parts. The former part defines a grammatical representation, called an *analysis tree*, for example,

S2. If $\zeta \in P_{CN}$, then $F_0(\zeta) \in P_T \ldots$

and the latter part sugars this tree into a string,

$\ldots$ where $F_0(\zeta) = \mathbf{every}\ \zeta$.

The level of analysis trees is important to recognize, since it is to analysis trees that *semantics* applies, not to strings of English words (Figure 1.6).

1.8 Formalization and sugaring in informal grammar

The 'informal' style of grammatical research, which is prominent in linguistic discussion, does not work with a delimited fragment. It is not formally specified what expressions of English fall within the treatment, and what cannot be treated. The treatment is not algorithmic, but creative, involving the grammarian's linguistic understanding. But even the 'informal' grammarian employs a formalism, in the sense of a system of forms that he imposes on the expressions he studies.

The directions of generation and formalization thus make sense here, too. For instance, parsing Latin sentences on the basis of school grammar is an informal activity of formalization. So is translation into a logical formalism, as practised by philosophers before and after Montague. The following questions, of increasing generality, are typical of the informal formalizing point of view.

What is the logical form of the sentence *Tom bakes a cake?*
How are complex sentences formed by *when* formalized?
What is the logical basis of progression in text?

Not so frequent, but clearly meaningful, is the informal sugaring point of view. One starts with what is provided by a formalism and asks how it is manifested in a natural language.

How is the proposition $(\forall x)(s(x) > x)$ expressed in English?
In what ways does English express universal quantification?
Can all propositions of Peano arithmetic be expressed by unambiguous English sentences?

As English is given to us independently of grammars, there is always an informal aspect in grammatical research, concerning the justification of the suggested rules. Even a claim of the form 'this grammar G generates all sentences of English' would need an informal justification, because it says something about all sentences of English, which is not a formally delimited totality.

In practice, the grammarian is quite aware of the partiality of his methods, and knows that the linguistic interest is not delimited to any particular fragment. He knows that expressions may fall outside his fragment, and that the analysis he manages to give to the expressions inside the fragment does not cover all of the aspects they have as expressions of natural language.

The emphasis of this book is on informal grammar, largely in the direction of sugaring. That is, we shall investigate the ways in which type-theoretical structures manifest themselves in English. But as shown by the titles of some chapters (Anaphoric expressions, Temporal reference, Text and discourse), we shall also take under discussion informally defined topics and see how they are understood in type theory.

The word *compositional* is used in informal grammar in a sense different from Section 1.6. One says, for instance, that predicate calculus cannot treat the sentence

if John owns a donkey he beats it

in a compositional way. By this it is meant that the implicans *John owns a donkey* is formalized as the proposition

$$(\exists x)(donkey(x)\,\&\,own(John,x))$$

but the whole sentence is formalized as the proposition

$$(\forall x)(donkey(x)\,\&\,own(John,x) \supset beat(John,x))$$

of which the formalization of the implicans is not a constituent. No formally specified syntactic structure is assumed. Formally, there is just a string of words and a segment of it. One does not demand that all segments should be formalized as constituents. What is in question is compositionality with respect to the string *John owns a donkey* as occurring in the string *if John owns a donkey he beats it*. This fails, but compositionality with respect to *John owns a donkey* as occurring in *if John owns a donkey he is busy* can be satisfied.

Compositionality in the present sense is thus relative to the formalism, to the expression, and to the place of occurrence. We say that the formalization of A, as occurring in $---A---$, is compositional in the formalism F, if the formalization of A alone in F is a constituent of the formalization of $---A---$ in F. In informal grammar, we try to satisfy compositionality with respect to what we intuitively regard as constituent, but there is no formal definition of this.

1.9 Notation for functions and patterns

Categorial grammars, on which logical formalisms are based, analyse expressions into functions and arguments. The *general functional notation* writes

$f(a, ..., b)$ for the function f applied to the arguments $a, ..., b$.

The functional structure can, however, be perceived in expressions of many different forms. Thus we may see the sentence *John loves Mary* as consisting of the function *love* applied to the arguments *John* and *Mary*. The *infix* notation (*John loves Mary*) shows this structure quite as well as the general functional notation *love*(*John, Mary*). We shall use parentheses, as required, to delimit strings of words treated as constituent expressions. (It was Frege, in *Begriffsschrift*, §9, who introduced the notion of function as a pattern that can be seen in a sentence.)

In the first six chapters we shall often use the infix notation instead of the general functional notation. In the formalizing point of view, this is the natural choice, for one then starts by finding the outermost form of the English expression, and proceeds in depth to some point only. One need not even assume there to be any atoms, any ultimate level of formalization. For instance, the sentence

every man loves a woman

is first analysed as

$(\forall x : man)(x \text{ loves a woman}).$

One can be satisfied with this analysis, without going deeper. The infix notation is then much more natural than, for example,

$(\forall x : man)love\text{-}a\text{-}woman(x).$

This pattern would, moreover, have to be broken if one later took the step of further analysis into

$$(\forall x \: : \: man)(\exists y \: : \: woman)love(x, y).$$

Formalization, in the informal sense, is not really translation into a formal language, but rearrangement of expressions making their structures explicit.

In generative grammar we have a fully specified formal language, whose expressions are built from atomic expressions. For atomic function expressions, the general functional notation is customary. Thus we shall use it in the last two chapters.

The sentences

John loves Mary,
John loves her,

have the common pattern x *loves* y, where a term denoting a man can be substituted for x, and a term denoting a woman for y. Now *John* denotes a man and *Mary* a woman. The pronoun *she* is, in many contexts, also usable as a term denoting a woman. But to use it in the present pattern, it must be turned into the accusative (objective) case, ACC(*she*) = *her*. That the second argument has this case is part of the pattern of the verb *love*. The pattern is thus not x *loves* y, but

$$x \text{ } loves \text{ ACC}(y).$$

We shall use combinations of capital letters as abbreviations of *morphological operations*. In English, they are far less prominent than in German, Latin, or Finnish.

The general applicability of a pattern often requires us to treat even prepositions as morphological operators rather than separate words. The common pattern in the sentences

John is married to Mary,
John is married,

cannot be x *is married to* ACC(y), as the preposition *to* does not occur in the latter sentence. But if we take the pattern to be

$$x \text{ } is \text{ } married \text{ TO}(y)$$

we can derive the latter sentence from *John is married* TO(Ø), where Ø is the zero sign (cf. Section 4.11).

We shall use the italic type style for English expressions when displayed, when quoted in text, and when occurring in formulae. Italics are also used for one-letter symbols, but multiletter symbols, like ACC, are usually set in roman type.

1.10 Notation for grammatical rules

We shall use expressions of the form

$$F \; \triangleright \; E$$

to say that

F can be sugared into E.

This is not to be understood procedurally, as the statement of a sugaring rule, but as a description about how the type-theoretical expression F can be expressed in English. A sugaring rule proper has the form

$$S(F) = E,$$

that is, it is a clause defining a function S for a form of type-theoretical expression (see Section 8.11).

An expression of the reverse form

$$F \; \triangleleft \; E$$

means that E is obtained by sugaring from F. It can also be read

E can be formalized as F.

In neither form of expression is it required that F be an expression of a fully formalized language. F will generally just be more explicit in type-theoretical form than E.

For those trained in logic, the natural deduction rule form

$$\frac{J_1 \ldots J_n}{J}$$

will be familiar. A rule of this form means that

From the premises $J_1, \ldots, J_n$ you may conclude J.

In linguistics, this format is used in categorial grammar; for example, in the application rule

$$\frac{f \; : \; (\alpha)\beta \quad a \; : \; \alpha}{f(a) \; : \; \beta}$$

which is read

if you have formed an expression f of category $(\alpha)\beta$ and an expression a of category α, then you may form the expression $f(a)$ of category β.

Rewrite rules used in phrase structure grammar can also be written in this format; for example,

$$S \rightarrow NP + VP$$

can be written

$$\frac{a \; : \; NP \quad b \; : \; VP}{a + b \; : \; S}.$$

But rewrite rules representing combinations of expressions by other means than concatenation would look strange. For instance, the application rule would become

$$\beta \rightarrow (\alpha)\beta(\alpha).$$

The strange thing about rewrite rules is that they look like rules for combining categories, even though they are rules for combining expressions of these categories. From the type-theoretical point of view, the situation is analogous to the situation with rules of inference. A rule of natural deduction, say, the rule of conjunction introduction,

$$\frac{A \quad B}{A\&B}$$

looks like a rule for combining the propositions A and B into the proposition $A\&B$, even though it is a rule for combining a proof of A with a proof of B into a proof of $A\&B$,

$$\frac{a \,:\, A \quad b \,:\, B}{(a,b) \,:\, A\&B}.$$

Note. With proofs explicit, it makes sense to order the premises progressively, to formulate the introduction rule for progressive conjunction,

$$\frac{a \,:\, A \quad b \,:\, B(a)}{(a,b) \,:\, (\Sigma x \,:\, A)B(x)}.$$

Progressive sequences of premises are very natural in rules like

$$S \rightarrow NP + VP,$$

where the choice of VP (its number, gender, etc.) depends on the choice of NP. A progressive version of the rule is

$$\frac{a \,:\, NP \quad b \,:\, VP(a)}{a + b \,:\, S}.$$

Definite clause grammar (see e.g. Pereira and Warren 1980) expresses the dependence by making both the NP and the VP depend on a variable n of type Number,

$$S \rightarrow NP(n) + VP(n).$$

This solution is analogous to the use of the formula

$$(\exists x)(A(x)\&B(x))$$

where we would use the progressive conjunction $(\Sigma x \,:\, A)B(x)$; cf. Section 3.5 below. The formula used, just like the definite clause rule, leaves the type of the variable unexpressed. An explicit formulation of the definite clause rule is

$$\frac{n \,:\, \text{Number} \quad a \,:\, NP(n) \quad b \,:\, VP(n)}{a + b \,:\, S}.$$

But this is not an accurate expression of the principle that the number of the verb phrase depends on the noun phrase. It rather says that the numbers of them both depend on some third factor.

2

GRADUAL INTRODUCTION TO TYPE THEORY

Martin-Löf designed his type theory to be a language usable in mathematics. His motivation was 'to make explicit what is usually implicitly taken for granted' (Martin-Löf 1984, pp. 3–4). The contrast indicated by 'usually' is the metamathematical treatment of logic:

> in the metamathematical tradition ... judgements and inferences are only partially and formally represented in the so-called object language, while they are implicitly used, as in any other branch of mathematics, in the so-called metalanguage. (ibid.)

This motivation of Martin-Löf's is on the lines of *Begriffsschrift*, the original version of predicate calculus. Frege did not leave things to be specified in a metalanguage; he wanted to formalize mathematical reasoning entirely.

> Alles, was für eine richtige Schlussfolge nöthig ist, wird voll ausgedrückt; was aber nicht nöthig ist, wird meistens auch nicht angedeutet; *nichts wird dem Errathen überlassen.*
>
> (*Begriffsschrift*, §3: Everything necessary for a correct inference is expressed in full, but what is not necessary is generally not indicated; *nothing is left to guesswork.*)

At the present time, when formalisms are not only used by intelligent agents, who have the background knowledge spelt out in the metalanguage, but also run in computers, there is a new need of explicitness, up to Frege's standard of leaving no room for guesswork. This has been realized in programming languages. In contemporary logic, the first explicit formalisms were the Automath languages designed by de Bruijn for the purpose of computerized mathematical reasoning (see de Bruijn 1970). Automath comprises classical logic, but it shows some central features of constructive type theory, such as a version of the propositions as types principle, and a notation for assertions in addition to propositions.

The *decidability of judgements* is a fundamental principle in the design of type theory. That is, the basic forms of expression, the forms of judgement, are such that it is always possible to tell whether an expression of that form is justified. This principle is essential in the mechanical checking of proofs. It should be noted that the only form of judgement that Frege used, $\vdash A$, to the effect that the proposition A is true, is not decidable in general, because it is not always decidable whether a proposition is true.

2.1   Predicate calculus as a meaningful formalism

If we are to compare constructive type theory with predicate calculus, we must consider both syntax and semantics. In its contemporary form, the syntax of predicate calculus does not make explicit everything that is semantically significant. We must look into the metalevel to reconstruct what has been left implicit. Having made such changes in the syntax of predicate calculus, we shall have a language to be called *explicit predicate calculus*, which is not very much different from type theory. Full type theory is then obtained by adding the propositions as types principle.

Presentations of predicate calculus as a meaningful formalism in the style of Martin-Löf's type theory have been given by Martin-Löf (1984, 1985, 1987) and Sundholm (1986). My indebtedness to these treatises in various details will not be indicated.

What we do in the first twelve sections is neutral between classical and intuitionistic predicate calculus. We shall speak of propositions as what is explained by Tarski-style truth definitions, which as such neither justify nor refute the law of the excluded middle or any alternative one of the crucial rules of inference whose adoption makes the calculus classical.

Consider now the syntax and semantics of predicate calculus. The *syntax* defines *singular terms* and *formulae*. In the *semantics*, a *model* is defined by laying down a *domain of individuals* and some *propositions* about the individuals. What is produced by the syntax is *interpreted* in the model. Singular terms are interpreted as individuals of the domain. Formulae are interpreted as propositions true or false in the model. For instance, in the standard model of arithmetic,

the domain is the set N of natural numbers,
the singular term $\underline{0}$ is interpreted as the individual 0 of the domain N,
the formula $P(t)$ is interpreted as the proposition that the interpretation t' of the term t is prime.

Any language presented in predicate calculus admits of several interpretations in various models. This is because the language is not explicit in meaning by itself, but only when endowed with an interpretation. We shall now show how to make the crucial things given in the interpretation explicit in the formalism itself.

2.2   Domains of individuals

Frege did not need to indicate domains of individuals in the *Begriffsschrift*, for he held there to be one domain of all individuals, of which the formalism speaks. In the contemporary syntax of predicate calculus, Frege's practice of not specifying domains has been retained, even though a specification would now be needed to make the formalism explicit. For, the 'domain of all individuals' has not been made mathematical sense of, and semantics introduces a *set* as the domain. In general, we must rely on an informal notion of set, to give an interpretation of formal set theory among other things. Thus we do not assume any formal set theory here.

Type theory uses the form of expression

$$A : \text{set}$$

to make the judgement that A is a set. What exactly it means to be a set need not concern us yet. All we need is that if A is a set we can make sense of saying that

$$a \text{ is an element of } A$$

and that

$$a \text{ and } b \text{ are equal elements of } A.$$

These judgements are written in our formalism

$a : A,$
$a = b : A,$

respectively. These judgements are meaningful only if A is a set; in other words, they *presuppose* the judgement A : set. The judgement $a = b : A$ moreover presupposes $a : A$ and $b : A$.

Martin-Löf 1984 uses the variants A set, $a \in A$, and $a = b \in A$ of these three forms of judgement. The colon : has replaced $\in$ for typographical reasons. Moreover, it is not used for set membership only, but for *typing* in the general sense in which the judgement A : set is read as saying that A is an *object of type set* (cf. Chapter 8).

Judgements of the forms $a : A$ and $a = b : A$, even though absent from the formalism of predicate calculus, appear in the metalanguage, for example, when quantifiers and functions are explained,

$(\exists x)B(x)$ is true if $B(a)$ is true for some $a : D$,
f is a function from A to B if $f(a) : B$ provided $a : A$, and if
$f(a) = f(b) : B$ provided $a = b : A$.

A very simple method of defining a set is to *enumerate* its elements. To define a set A of n elements, n judgements of the form $a : A$ are needed. For instance, to define the set continent of the five continents *Africa*, *America*, *Asia*, *Australia*, and *Europe*, five judgements are needed,

Africa : *continent*,
America : *continent*,
Asia : *continent*,

Australia : *continent,*
Europe : *continent.*

The elements of the set N of natural numbers cannot be enumerated. To define N, we need a *recursive rule*, which generates more and more elements of N, *ad infinitum*. We also need a *base element* 0, from which the generation starts.

$$0 : N, \qquad \frac{a : N}{s(a) : N}.$$

These rules generate the elements $0 : N$, $s(0) : N$, $s(s(0)) : N$, etc.

There are operators that form sets from given sets. Such an operator is defined by defining the complex set under the assumption that its constituent sets have been defined. For instance, the cartesian product $A \times B$ is a set for any given sets A and B. This is expressed by the rule

$$\frac{A : \text{set} \quad B : \text{set}}{A \times B : \text{set}}.$$

Elements of $A \times B$ are pairs (a, b) where $a : A$ and $b : B$. This is expressed by the rule

$$\frac{a : A \quad b : B}{(a, b) : A \times B}.$$

The rules that define a set by generating its elements are called the *introduction rules* of the set. To be precise, the definition of a set must also tell what elements are equal. To the three groups of introduction rules above, we have to add rules that introduce equal elements.

Africa = *Africa* : *continent,*
America = *America* : *continent,*
Asia = *Asia* : *continent,*
Australia = *Australia* : *continent,*
Europe = *Europe* : *continent;*

$$0 = 0 : N, \qquad \frac{a = b : N}{s(a) = s(b) : N};$$

$$\frac{a = c : A \quad b = d : B}{(a, b) = (c, d) : A \times B}.$$

But the definitions of equal elements will usually be left implicit, as they follow from the principle that every introductory operator produces equal elements from equal arguments and only from equal arguments.

To make rules for sets efficiently usable in combination with logical rules, type theory uses the rule notation in defining sets. But it is possible to define an equivalent curly bracket notation, in which one writes, for instance,

$continent = \{Africa, America, Asia, Australia, Europe\}$: set,
$N = \{0, s(a) \ (a : N)\}$: set,
$A \times B = \{(a, b) \ (a : A, b : B)\}$: set.

2.3   Functions

In addition to judgements of the form $a : A$, which introduces an element
of a set A, there are judgements of the form

$$f(x) : B \ (x : A),$$

which introduces a *function* from A to B. The singular term x is a *variable*,
and its occurrence in parentheses in $f(x)$ indicates that it may occur *free*
in $f(x)$. The judgement $x : A$, which introduces a variable, is a *hypothesis*,
and the whole $f(x) : B \ (x : A)$ is a *hypothetical judgement*. It can be read
in several ways, for example,

$f(x) : B$ for arbitrary $x : A$,
$f(x) : B$ under the hypothesis $x : A$,
$f(x) : B$ provided $x : A$,
$f(x) : B$ given $x : A$,
$f(x) : B$ if $x : A$,
$f(x) : B$ in the context $x : A$.

The meaning of this hypothetical judgement is that whatever element a
of A is substituted for x in $f(x)$, an element $f(a)$ of B results, and that
substitutions of equal elements of A result in equal elements of B. These
conditions can be expressed in the form of the *substitution rules*

$$\frac{(x : A) \atop f(x) : B \quad a : A}{f(a) : B}, \qquad \frac{(x : A) \atop f(x) : B \quad a = b : A}{f(a) = f(b) : B}.$$

In the rule notation, the hypothesis belonging to a premise that is a hypothetical judgement is written above instead of on the right; cf. Section 2.8
for an explanation of this convention.

   For instance, the square of a natural number is introduced by the hypothetical judgement

$$x^2 : N \ (x : N).$$

Functions of more than one variable are given by hypothetical judgements
of more than one hypothesis, for example,

$x + y : N \ (x : N, y : N)$,
$x + y * z : N \ (x : N, y : N, z : N)$.

The list of hypotheses in a hypothetical judgement is called a *context*. A
judgement made in the *empty context*, that is, without hypotheses, is a
categorical judgement.

The elements introduced by the introduction rules of a set are called the *canonical* elements of the set. Elements given otherwise, for example, the elements $3 : N$ and $2 + 3 : N$, are *non-canonical*, and they must be defined in terms of canonical elements. Thus we have a series of explicit definitions

$$1 = s(0) : N,$$
$$2 = s(1) : N,$$
$$3 = s(2) : N,$$

by which the non-canonical element $3 : N$ can be brought into the canonical form $s(s(s(0)))$, and a pair of recursion equations

$$\begin{cases} a + 0 = a : N, \\ a + s(b) = s(a + b) : N, \end{cases}$$

by which the sum $2 + 3$ can be brought into the form $s(s(s(s(s(0)))))$.

We shall not make any formal distinction between variables and constants. Any expression that has not been specified as a canonical or non-canonical element of a set may be used as a variable ranging over the elements of that set. But in the formulation of rules, it is customary to use x, y, z, x_1, x_2, etc., as variables introduced in hypotheses, and a, b, c, a_1, a_2, etc., as schematic letters free for any terms of appropriate types.

2.4   Propositions and propositional functions

In addition to domains of individuals, an interpretation of predicate calculus needs *propositions*. They are introduced by giving *truth conditions*: to introduce a proposition you must tell what it is for it to be *true*. We write

$$A : \mathrm{prop}$$

to formalize the judgement that A is a proposition. A very simple proposition is the *absurdity* $\bot$, which is explained by telling that it is true under no condition. The judgement that $\bot$ is a proposition is formally written

$$\bot : \mathrm{prop}.$$

Propositions are often formed by applying *propositional functions* to individuals. Propositional functions are introduced by hypothetical judgements of the form

$$B(x) : \mathrm{prop} \ (x : A)$$

where $A : \mathrm{set}$. The following rules of substitution hold for propositional functions.

$$\frac{\begin{array}{c}(x : A)\\ B(x) : \mathrm{prop} \quad a : A\end{array}}{B(a) : \mathrm{prop}},\qquad \frac{\begin{array}{c}(x : A)\\ B(x) : \mathrm{prop} \quad a = b : A\end{array}}{B(a) = B(b) : \mathrm{prop}}.$$

The *Begriffsschrift* did not make judgements of the form A : prop explicit, but just explained informally what it is to be a proposition, or a *beurtheilbarer Inhalt*, and prescribed that only such things can be judged to be true (op. cit. §2). In contemporary predicate calculus, the judgement is made on the metalevel, in the form

A is a well-formed formula.

Making the judgement explicit in the formalism is part of the general spirit of type theory. But as we shall see, it also adds to the expressive power of the theory.

2.5 Polymorphism and overloading

The ordinary interpretation of predicate calculus uses only one domain of individuals, and all functions can be applied to all individuals. If domains are made explicit, every function is defined for some particular domain, and it is only applicable to the individuals of that domain. For instance, the property of being prime is a propositional function over the set of natural numbers,

$$prime(x) : \text{prop} \ (x : N).$$

This function cannot be applied to the individuals of any other domain.

In informal language, a function often appears to be defined for several different domains. In careful formalization, different symbols must be used for each domain. For instance, the sum of natural numbers and the sum of real numbers are distinct functions,

$$x +_N y : N \ (x : N, y : N),$$
$$x +_R y : R \ (x : R, y : R).$$

The type ambiguity of expressions of informal language is the result of sugaring procedures, such as

$$x +_N y \ \triangleright \ x + y.$$

The use of a common symbol for several operators of different types, like $+$ above, is called *overloading* in computer science. A more general kind of type ambiguity arises from operators that are defined uniformly for elements of any sets, like the identity predicate

$$I(A, x, y) : \text{prop} \ (x : A, \ y : A)$$

which is true of equal elements a and b of any set A. The sugaring of such an expression by omission of the set argument produces a *polymorphic* function expression. The identity symbol $=$ is typically used polymorphically in informal mathematics,

$$(x = y) : \text{prop} \ (x : A, \ y : A).$$

Thus
$$I(A, a, b) \; \triangleright \; a = b.$$

Certain propositional functions of everyday language are notoriously relative to domain. For instance, 'good' applies differently to individuals of different domains, and so does 'big'. Their proper syntax is, in analogy with the identity predicate,

$good(A, x)$: prop $(x : A)$,
$big(B, x)$: prop $(x : B)$,

where A is any domain in which goodness is defined, and B any domain in which bigness is defined. Thus to say of c that he is a good cobbler (example from Aristotle's *De Interpretatione*, 20b35–40), we shall not say anything like
$$cobbler(c) \& good(c)$$
but
$$good(Cobbler, c).$$

(Observe that $cobbler(x)$ is a one-place predicate but *Cobbler* is a set term, with no argument place. There may still be a connection between them, for example, $Cobbler = \{x : man \mid cobbler(x)\}$: set; cf. Section 2.12.)

It may be, of course, that 'good' has even more hidden arguments, for example, one for the purpose for which goodness is evaluated. Moreover, by calling a man a good cobbler we may also mean that he is a cobbler and a good man,
$$cobbler(c) \& good(man, c),$$
since the sugared version we use in English does not uniquely determine the dropped set argument.

2.6   Connectives and quantifiers

Complex propositions are formed by means of *logical operators—connectives* and *quantifiers*. We shall use the connectives *conjunction* &, *disjunction* $\vee$, and *implication* $\supset$, each of which combines two propositions, and *negation* $\sim$, which is applied to one proposition.

$$A \& B : \text{prop if } A : \text{prop and } B : \text{prop},$$
$$A \vee B : \text{prop if } A : \text{prop and } B : \text{prop},$$
$$A \supset B : \text{prop if } A : \text{prop and } B : \text{prop},$$
$$\sim A : \text{prop if } A : \text{prop}.$$

As prop is not a set, we cannot formulate these clauses as hypothetical judgements, like

$$(X \& Y) : \text{prop} \quad (X : \text{prop}, \; Y : \text{prop}).$$

But they can be written as *proposition formation rules*, in this case,

$$\frac{A : \text{prop} \quad B : \text{prop}}{A\&B : \text{prop}}.$$

The *universal quantifier* $\forall$ combines a set and a propositional function over that set. So does the *existential quantifier* $\exists$.

$$(\forall x : A)B(x) : \text{prop} \quad \text{if} \quad A : \text{set and } B(x) : \text{prop} \quad (x : A),$$
$$(\exists x : A)B(x) : \text{prop} \quad \text{if} \quad A : \text{set and } B(x) : \text{prop} \quad (x : A).$$

The proposition formation rules correspond to the rules of formation of well-formed formulae, which in ordinary predicate calculus are presented on the metalevel. Even *Begriffsschrift* left these rules implicit. In type theory, where the formation rules belong to the calculus itself, their use may be combined with the use of ordinary rules of inference when propositions are formed.

Complex propositions are explained semantically by explaining their truth conditions under the assumption that their immediate constituents have been explained, in the style of Tarski (1935, §3).

$$A\&B \text{ is true} \quad \text{if} \quad A \text{ is true and } B \text{ is true},$$
$$A \vee B \text{ is true} \quad \text{if} \quad A \text{ is true or } B \text{ is true},$$
$$A \supset B \text{ is true} \quad \text{if} \quad B \text{ is true provided } A \text{ is true},$$
$$\sim A \text{ is true} \quad \text{if} \quad \perp \text{ is true provided } A \text{ is true},$$
$$(\forall x : A)B(x) \text{ is true} \quad \text{if} \quad B(x) \text{ is true provided } x : A,$$
$$(\exists x : A)B(x) \text{ is true} \quad \text{if} \quad B(a) \text{ is true for some } a : A.$$

2.7 Assertions

In the truth definition of Tarski style, there occur judgements of the form

$$A \text{ is true},$$

where A is a proposition. Such a judgement can be called an *assertion* of the proposition A. In type theory, it is formally written either

$$A \text{ true}$$

or, using Frege's *judgement stroke* (*Begriffsschrift*, §2),

$$\vdash A.$$

By means of the judgement stroke, Frege distinguished between asserted and unasserted occurrences of propositions. The proposition A occurs unasserted, for instance,

when it is a constituent of another proposition (e.g. in the assertion $\vdash A \supset B$),

in the judgement A : prop,
inside the question whether A is true.

But when A occurs in a mathematical proof, as a premise or as the conclusion of an inference, it occurs asserted, and the explicit formalism will mark it with the assertion sign, writing $\vdash A$, or, as we shall usually do, A true.

In Frege, the sign $\vdash$ carries an *epistemic force*, so that Frege only prefixes it to propositions he himself asserts categorically. In type theory, assertions will also occur as hypotheses. Thus the assertion sign is not a sign of force, in the sense of Frege (cf. Dummett, 1973, chapter 10), but rather of *mood*, similar to what Stenius (1967) calls the *indicative mood* and contrasts to the *interrogative mood*, the *imperative mood*, etc. The mood does not belong to the *descriptive content*, that is, to the proposition. The linguist may be familiar with the notions of *modus* and *dictum*, which Bally (1944, §28) finds in every phrase of language.

Logical mood does not relate to grammatical mood (the indicative, imperative, subjunctive, etc., forms of the verb) in any simple fashion, as already observed by Apollonius Dyscolus (see the *Syntaxis*, book III, and the preface by Householder, 1981, p. 10).

The contemporary notation of predicate calculus does not indicate mood, partly because it only makes explicit judgements in the assertive mood. If there were not only assertions, but questions as well, mood operators would have to be introduced. To suppress the sign of assertion—which is, of course, a possible convention—would give the false impression that a sentence in any other mood has an assertion as a part.

To make the mood into an additional part of the proposition, by means of operators like

(I *assert* A) : prop if A : prop,
(I *ask whether* A) : prop if A : prop,

(cf. Lewis 1972, pp. 39–42), makes mood into a part of propositional content. It is of course possible to define such operators, but they do not capture the phenomenon of mood. In other words, they cannot distinguish the *performative* use of language from reports about performative use. To reduce mood into such operators is an instance of what Austin calls the *descriptive fallacy* (1962, p. 100).

Judgements of the form A true can occur as hypotheses; another judgement J can be made under the hypothesis that the proposition A is true. The corresponding rule of substitution is

$$\frac{\overset{(A\ \text{true})}{J} \qquad A\ \text{true}}{J}.$$

A typical instance of a hypothetical judgement of this form is

$$B \text{ true } (A \text{ true}),$$

to the effect that the truth of B follows from the truth of A, that is, that B is a *consequence* of A. The general case with n hypotheses,

$$A \text{ true } (A_1 \text{ true}, \ldots, A_n \text{ true}),$$

corresponds to the *sequent*

$$A_1, \ldots, A_n \rightarrow A$$

of Gentzen (1934). The context

$$A_1 \text{ true}, \ldots, A_n \text{ true},$$

corresponds to the antecedent

$$A_1, \ldots, A_n$$

of the sequent.

But we can also make judgements of the form

$$B : \text{prop } (A \text{ true}),$$

to the effect that B is a proposition if A is true. It expresses what is often called *presupposition* in linguistics and spelt out by saying that some sentence makes sense under the assumption that some other sentence is true. But observe that it is not a presupposition in the technical sense of type theory, in which $B : \text{prop}$ has no presuppositions, and the presupposition of A true is $A : \text{prop}$.

An example of presupposition in the linguistic sense is that it makes sense to say that John stops smoking provided he smokes,

$$(\textit{John stops smoking}) : \text{prop } ((\textit{John smokes}) \text{ true}).$$

The propositional function introducing the verb *stop smoking* has a context with hypotheses of both forms, which is, moreover, *progressive* in the sense that the latter hypothesis contains the variable introduced by the former hypothesis.

$$(\textit{x stops smoking}) : \text{prop } (x : \textit{man}, (\textit{x smokes}) \text{ true}).$$

Observe that the rule of permutation of hypotheses (Gentzen 1934, III §1.21) is not valid for progressive contexts.

2.8   Rules of the explicit predicate calculus

The explanations of judgements and propositions given above justify a system of inference rules. This system is an explicit version of predicate calculus, very much reminiscent of Martin-Löf's type theory.

For each logical operator, there is a *formation (F) rule* which tells that a proposition can be formed by means of the operator, given such and such premises. *Introduction (I) rules* state for any proposition formed by means of each operator the condition of judging it true. *Elimination (E) rules* are justified by the necessity of these conditions. Introduction and elimination rules can also be seen as expressions in rule form for Tarski's truth definition, so that the introduction rules are obtained by turning the table one right angle counterclockwise (cf. Martin-Löf 1987), and the elimination rules by turning them clockwise. The limitations of the rule notation make this procedure a little complicated, especially for the elimination rules.

For instance, consider the truth condition for conjunction,

$A\&B$ is true if A is true and B is true.

Turned counterclockwise, it gives the conjunction introduction rule

$$\frac{A\ \text{true}\quad B\ \text{true}}{A\&B\ \text{true}}\ \&I.$$

Turned clockwise, it would give a rule with two conclusions. As this is against the conventions of rule notation, the same idea is expressed by two rules with one and the same premise,

$$\frac{A\&B\ \text{true}}{A\ \text{true}}\ \&E, \qquad \frac{A\&B\ \text{true}}{B\ \text{true}}\ \&E.$$

Or consider universal quantification,

$(\forall x\ :\ A)B(x)$ is true if $B(x)$ is true provided $x\ :\ A$.

This gives an introduction rule with a hypothetical premise,

$$\frac{\begin{array}{c}(x\ :\ A)\\ B(x)\ \text{true}\end{array}}{(\forall x\ :\ A)B(x)\ \text{true}}\ \forall I.$$

In order for $(\forall x\ :\ A)B(x)$ to be true, $B(x)$ must be true for an arbitrary element x of A. This means that nothing else is assumed about x but $x\ :\ A$. For the proper use of the $\forall I$ rule, this means that the premise may not depend on any other hypothesis in which x is free. This is the semantical explanation of the *variable restriction* belonging to the $\forall I$ rule. As for $\forall$ elimination, the truth condition is read as saying that if $(\forall x\ :\ A)B(x)$ is true then $B(x)$ is true given $x\ :\ A$. The rule notation does not permit hypothetical conclusions, but the same effect is attained by lifting the hypothesis into a premise,

$$\frac{(\forall x\ :\ A)B(x)\ \text{true}\quad a\ :\ A}{B(a)\ \text{true}}\ \forall E.$$

In addition to the formation, introduction, and elimination rules, the full system comprises the *structural rules* of *reflexivity*, *symmetry*, and *transitivity* of equality judgements, as well as the rules of *extensionality of sets*, and rules of *substitution*. In the first rule of substitution, $J(x)$ stands for a judgement of any form, such that x may occur free in it. (See Martin-Löf 1984, pp. 19–20 or Nordström *et al.* 1990, pp. 35–38 for substitution with several hypotheses.)

Every inference rule here formulated for categorical judgements relativizes to judgements made in arbitrary contexts. The conclusion then depends on all of the hypotheses of the premises, except those that are *discharged* at the application of the rule. Licence to discharge one or more hypotheses of a premise is indicated by writing the hypotheses in parentheses above the premise.

If a discharged hypothesis introduces a variable, like in the $\forall I$ rule, the variable becomes *bound* in the conclusion. The variable that becomes bound may not occur free in any hypothesis on which the conclusion still depends. Semantically speaking, one discharges the hypothesis $x : A$ when one has proved something for an arbitrary element of A. In such a proof, one must not assume anything more about x than that it is an element of A.

$$\bot : \text{prop} \; {}^{\bot F} \qquad\qquad \frac{\bot \; \text{true}}{A \; \text{true}} \; {}^{\bot E}$$

$$\frac{A : \text{prop} \quad B : \text{prop}}{A\&B : \text{prop}} \; {}^{\&F} \qquad \frac{A \; \text{true} \quad B \; \text{true}}{A\&B \; \text{true}} \; {}^{\&I}$$

$$\frac{A\&B \; \text{true}}{A \; \text{true}} \; {}^{\&E} \qquad \frac{A\&B \; \text{true}}{B \; \text{true}} \; {}^{\&E}$$

$$\frac{A : \text{prop} \quad B : \text{prop}}{A \vee B : \text{prop}} \; {}^{\vee F}$$

$$\frac{A \; \text{true}}{A \vee B \; \text{true}} \; {}^{\vee I} \qquad \frac{B \; \text{true}}{A \vee B \; \text{true}} \; {}^{\vee I}$$

$$\frac{A \vee B \; \text{true} \quad \overset{(A \; \text{true})}{C \; \text{true}} \quad \overset{(B \; \text{true})}{C \; \text{true}}}{C \; \text{true}} \; {}^{\vee E}$$

$$\frac{A : \text{prop} \quad B : \text{prop}}{A \supset B : \text{prop}} \; {}^{\supset F} \qquad \frac{\overset{(A \; \text{true})}{B \; \text{true}}}{A \supset B \; \text{true}} \; {}^{\supset I}$$

$$\frac{A \supset B \; \text{true} \quad A \; \text{true}}{B \; \text{true}} \; {}^{\supset E}$$

$$\frac{A \,:\, \text{prop}}{\sim A \,:\, \text{prop}} \sim F \qquad \frac{\overset{(A \text{ true})}{\perp \text{ true}}}{\sim A \text{ true}} \sim I$$

$$\frac{\sim A \text{ true} \quad A \text{ true}}{\perp \text{ true}} \sim E$$

$$\frac{A \,:\, \text{set} \quad \overset{(x \,:\, A)}{B(x) \,:\, \text{prop}}}{(\forall x \,:\, A)B(x) \,:\, \text{prop}} \forall F \qquad \frac{\overset{(x \,:\, A)}{B(x) \text{ true}}}{(\forall x \,:\, A)B(x) \text{ true}} \forall I$$

$$\frac{(\forall x \,:\, A)B(x) \text{ true} \quad a \,:\, A}{B(a) \text{ true}} \forall E$$

$$\frac{A \,:\, \text{set} \quad \overset{(x \,:\, A)}{B(x) \,:\, \text{prop}}}{(\exists x \,:\, A)B(x) \,:\, \text{prop}} \exists F \qquad \frac{a \,:\, A \quad B(a) \text{ true}}{(\exists x \,:\, A)B(x) \text{ true}} \exists I$$

$$\frac{(\exists x \,:\, A)B(x) \text{ true} \quad \overset{(x \,:\, A, \, B(x) \text{ true})}{C \text{ true}}}{C \text{ true}} \exists E$$

$$\frac{A \,:\, \text{set}}{A = A \,:\, \text{set}} \text{ refl.} \qquad \frac{A = B \,:\, \text{set}}{B = A \,:\, \text{set}} \text{ symm.}$$

$$\frac{A = B \,:\, \text{set} \quad B = C \,:\, \text{set}}{A = C \,:\, \text{set}} \text{ trans.}$$

$$\frac{a \,:\, A}{a = a \,:\, A} \text{ refl.} \qquad \frac{a = b \,:\, A}{b = a \,:\, A} \text{ symm.}$$

$$\frac{a = b \,:\, A \quad b = c \,:\, A}{a = c \,:\, A} \text{ trans.}$$

$$\frac{A = B \,:\, \text{set} \quad a \,:\, A}{a \,:\, B} \text{ ext.} \qquad \frac{A = B \,:\, \text{set} \quad a = b \,:\, A}{a = b \,:\, B} \text{ ext.}$$

$$\frac{a \,:\, A \quad \overset{(x \,:\, A)}{J(x)}}{J(a)} \text{ subst.} \qquad \frac{a = c \,:\, A \quad \overset{(x \,:\, A)}{B(x) \,:\, \text{set}}}{B(a) = B(c) \,:\, \text{set}} \text{ subst.}$$

$$\frac{a = c \,:\, A \quad \overset{(x \,:\, A)}{b(x) \,:\, B(x)}}{b(a) = b(c) \,:\, B(a)} \text{ subst.}$$

2.9 Examples of proofs in the explicit predicate calculus

The system of rules can be used for proving judgements of all of the six forms A : set, $A = B$: set, a : A, $a = b$: A, A : prop, and A true. Proofs will be written in the tree form induced by the rules. Discharges of hypotheses will be indicated by numerals both above the discharged occurrences of hypotheses and beside the inference lines at which the discharges are made.

Prove first (Figure 2.1) that

$$(\forall x \; : \; A)(B(x) \supset C(x))$$

is a proposition if

$$A \; : \; \text{set}, B(x) \; : \; \text{prop} \; (x \; : \; A), C(x) \; : \; \text{prop} \; (x \; : \; A).$$

Parentheses are used for indicating constituent structure at need.

$$
\cfrac{A \; : \; \text{set} \quad \cfrac{\cfrac{(x \; : \; A) \quad \quad 1. \\ B(x) \; : \; \text{prop} \quad x \; : \; A}{B(x) \; : \; \text{prop}} \; subst \quad \cfrac{\cfrac{(x \; : \; A) \quad \quad 1. \\ C(x) \; : \; \text{prop} \quad x \; : \; A}{C(x) \; : \; \text{prop}} \; subst}{B(x) \supset C(x) \; : \; \text{prop}} \; \supset F}{(\forall x \; : \; A)(B(x) \supset C(x)) \; : \; \text{prop}} \; \forall F, 1.
$$

Figure 2.1

Prove then (Figure 2.2) the implication

$$(\forall x \; : \; A)(B(x) \supset C(x)) \supset ((\exists x \; : \; A)B(x) \supset (\exists x \; : \; A)C(x)) \text{ true.}$$

This proof tree, unlike the previous one, has a counterpart in the ordinary predicate calculus.

$$
\cfrac{(\exists x : A)B(x) \text{ true} \quad \cfrac{\cfrac{\cfrac{(\forall x : A)(B(x) \supset C(x)) \text{ true} \quad x : A}{((B(x) \supset C(x)) \text{ true}} \forall E \quad B(x) \text{ true}}{C(x) \text{ true}} \supset E}{(\exists x : A)C(x) \text{ true}} \exists I}{\cfrac{\cfrac{(\exists x : A)C(x) \text{ true}}{(\exists x : A)B(x) \supset (\exists x : A)C(x) \text{ true}} \supset I, 3.}{(\forall x : A)(B(x) \supset C(x)) \supset ((\exists x : A)B(x) \supset (\exists x : A)C(x)) \text{ true}} \supset I, 4.}
$$

Figure 2.2

2.10   Intuitionistic and classical logic

The system of rules laid down above is exactly Gentzen's system of Natural Deduction for intuitionistic predicate calculus (Gentzen 1934, II §2.21) made explicit in accordance with the principles of type theory. Classical predicate calculus is obtained by adding to the intuitionistic calculus any one of the rules *excluded middle* (*EM*), *double negation elimination* (*DN*), *classical $\perp$ elimination* ($\perp C$).

$$A \vee \sim A \text{ true } EM, \qquad \frac{\sim \sim A \text{ true}}{A \text{ true}} DN, \qquad \frac{\begin{array}{c}(\sim A \text{ true})\\ \perp \text{ true}\end{array}}{A \text{ true}} \perp C.$$

The first two alternatives were suggested by Gentzen himself (op. cit., §5.3). As noted by him, they involve a departure from the balance between introduction and elimination rules. By choosing the third rule—which makes the weaker rule $\perp E$ unnecessary—and limiting its use to atomic formulae, Prawitz (1965) succeeded in restoring the balance so as to be able to prove his normalization theorem even for classical predicate calculus.

The crucial laws of classical logic cannot be derived from the Tarski-style truth definitions for logical operators. To make the truth definition justify any of the three rules characteristic of classical logic, we must add an extra principle such as one of the following.

A is true or A is false,
A is true or $\sim A$ is true,
A is true if $\sim A$ is false.

Notes. It is easy to prove *DN* and $\perp C$ from each other and from *EM*. To prove *EM* from *DN*, one can first prove the double negation of *EM* constructively.

Observe that even though the laws *EM* and *DN* can be derived from each other, the propositions $A \vee \sim A$ and $\sim \sim A \supset A$ are not always equivalent. If they were, we could prove

$$\sim A \vee \sim \sim A,$$

because we can prove

$$\sim \sim \sim A \supset \sim A.$$

2.11   Substantival and adjectival terms

In ordinary predicate calculus, both adjectives, verbs, and common nouns are formalized as predicates, over the one and only domain D of individuals, for example,

$(x \text{ is black}) : \text{prop } (x : D),$

$(x\ walks)$: prop $(x\ :\ D)$,
$(x\ is\ a\ raven)$: prop $(x\ :\ D)$.

The explicit predicate calculus makes a distinction between sets and propositional functions. This distinction provides a counterpart of the distinction between common nouns, on the one hand, and verbs and adjectives, on the other. Thus there are two forms of judgement used for the 'predication'

$$a\ is\ B.$$

The first form says that a is an element of the set B,

$$a\ :\ B.$$

The second form says, of an element a of a set A, that it has the property B, where $B(x)$: prop $(x\ :\ A)$.

$$B(a)\ \text{true.}$$

In their discussion of Aquinas, Anscombe and Geach (1961) introduce the distinction between *substantival* and *adjectival* terms. Substantival terms serve as the basis of counting and thus of quantification. This is what is guaranteed to a set term by the definition of equality of its elements; cf. Section 2.2 above. Propositional functions can only be defined over sets already defined. A set is, like a type in Russell, the range of significance of a propositional function (see *Principia*, Introduction, chapter II).

In ordinary predicate calculus, there are no expressions that correspond to English quantifier phrases like *every A*, where A is a substantival term. Such phrases are dissolved by using connectives, so that one simulates

$$(\forall x\ :\ A)B(x)\ \text{with}\ (\forall x)(A(x) \supset B(x)),$$
$$(\exists x\ :\ A)B(x)\ \text{with}\ (\exists x)(A(x)\&B(x)).$$

In English, sentences corresponding to quantified propositions of ordinary predicate calculus never occur. If you try to read aloud the formula

$$(\forall x)((x\ is\ a\ raven) \supset (x\ is\ black))$$

you cannot avoid using a substantival term,

every **raven** *is black,*
if some **entity** *is a raven it is black,*
for every **x**, *if x is a raven it is black.*

In the third sentence, x is used as a common noun; it is not possible to understand it as a singular term, for you cannot form phrases like *every Africa*. In the explicit predicate calculus, we can formalize the sentence *every raven is black* as the proposition

$$(\forall x\ :\ raven)(x\ is\ black).$$

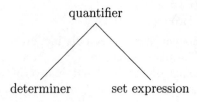

Figure 2.3

Note that this proposition cannot be converted to anything like

$$(\forall x)(\sim (x \text{ is black}) \supset \sim (x \text{ is a raven})),$$

because there are no such sets as complements of given sets. (The problems created by this conversion were observed by Hempel (1945).)

In their theory of *generalized quantifiers*, Barwise and Cooper (1981) start from the observation that *quantifiers* in English really have the form shown in Figure 2.3, that is, they are like $(\forall x : A)$ and unlike $(\forall x)$. But instead of revising the formalism of predicate calculus, they introduce real quantifiers in their metalanguage only.

The use of quantifiers restricted by set terms is particularly important in the formalization of most-sentences, such as

most ravens are black.

For if we interpret *raven* as a propositional function over a domain A, we cannot express the meaning of this sentence by quantification over A. The closest we get is

$$(\mathrm{W}x)((x \text{ is a raven}) \supset (x \text{ is black})),$$

(W is the inverted M) which is vacuously true if most elements of A are not ravens, as observed by Rescher (1962). We must quantify over ravens only,

$$(\mathrm{W}x : \text{ raven})(x \text{ is black}).$$

Wallace (1965) gave a solution along these lines in predicate calculus. Sundholm (1989) has defined the quantifier W in type theory, as well as some other 'generalized quantifiers'.

2.12   Separated subsets

In English, complex common nouns can be formed by *modifying* given common nouns, for example, by relative clauses and by adjectival attributes. This can be modelled by the formation of *subsets* by *separation*. Elements of the new set are those elements of the old set that have the separating property.

$$\frac{\displaystyle \begin{array}{c} (x \,:\, A) \\ A \,:\, \mathrm{set} \quad B(x) \,:\, \mathrm{prop} \end{array}}{\{x \,:\, A \mid B(x)\} \,:\, \mathrm{set}} \; , \qquad \frac{a \,:\, A \quad B(a) \; \mathrm{true}}{a \,:\, \{x \,:\, A \mid B(x)\}} \, .$$

This explanation of subsets also justifies the following rules.

$$\frac{a \,:\, \{x \,:\, A \mid B(x)\}}{a \,:\, A} \; , \qquad \frac{a \,:\, \{x \,:\, A \mid B(x)\}}{B(a) \; \mathrm{true}} \, .$$

Observe that the curly bracket notation here adopted for subsets is distinct from the notation used for definitions of sets in Section 2.2. Defining subsets by using the latter, we would write

$$\{x \,:\, A \mid B(x)\} = \{a \; (a \,:\, A, \; B(a) \; \mathrm{true})\} \,:\, \mathrm{set}.$$

Common nouns modified adjectivally or by relative clauses can now be formalized as sets formed by separation,

$(black\ raven) = \{x \,:\, raven \mid (x\ is\ black)\} \,:\, \mathrm{set},$
$(man\ who\ owns\ a\ donkey)$
$$= \{x \,:\, man \mid (\exists y \,:\, donkey)(x\ owns\ y)\} \,:\, \mathrm{set}.$$

Separated sets are indispensable as domains of most-quantification. For instance, to formalize the sentence

most young ravens are black,

the proposition

$$(\mathsf{W}x \,:\, raven)((x\ is\ young) \supset (x\ is\ black)),$$

which dissolves the complex common noun, is inadequate, and

$$(\mathsf{W}x \,:\, \{y \,:\, raven \mid (y\ is\ young)\})(x\ is\ black)$$

must be used.

Example. We can now formalize the sentences

every man who owns a donkey is busy,
some man who owns a donkey is busy,

in a compositional way, so that the common noun phrase *man who owns a donkey* is treated as a constituent of both of them. But we cannot formalize

every man who owns a donkey beats it,
some man who owns a donkey beats it,

in this way.

$$\dfrac{A : \text{set} \qquad \dfrac{\dfrac{\begin{array}{c}(x : A)\\ B(x) : \text{set}\end{array} \quad \begin{array}{c}2.\\ x : A\end{array}}{B(x) : \text{set}}\,\mathit{subst} \qquad \dfrac{\begin{array}{c}(x : A,\ y : B(x))\\ C(x,y) : \text{prop}\end{array} \quad \begin{array}{c}2.\\ x : A\end{array} \quad \begin{array}{c}1.\\ y : B(x)\end{array}}{C(x,y) : \text{prop}}\,s.}{(\exists y : B(x))C(x,y) : \text{prop}}\,\exists F, 1.}{(\forall x : A)(\exists y : B(x))C(x,y) : \text{prop}}\,\forall F, 2.$$

Figure 2.4

2.13 Families of sets

A *family of sets* over a given set is a set-valued function, given in a hypothetical judgement of the form

$$B(x) : \text{set}\ \ (x : A).$$

For instance, the indications of calendar time form a system of progressively dependent sets. The set of years can be formed independently of any hypotheses. So can the set of the twelve months in the Gregorian calendar, but in the Islamic calendar, some years have twelve months, some thirteen. The set of days depends, because of leap years, both on the year and on the month. The set of hours varies in accordance with adjustments of summer and winter time.

Gregorian calendar.
$\mathit{year} : \text{set}$,
$\mathit{month} : \text{set}$,
$\mathit{day}(y, m) : \text{set}\ \ (y : \mathit{year},\ m : \mathit{month})$,
$\mathit{hour}(y, m, d) : \text{set}\ \ (y : \mathit{year},\ m : \mathit{month}, d : \mathit{day}(y, m))$.
Islamic calendar.
$\mathit{year} : \text{set}$,
$\mathit{month}(y) : \text{set}\ \ (y : \mathit{year})$,
$\mathit{day}(y, m) : \text{set}\ \ (y : \mathit{year},\ m : \mathit{month}(y))$,
$\mathit{hour}(y, m, d) : \text{set}\ \ (y : \mathit{year},\ m : \mathit{month}(y), d : \mathit{day}(y, m))$.

Families of sets give rise to propositions with progressively ordered quantifier prefixes, but they can be formed by the rules we already have, relativizing them to contexts. Assuming

$A : \text{set}$,
$B(x) : \text{set}\ \ (x : A)$,
$C(x, y) : \text{prop}\ \ (x : A, y : B(x))$,

we can form the proposition $(\forall x : A)(\exists y : B(x))C(x, y)$ as shown in Figure 2.4.

Progressive quantifier prefixes are indispensable in the formalization of such sentences as *every man admires most of his brothers*, as

$$(\forall x : man)(Wy : (brother\ of\ x))(x\ admires\ y).$$

2.14 The classical notion of proposition

As we observed in Section 2.10, classical logic differs from intuitionistic logic in that it assumes principles that go beyond the straightforward Tarski-style explanations of logical constants. Consider one of the equivalent extra principles, the principle of *bivalence*,

> every proposition is true or false.

There is an established tradition of logic that regards this principle as un-problematic. It seems to have been assumed already by Aristotle in *De Interpretatione*. In *Grundgesetze*, Frege gave it a mathematical formulation according to which sentences like $2 + 3 = 5$ denote (*bezeichnen*) truth values, of which there are two, the True and the False. This idea of Frege's has been accepted in modern mathematical logic and in formal linguistics (e.g. in Montague) as the standard interpretation of formulae. Where singular terms are interpreted as individuals of the domain, formulae are interpreted as individuals of another domain, the set Bool of truth values, whose elements are True and False, or, by more succinct names, 0 and 1. One then defines prop as the set Bool,

$$prop = Bool : set.$$

Logical operators are Boolean-valued functions of Boolean arguments, such as

$(X\&Y) : Bool\ (X : Bool,\ Y : Bool),$
$(\forall x : A)B(x) : Bool$ if $A : set$ and $B(x) : Bool\ (x : A).$

As every proposition is an element of Bool, every proposition must be equal to either True or False. The assertion that A is true comes to mean that A is equal to True.

A more moderate version of bivalent semantics does not define propositions as truth values, but introduces a valuation function

$$V(A) : Bool\ \text{if}\ A : prop,$$

which to each proposition assigns a truth value, propositions themselves being something else. Bivalence then does not mean that every proposition is equal to True or False, but only that every proposition has True or False as its value.

As True and False are the only canonical elements of the set Bool, both $(A\&B)$ and $V(a)$ are non-canonical, and must be defined as either True or

False. Thus we have, for example,

$$(\text{True\&False}) = \text{False} : \text{Bool}.$$

The conjunction of two canonical truth values can, indeed, always be computed into a canonical truth value, and this justifies the introduction of conjunction as a Boolean-valued function of Boolean arguments. This justification extends to $\vee$, $\supset$, and $\sim$ by the truth table method.

But a non-canonical truth value formed by quantification,

$$(\forall x : A)B(x) : \text{Bool},$$

cannot, for all A : set, $B(x)$: Bool $(x : A)$, be computed into a canonical truth value in the intended way, which is to go through all instances $B(a)$ where $a : A$, as A may be infinite. If we require that non-canonical elements must be effectively computable into canonical elements, the introduction of a universally quantified proposition as a truth value is unjustified.

The classical 'computation rule' for $\forall$,

$$(\forall x : A)B(x) = \begin{cases} \text{True if } B(a) = \text{True for every } a : A, \\ \text{False otherwise,} \end{cases}$$

provides an example of a definition that is not *effective*. In constructive type theory, definitions are required to be effective in the sense that it is always possible to reduce a defined term into its definiens. It follows from this requirement that non-canonical expressions are effectively computable into canonical ones, and, furthermore, that all functions are effectively computable, because a functional application $f(a)$ is nothing but a non-canonical element of the goal set.

The requirement of effectiveness of definitions has been debated in the foundations of mathematics since it was violated by Weierstrass, Dedekind, and Cantor. As reported by Kleene (1952, p. 46), Kronecker objected that 'their fundamental definitions are only words, since they do not enable one in general to decide whether a given object satisfies a definition.' The principle that definitions must be effective turns out to be what makes the difference between intuitionistic and classical logic. The failure of bivalence is just one consequence of it. The principle of effective definitions itself is one instance of the requirement of decidability of judgements.

2.15   The intuitionistic notion of proposition

Combined with the principle of bivalence, the requirement that definitions be effective is only tenable at the cost that there can no longer be undecidable propositions, like those formed by quantification over infinite domains. This was, indeed, the verificationist position of the 1920s. (See e.g. Waismann 1931.) Postverificationist analytic philosophy has usually avoided this disastrous consequence by giving up the effectivity of definitions, while intuitionistic mathematics has considered bivalence the less important principle. Intuitionism has thus been faced with the task of finding a notion of proposition free from the assumption of bivalence, but as clear as the notion of truth value.

Heyting (1931) gave an account of propositions (*Aussagen*) based on Husserl's *Logical Investigations*. A proposition is an *expectation* (*Erwartung*). To understand a proposition is to understand what would *fulfil* (*erfüllen*) the expectation. To take Heyting's own example, the proposition

Euler's constant C is rational

is fulfilled by a pair of integers a and b such that $C = a/b$. Assertions of the form

the proposition A is true

now come to mean

the expectation A is fulfilled.

It is possible to know what expectation A is, that is, what it is for it to be fulfilled, without knowing whether it can be fulfilled.

Heyting gave a full account of logical constants in terms of expectations and fulfilment in his book of 1956. But this account was preceded by Kolmogorov's semantics of propositional calculus in terms of *problems* and *solutions*, corresponding to expectations and fulfilments, respectively (Kolmogorov 1932). So one interprets A is true as

the problem A has a solution.

Heyting's semantics was also preceded by Gentzen's conception of introduction rules as the definitions of logical constants (Gentzen 1934, II §5.13). Introduction rules state the conditions for *proofs* that fulfil the expectations expressed by the propositions. The word proof has, quite naturally, become standard for fulfilment in later intuitionistic accounts. Thus Heyting (1956, pp. 102–107) explains the logical operators by telling what proofs are called for by propositions formed by means of them. Heyting's explanations are summarized in Table 2.1.

This table entails the Tarski-style truth definition, if one understands true as having a proof. But it does not entail the law of the excluded middle, for neither a proof of A nor a proof of $\sim A$ is available in general.

2.16 The propositions as types principle

Martin-Löf's type theory follows the *propositions as types principle*, according to which propositions are sets, and proofs are elements. That a proposition is true means that the set has an element. We have, at least, four alternative terminologies in which to read judgements of the forms $a : A$ and A true (Table 2.2).

proposition	is proved by
$\perp$	—
$A\&B$	a proof of A and a proof of B
$A \vee B$	a proof of A or a proof of B
$A \supset B$	a method for obtaining a proof of B from any proof of A
$\sim A$	a method for obtaining a proof of $\perp$ from any proof of A
$(\forall x : A)B(x)$	a method for obtaining a proof of $B(a)$ from any $a : A$
$(\exists x : A)B(x)$	an element $a : A$ and a proof of $B(a)$

Table 2.1

$a : A$	A true
a is an element of the set A	A has an element
a is a proof of the proposition A	A is true
a fulfils the expectation A	A is fulfilled
a is a solution to the problem A	A has a solution

Table 2.2

The proofs of complex propositions are defined as certain complexes of proofs of their constituent propositions, as shown in Table 2.3.

The proposition $\perp$ is thus the *empty set*, $A\&B$ is the *cartesian product* of A and B, $A \vee B$ is the *disjoint union* of A and B. $A \supset B$ is the *function space* from A to B. Proofs of the forms prescribed in the table are *canonical*, as they are canonical elements of the sets in question. Non-canonical proofs must be effectively computable into canonical proofs.

The proofs of a proposition, as the elements of a set, are individual

Proofs of	have the form of
$\perp$	—
$A\&B$	a pair (a, b) where $a : A$ and $b : B$
$A \vee B$	a canonical injection $i(a)$ where $a : A$ or $j(b)$ where $b : B$
$A \supset B$	a λ abstract $(\lambda x)b(x)$ where $b(x) : B$ $(x : A)$
$\sim A$	a λ abstract $(\lambda x)b(x)$ where $b(x) : \perp$ $(x : A)$
$(\forall x : A)B(x)$	a λ abstract $(\lambda x)b(x)$ where $b(x) : B(x)$ $(x : A)$
$(\exists x : A)B(x)$	a pair (a, b) where $a : A$ and $b : B(a)$

Table 2.3

$$
\left.
\begin{array}{c}
x \, : \, A \\
\vdots \\
\dfrac{b(x) \, : \, B}{\underbrace{(\lambda x)b(x)} \, : \, A \supset B}
\end{array}
\right\} \text{proof process}
$$

proof object

Figure 2.5

objects. They must be distinguished from *proof processes*, in which such elements are found. For instance, if I prove $A \supset B$ by proceeding from the hypothesis $x \, : \, A$ to the judgement $b(x) \, : \, B$ and then discharging the hypothesis, this complex action is the proof process in which I find the *proof object* $(\lambda x)b(x)$ of the proposition $A \supset B$ (see Figure 2.5).

It is easy to conceive any element of any set A as a proof of a certain proposition, namely of the proposition that

there is an element of A.

The propositions as types principle has a twofold history. On the one hand, there was the observation by Curry, that implications $A \supset B$ can be interpreted as function types $A' \to B'$, where A' and B' are the interpretations of A and B, respectively, so that proofs of $A \supset B$ are interpreted as functions from A' to B' (Curry and Feys 1958, pp. 312–315). This interpretation was extended to first-order arithmetic in the late 1960s by Howard (see Howard 1980). On the other hand, there was Heyting's explanation of propositions as expectations. In this philosophical tradition, Dummett (1975) and Prawitz (1977) made a distinction between canonical and non-canonical proofs and suggested that propositions be explained by telling what their canonical proofs are. But they did not distinguish between proof objects and proof processes.

In his type theory, Martin-Löf united the informal intuitionistic explanation of propositions and the formal interpretation of formulae as types in an identification of propositions and types (Martin-Löf 1975). In Martin-Löf 1984, the word 'type' was changed into the word 'set' and given a new meaning itself; see op. cit., pp. 21–23, as well as Section 8.1 below.

Judgement	where	means
A : set	—	A is a set
$A = B$: set	A : set, B : set	A and B are equal sets
$a : A$	A : set	a is an element of A
$a = b : A$	A : set, $a : A$, $b : A$	a and b are equal elements of A

Table 2.4

2.17   Logic in type theory

Making no distinction between propositions and sets, intuitionistic type theory has only four forms of judgement (Table 2.4) The first two forms of judgement have the notational variants A : prop and $A = B$: prop, respectively. The form $\vdash A$, or A true, is an abbreviation of $a : A$ obtained by suppressing the proof a. The judgement A true can only be made derivatively of a judgement $a : A$ that makes a proof explicit. Moreover, it makes a departure from the general principle that judgements are decidable. It is always decidable whether a given a is a proof of the proposition A, but it is not always decidable whether a given proposition A has a proof.

In type theory, proposition-forming operators are set-forming operators. They are given in *formation rules*. Such an operator is explained by giving the *introduction rules* of the new set, assuming the constituent sets are defined. The introduction rules of each set prescribe how its canonical elements are formed. The operators by which canonical elements are formed from their immediate constituents are called the *constructors* of the set in question. The constructors of the set N, for instance, are 0 and s. The constructor of the cartesian product $A \times B$ is the pairing operator.

The *elimination rules* of each set tell how functions are defined on that set. They give operators called *selectors*, in terms of which other functions can be defined. The *equality rules* justify the elimination rules by showing how the selectors operate on canonical arguments. For the cartesian product $A \times B$, we can define as selectors the *projections p* and *q*, which select the left and the right constituent of a pair, respectively.

Let us summarize the rules of the cartesian product.

$$\frac{A : \text{set} \quad B : \text{set}}{A \times B : \text{set}} \times F, \qquad \frac{a : A \quad b : B}{(a,b) : A \times B} \times I,$$

$$\frac{c : A \times B}{p(c) : A} \times E, \qquad \frac{c : A \times B}{q(c) : B} \times E,$$

$$\frac{a : A \quad b : B}{p((a,b)) = a : A} \times eq, \qquad \frac{a : A \quad b : B}{q((a,b)) = b : B} \times eq.$$

The introduction rules of a set A are a kind of an *inductive definition* of that set. There is a corresponding principle of *inductive proof* over the elements of A, which is at the same time the most general elimination rule for A. This rule has one *major premise* of the form $c : A$, and a number of *minor premises*, one for each introduction rule. The minor premises prove the propositional function

$$C(z) : \text{prop} \ (z : A)$$

for each form a canonical element of A may have. For the cartesian product $A \times B$, the principle of inductive proof is the rule

$$\frac{c : A \times B \quad \overset{(x \,:\, A, \ y \,:\, B)}{d(x,y) : C((x,y))}}{E(c,(x,y)d(x,y)) : C(c)} \times E.$$

In type theory, a hypothesis always has the form $x : A$. The hypothesis A true has this form by the propositions as types principle. When a hypothesis is discharged, the variable gets bound in the conclusion. This is indicated in various ways in the operators introduced in rules that allow discharges. In the $\times E$ rule, the variables x and y bound in the subexpression $d(x,y)$ are written in parentheses preceding $d(x,y)$.

The rule $\times E$ is justified by the equality rule

$$\frac{a : A \quad b : B \quad \overset{(x \,:\, A, \ y \,:\, B)}{d(x,y) : C((x,y))}}{E((a,b),(x,y)d(x,y)) = d(a,b) : C((a,b))} \times eq.$$

The projections can be defined in terms of E, as follows.

$$p(c) = E(c,(x,y)x) : A \ \text{ for } c : A \times B,$$
$$q(c) = E(c,(x,y)y) : B \ \text{ for } c : A \times B.$$

Example. If one needs the set $A * B * C$ of triples, one can either define it as $A \times (B \times C)$, or introduce it from scratch, by giving introduction rules for triples, and go on by formulating corresponding elimination and equality rules. Direct formulation is perhaps more in the spirit of type theory than explicit definition.

2.18 Existential quantification, conjunction, and subset separation

The operator Σ, which forms the *disjoint union of a family of sets*, generalizes the cartesian product of two sets by allowing the second set to depend on the element of the first set.

$$\frac{A : \text{set} \quad \overset{(x \,:\, A)}{B(x) : \text{set}}}{(\Sigma x : A)B(x) : \text{set}} \Sigma F, \qquad \frac{a : A \quad b : B(a)}{(a,b) : (\Sigma x : A)B(x)} \Sigma I,$$

$$\frac{c \;:\; (\Sigma x \;:\; A)B(x)}{p(c) \;:\; A}\; \Sigma E, \qquad \frac{c \;:\; (\Sigma x \;:\; A)B(x)}{q(c) \;:\; B(p(c))}\; \Sigma E,$$

$$\frac{a \;:\; A \quad b \;:\; B(a)}{p((a,b)) \;=\; a \;:\; A}\; \Sigma eq, \qquad \frac{a \;:\; A \quad b \;:\; B(a)}{q((a,b)) \;=\; b \;:\; B(a)}\; \Sigma eq.$$

In the rule ΣF, the variable x gets bound in $B(x)$.

Σ sets have one constructor, the pairing operation. The principle of inductive proof and the corresponding equality rule are generalizations of the rules for $\times$.

$$\frac{c \;:\; (\Sigma x \;:\; A)B(x) \quad \overset{(x \;:\; A,\; y \;:\; B(x))}{d(x,y) \;:\; C((x,y))}}{E(c,(x,y)d(x,y)) \;:\; C(c)}\; \Sigma E,$$

$$\frac{a \;:\; A \quad b \;:\; B \quad \overset{(x \;:\; A,\; y \;:\; B(b))}{d(x,y) \;:\; C((x,y))}}{E((a,b),(x,y)d(x,y)) \;=\; d(a,b) \;:\; C((a,b))}\; \Sigma eq.$$

The projections can be defined in terms of E, like before. Observe that the type of $q(c)$ depends on $p(c)$.

$p(c) \;=\; E(c,(x,y)x) \;:\; A$ for $c \;:\; (\Sigma x \;:\; A)B(x)$,
$q(c) \;=\; E(c,(x,y)y) \;:\; B(p(c))$ for $c \;:\; (\Sigma x \;:\; A)B(x)$.

As a proposition, $(\Sigma x \;:\; A)B(x)$ corresponds to both conjunction and existential quantification, as suggested by Table 2.3 in Section 2.16. We define

$A\&B \;=\; (\Sigma x \;:\; A)B \;:\; \text{prop}$ for $A \;:\; \text{prop}, B \;:\; \text{prop},$
$(\exists x \;:\; A)B(x) \;=\; (\Sigma x \;:\; A)B(x) \;:\; \text{prop}$
  for $A \;:\; \text{set}, B(x) \;:\; \text{prop} \;(x \;:\; A)$.

By suppressing elements of sets understood as propositions, we obtain from the Σ rules the $\&$ and $\exists$ rules of predicate calculus. The customary $\exists E$ rule corresponds to the rule that introduces the selector E. The customary $\&E$ rules correspond to the projection rules. The rule for the selector E gives, for $\&$ defined as above, the rule

$$\frac{A\&B \text{ true} \qquad \overset{(A \text{ true},\; B \text{ true})}{C \text{ true}}}{C \text{ true}},$$

which is of the general form of elimination rules, corresponding to the principle of inductive proof, studied by Schroeder-Heister (1984).

The rule of Σ equality for the selector E corresponds to the operation of $\exists$ *reduction* of Prawitz (1965, pp. 37–38), which reduces a derivation

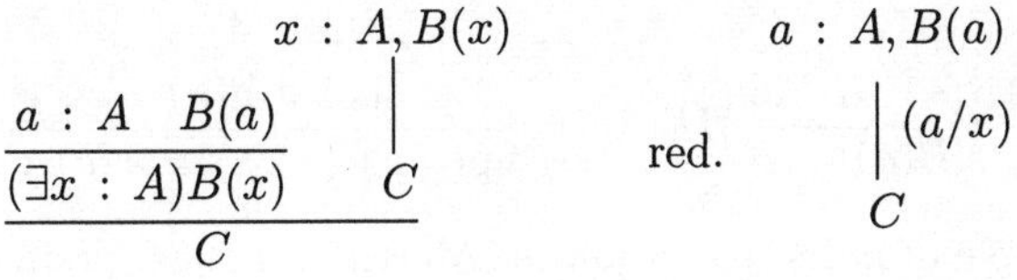

$$
\begin{array}{cc}
& x \; : \; A, B(x) \\
\dfrac{a \; : \; A \quad B(a)}{(\exists x \; : \; A)B(x)} \quad \Big| \quad C \\
\hline
\multicolumn{2}{c}{C}
\end{array}
\qquad \text{red.} \qquad
\begin{array}{c}
a \; : \; A, B(a) \\
\Big| \; (a/x) \\
C
\end{array}
$$

Figure 2.6

terminating in an instance of ∃ elimination immediately preceded by an instance of ∃ introduction into a derivation without this detour (Figure 2.6).

As a set, $(\Sigma x \; : \; A)B(x)$ corresponds to the set of elements of

$$A \text{ such that } B;$$

to introduce an element $a \; : \; A$ such that $B(a)$, we need both an element a of A and a proof of the proposition $B(a)$. One could thus define

$$\{x \; : \; A \mid B(x)\} = (\Sigma x \; : \; A)B(x) \; : \; \text{set for } A \; : \; \text{set}, \; B(x) \; : \; \text{prop} \; (x \; : \; A).$$

The Σ rules can then be seen as type-theoretical versions of the subset rules of Section 2.12 above.

We shall avoid the notation $\{x \; : \; A \mid B(x)\}$ in type theory. Nordström *et al.* 1990 use it for subsets of A whose elements are bare elements of A. Such subsets involve a departure from the type-theoretical standard of making all proofs explicit. The set membership judgement

$$c \; : \; \{x \; : \; A \mid B(x)\}$$

is not generally decidable. We shall not use these subsets, for this reason and for some other reasons to be discussed in Section 3.3.

2.19   Universal quantification and implication

The operator Π forms *the cartesian product of a family of sets*. Elements of a Π set are λ abstracts of functions.

$$
\dfrac{\begin{array}{c}(x \; : \; A)\\ A \; : \; \text{set} \quad B(x) \; : \; \text{set}\end{array}}{(\Pi x \; : \; A)B(x) \; : \; \text{set}} \; \Pi F,
\qquad
\dfrac{\begin{array}{c}(x \; : \; A)\\ b(x) \; : \; B(x)\end{array}}{(\lambda x)b(x) \; : \; (\Pi x \; : \; A)B(x)} \; \Pi I.
$$

In the rule ΠF, the variable x gets bound in $B(x)$, and in ΠI, also in $b(x)$.

The selector ap is used for *applying* an element of $(\Pi x \; : \; A)B(x)$ to an argument $a \; : \; A$. The application of a λ abstract $(\lambda x)b(x)$ to an argument

a is computed by substituting a for x in $b(x)$.

$$\frac{c \,:\, (\Pi x \,:\, A)B(x) \quad a \,:\, A}{\mathrm{ap}(c, a) \,:\, B(a)} \ \Pi E, \qquad \frac{\begin{array}{c}(x \,:\, A)\\ b(x) \,:\, B(x) \quad a \,:\, A\end{array}}{\mathrm{ap}((\lambda x)b(x), a) \;=\; b(a) \,:\, B(a)} \ \Pi eq.$$

For the principle of inductive proof, see Martin-Löf 1984, preface, or Nordström *et al.* 1990, section 7.2.

Implication and universal quantification are defined in terms of Π, as suggested by Table 2.3 in Section 2.16.

$A \supset B = (\Pi x \,:\, A)B \,:\, \text{prop for } A \,:\, \text{prop}, \ B \,:\, \text{prop},$
$(\forall x \,:\, A)B(x) = (\Pi x \,:\, A)B(x) \,:\, \text{prop}$
$\quad \text{for } A \,:\, \text{set}, \ B(x) \,:\, \text{prop} \ (x \,:\, A).$

The $\supset$ and $\forall$ rules of predicate calculus are now obtained as special cases of the Π rules of type theory.

Example. The branching quantifier proposition

$$\begin{array}{c} (\forall x)(\exists y) \\[4pt] \\[4pt] (\forall u)(\exists v) \end{array} \Big\rangle\!\!\!\longrightarrow H(x, y, u, v)$$

has no equivalent in first-order predicate calculus, but it does have an interpretation in second-order predicate calculus, in terms of Skolem functions:

$$(\exists f)(\exists g)(\forall x)(\forall u)H(x, f(x), u, g(u)).$$

This interpretation can be made in type theory as well, by existential quantification over sets of functions (cf. Ranta 1988). Moreover, there is an immediate progressive generalization of the branching quantifier proposition,

$$\begin{array}{c} (\forall x \,:\, A)(\exists y \,:\, B(x)) \\[4pt] \\[4pt] (\forall u \,:\, C)(\exists v \,:\, D(u)) \end{array} \Big\rangle\!\!\!\longrightarrow H(x, y, u, v).$$

2.20   Disjunction

The *disjoint union of two sets*, $A + B$, has as its proofs canonical injections of elements of both constituent sets. The principle of inductive proof says that a function can be defined on $A + B$ if it can be defined separately on both A and B.

$$\frac{A \ : \ \mathrm{set} \quad B \ : \ \mathrm{set}}{A + B \ : \ \mathrm{set}} + F,$$

$$\frac{a \ : \ A}{i(a) \ : \ A + B} + I, \qquad \frac{b \ : \ B}{j(b) \ : \ A + B} + I,$$

$$\frac{c \ : \ A + B \quad \overset{(x \ : \ A)}{d(x) \ : \ C(i(x))} \quad \overset{(y \ : \ B)}{e(y) \ : \ C(j(y))}}{D(c, (x)d(x), (y)e(y)) \ : \ C(c)} + E,$$

$$\frac{a \ : \ A \quad \overset{(x \ : \ A)}{d(x) \ : \ C(i(x))} \quad \overset{(y \ : \ B)}{e(y) \ : \ C(j(y))}}{D(i(a), (x)d(x), (y)e(y)) \ = \ d(a) \ : \ C(i(a))} + eq,$$

$$\frac{b \ : \ B \quad \overset{(x \ : \ A)}{d(x) \ : \ C(i(x))} \quad \overset{(y \ : \ B)}{e(y) \ : \ C(j(y))}}{D(j(b), (x)d(x), (y)e(y)) \ = \ e(b) \ : \ C(j(b))} + eq.$$

In the rules $+E$ and $+eq$, the variable x gets bound in $d(x)$ and the variable y in $e(y)$.

The disjunction of two propositions is defined as their disjoint union,

$$A \vee B \ = \ A + B \ : \ \text{prop for } A \ : \ \text{prop,} \quad B \ : \ \text{prop.}$$

2.21   Absurdity and negation

To finish the type-theoretical interpretation of predicate calculus, introduce the empty set $\emptyset$, which has no introduction rules and thus needs no equality rule.

$$\emptyset \ : \ \mathrm{set} \ {}^{\emptyset F}, \qquad \frac{c \ : \ \emptyset}{\mathrm{case}_\emptyset(c) \ : \ C(c)} \ \emptyset E.$$

The absurdity $\perp$ is defined as the empty set. Negation is implication of absurdity.

$$\perp \ = \ \emptyset \ : \ \text{prop,}$$
$$\sim A \ = \ A \supset \perp \ : \ \text{prop for } A \ : \ \text{prop.}$$

The rule of absurdity elimination, or *ex falso quodlibet*,

$$\frac{\perp \ \text{true}}{C \ \text{true}} \ {\perp}E$$

is thus induction over the empty set, which is trivially justified.

$$\frac{f : (\forall x : A)(B(x) \supset C(x)) \quad x : A}{\mathrm{ap}(f, x) : ((B(x) \supset C(x)))} \forall E \quad y : B(x)$$

$$\frac{z : (\exists x : A)B(x) \quad \dfrac{x : A \quad \dfrac{\mathrm{ap}(f, x) : ((B(x) \supset C(x)))}{\mathrm{ap}(\mathrm{ap}(f, x), y) : C(x)} \supset E}{(x, y)(x, \mathrm{ap}(\mathrm{ap}(f, x), y)) : (\exists x : A)C(x)} \exists I}{E(z, (x, y)(x, \mathrm{ap}(\mathrm{ap}(f, x), y))) : (\exists x : A)C(x)} \exists E, 1., 2.$$

$$\frac{(\lambda z)E(z, (x, y)(x, \mathrm{ap}(\mathrm{ap}(f, x), y))) : (\exists x : A)B(x) \supset (\exists x : A)C(x)}{(\lambda f)(\lambda z)E(z, (x, y)(x, \mathrm{ap}(\mathrm{ap}(f, x), y))) :} \supset I, 3.$$

$$(\forall x : A)(B(x) \supset C(x)) \supset ((\exists x : A)B(x) \supset (\exists x : A)C(x))$$

Figure 2.7

2.22   Examples of proofs in type theory

The proof tree in Section 2.9 for the conclusion

$$(\forall x : A)(B(x) \supset C(x)) : \mathrm{prop}$$

under the assumptions

$$A : \mathrm{set}, \ B(x) : \mathrm{prop} \ (x : A), \ C(x) : \mathrm{prop} \ (x : A)$$

is as such a proof tree in type theory. The proof tree for the implication

$$(\forall x : A)(B(x) \supset C(x)) \supset ((\exists x : A)B(x) \supset (\exists x : A)C(x)) \ \mathrm{true}$$

is obtained from the type-theoretical proof tree by suppressing proof objects. The full type-theoretical tree is shown in Figure 2.7.

An example of a proposition not provable nor even expressible in predicate calculus is the *axiom of choice*,

$$(\forall x : A)(\exists y : B(x))C(x, y) \supset (\exists f : (\Pi x : A)B(x))(\forall x : A)C(x, \mathrm{ap}(f, x)),$$

whose proof

$$(\lambda z)((\lambda x)p(\mathrm{ap}(z, x)), (\lambda x)q(\mathrm{ap}(z, x)))$$

is constructed in Martin-Löf 1982, pp. 173–174, and in 1984, pp. 50–52. Martin-Löf's argument is given in text form, but it is easily converted into a tree.

Examples. It is easy to prove that the propositions

$$(\Pi x : A)(\Pi y : B(x))C(x, y),$$
$$(\Pi z : (\Sigma x : A)B(x))C(p(z), q(z))$$

are equivalent, that is, that either one of them implies the other. From this equivalence, one can obtain equivalences of predicate and propositional calculus, choosing $\forall, \supset, \sim, \exists, \&$ instead of Π and Σ and stripping out dependencies between A, $B(x)$, and $C(x, y)$ correspondingly. The least general equivalence obtained in this way is between

$$A \supset \sim B \text{ and } \sim (A \& B).$$

The proof objects establishing this equivalence are still the same as in the most general case.

2.23 Finite sets, truth values

Type theory is open for new forms of sets. We shall make use of enumerated sets, the set N of natural numbers, and the equality proposition $I(A, a, b)$.

The empty set $\emptyset$ is a special instance of the enumerated sets $\{a, \ldots, b\}$, where $a, \ldots, b$ are introduced as the canonical elements of the set. The selector $\text{case}_\emptyset$ is, correspondingly, an instance of the selector $\text{case}_{\{a, \ldots, b\}}$, which defines functions on $\{a, \ldots, b\}$ by cases, by going through all elements of $\{a, \ldots, b\}$. If no confusion can arise, we write simply case for $\text{case}_{\{a, \ldots, b\}}$.

The formation rule $\{a, \ldots, b\}F$ has no premises.

$$\{a, \ldots, b\} \ : \ \text{set} \ \{a, \ldots, b\}F.$$

There is an introduction rule without premises for each of the enumerated constants $a, \ldots, b$.

$$a \ : \ \{a, \ldots, b\} \ \{a, \ldots, b\}I, \quad \ldots \quad b \ : \ \{a, \ldots, b\} \ \{a, \ldots, b\}I.$$

The elimination rule has the major premise $c \ : \ \{a, \ldots, b\}$, and a minor premise for each of the elements $a, \ldots, b$.

$$\frac{c \ : \ \{a, \ldots, b\} \quad d \ : \ C(a) \quad \ldots \quad e \ : \ C(b)}{\text{case}_{\{a, \ldots, b\}}(c, d, \ldots, e) \ : \ C(c)} \ \{a, \ldots, b\}E.$$

Thus there is an equality rule for each of the elements $a, \ldots, b$.

$$\frac{d \ : \ C(a) \quad \ldots \quad e \ : \ C(b)}{\text{case}_{\{a, \ldots, b\}}(a, d, \ldots, e) \ = \ d \ : \ C(a)} \ \{a, \ldots, b\}eq,$$

$$\ldots$$

$$\frac{d \ : \ C(a) \quad \ldots \quad e \ : \ C(b)}{\text{case}_{\{a, \ldots, b\}}(b, d, \ldots, e) \ = \ e \ : \ C(b)} \ \{a, \ldots, b\}eq.$$

The set Bool of truth values is $\{\text{True}, \text{False}\}$. The rules for Bool are thus

$$\text{Bool} \ : \ \text{set} \ \text{Bool}F,$$

$$\text{True} \ : \ \text{Bool} \ \text{Bool}I, \qquad \text{False} \ : \ \text{Bool} \ \text{Bool}I,$$

$$\frac{c \ : \ \text{Bool} \quad d \ : \ C(\text{True}) \quad e \ : \ C(\text{False})}{\text{case}(c, d, e) \ : \ C(c)} \ \text{Bool}E,$$

$$\frac{d \ : \ C(\text{True}) \quad e \ : \ C(\text{False})}{\text{case}(\text{True}, d, e) \ = \ d \ : \ C(\text{True})} \ \text{Bool}eq,$$

$$\frac{d \; : \; C(\text{True}) \quad e \; : \; C(\text{False})}{\text{case}(\text{False}, d, e) \; = \; e \; : \; C(\text{False})} \; \text{Booleq}.$$

It is now possible to present classical logic in constructive type theory, defining its formulae as non-canonical truth values. The Boolean connectives are easily defined in terms of case. The Boolean quantifiers over enumerated sets are defined in terms of connectives. This definition does not, of course, extend to infinite sets, because conjunctions and disjunctions are finitely long.

$a \wedge b = \text{case}(a, b, \text{False}) \; : \; \text{Bool for } a, b \; : \; \text{Bool},$
$a \vee b = \text{case}(a, \text{True}, b) \; : \; \text{Bool for } a, b \; : \; \text{Bool},$
$a \rightarrow b = \text{case}(a, b, \text{True}) \; : \; \text{Bool for } a, b \; : \; \text{Bool},$
$\neg a = \text{case}(a, \text{False}, \text{True}) \; : \; \text{Bool for } a \; : \; \text{Bool},$
$(\bigwedge x : \{a \ldots b\}) f(x) = f(a) \wedge \ldots \wedge f(b) \; : \; \text{Bool}$
for $f(x) \; : \; \text{Bool} \; (x \; : \; \{a \ldots b\})$,
$(\bigvee x : \{a \ldots b\}) f(x) = f(a) \vee \ldots \vee f(b) \; : \; \text{Bool}$
for $f(x) \; : \; \text{Bool} \; (x \; : \; \{a \ldots b\})$.

For instance, $a \wedge b$ is computed in accordance with the rules Booleq by first computing a. If a is True, the value of $a \wedge b$ is the same as the value of b. If a is False, $a \wedge b$ is False outright. You need not compute b any more.

Example. The rules of the one-element set $\top = \{\dagger\}$ can be given in accordance with the above scheme. $\top$ functions as the true proposition *verum*, for which the following theorems can be proved.

$A \supset \top$,
$(\top \supset A) \supset A$.

2.24   Natural numbers

Natural numbers have the following rules.

$$N \; : \; \text{set} \; {}^{NF}, \qquad 0 \; : \; N \; {}^{NI}, \qquad \frac{a \; : \; N}{s(a) \; : \; N} \; NI,$$

$$\frac{c \; : \; N \quad d \; : \; C(0) \quad \begin{array}{c} (x \; : \; N, \; y \; : \; C(x)) \\ e(x, y) \; : \; C(s(x)) \end{array}}{R(c, d, (x, y)e(x, y)) \; : \; C(c)} \; NE,$$

$$\frac{d \; : \; C(0) \quad \begin{array}{c} (x \; : \; N, \; y \; : \; C(x)) \\ e(x, y) \; : \; C(s(x)) \end{array}}{R(0, d, (x, y)e(x, y)) \; = \; d \; : \; C(0)} \; Neq,$$

$$\frac{d \,:\, C(0) \qquad \begin{array}{c}(x \,:\, N, \quad y \,:\, C(x)) \\ e(x,y) \,:\, C(s(x)) \end{array}}{R(s(a), d, (x,y)e(x,y)) \;=\; e(a, R(a, d, (x,y)e(x,y))) \,:\, C(s(a))} \, Neq.$$

Canonical natural numbers are *zero* 0 and those of the *successor* form $s(a)$. The rule NE can be seen as the rule of the proof of a proposition $C(c)$ for arbitrary $c \,:\, N$ by *induction*, and as the rule of the definition of a function on N by *recursion*. For instance, addition and multiplication are defined as follows.

$$a + b \;=\; R(b, a, (x,y)s(y)) \,:\, N \text{ for } a, b \,:\, N,$$
$$a * b \;=\; R(b, 0, (x,y)(y + a)) \,:\, N \text{ for } a, b \,:\, N.$$

To see how this works, consider the computation of $a + b$. First compute b. If the value is 0, the value of $a + b$ is a. If the value is of the successor form $s(c)$, the value of $a + b$ is computed by computing $R(c, a, (x,y)s(y))$, that is, $a + c$, and taking the successor. This computational behaviour is exactly what is expressed by the customary pair of equations

$$\begin{cases} a + 0 = a, \\ a + s(b) = s(a + b). \end{cases}$$

The decimal notation, in which $1 = s(0) \,:\, N$, $2 = s(1) \,:\, N$, etc., will be used throughout this book.

Examples. The Boolean quantifiers

$$(\bigwedge x < n)f(x) \,:\, \text{Bool},$$
$$(\bigvee x < n)f(x) \,:\, \text{Bool},$$
$$(Most\ x < n)f(x) \,:\, \text{Bool},$$

for $n \,:\, N$, $f(x) \,:\, \text{Bool}\ (x \,:\, N)$, can be defined by recursion. The third of them is more complicated than the first two.

Natural numbers have a Boolean test of equality, that is, a function

$$\text{Eq}(x, y) \,:\, \text{Bool}\ (x \,:\, N, \ y \,:\, N),$$

whose value is True only if x and y are constructed from 0 by the same number of s operators. The recursion equations are easy to formulate, but the definition in terms of R is non-trivial.

The set of lists of elements of a set A is defined by two introduction rules,

$$\text{nil} \,:\, \text{List}(A), \qquad \frac{a \,:\, A \quad b \,:\, \text{List}(A)}{\text{cons}(a, b) \,:\, \text{List}(A)}.$$

In terms of the list elimination rule, one can define functions like append, which concatenates two lists, and rev, which reverses a list, as well as Boolean existential and universal quantifiers. If the set A has a Boolean test of equality, so does List(A), and one can define the Boolean-valued function occur, which checks whether an element occurs in a list, the function prune, which deletes repeated occurrences of an element, and the Boolean quantifier stating that most elements of a list have a given property.

Now we have considered three different ways of studying quantification over finite domains in type theory: enumerated sets, natural numbers up to a given n, and lists.

2.25   Equality propositions

The *equality proposition*, which corresponds to the identity predicate of predicate calculus, is the minimal reflexive relation in each set.

$$\frac{A \,:\, \text{set} \quad a \,:\, A \quad b \,:\, A}{I(A, a, b) \,:\, \text{set}} \, IF, \qquad \frac{a \,:\, A}{r(a) \,:\, I(A, a, a)} \, II,$$

$$\frac{a \,:\, A \quad b \,:\, A \quad c \,:\, I(A, a, b) \quad d(x) \,:\, C(x, x, r(x))}{J(a, b, c, (x)d(x)) \,:\, C(a, b, c)} \, IE,$$

$$\frac{a \,:\, A \quad d(x) \,:\, C(x, x, r(x))}{J(a, a, r(a), (x)d(x)) \,=\, d(a) \,:\, C(a, a, r(a))} \, Ieq.$$

Observe the distinction between the equality proposition $I(A, a, b)$ and the judgement $a = b : A$, which is not a proposition. The judgement $a = b : A$ can be called *definitional equality*, because it is the form in which explicit definitions, like abbreviations and computation rules of selectors are written. It is only transmitted by the rules of reflexivity, symmetry, and transitivity, and by substitutions of definitionally equals. The truth of the proposition $I(A, a, b)$ can be inferred from the definitional equality $a = b : A$, but not vice versa. We can also substitute b for a in a proposition $B(a)$ if $I(A, a, b)$ is true, and obtain an equivalent proposition $B(b)$. But $B(b)$ is not necessarily equal to $B(a)$ in the sense $B(a) = B(b) : \text{prop}$. We derive the rules

$$\frac{a \,:\, A \quad a = b \,:\, A}{I(A, a, b) \; \text{true}}, \qquad \frac{a \,:\, A \quad b \,:\, A \quad I(A, a, b) \; \text{true} \quad B(a) \; \text{true}}{B(b) \; \text{true}}$$

as follows (Figure 2.8 and Figure 2.9, respectively.)

As the latter principle is called Leibniz's law, we make the abbreviatory definition

Leibniz$(a, b, c, d) = \text{ap}(J(a, b, c, (x)(\lambda y)y), d) : B(b)$
    for $a : A$, $b : A$, $c : I(A, a, b)$, $d : B(a)$.

The current rules for the equality proposition differ from the version of type theory in Martin-Löf 1984, in which a stronger elimination rule is

$$\dfrac{A \,:\, \text{set} \quad a \,:\, A \quad x \,:\, A}{I(A,a,x) \,:\, \text{prop}} \, IF$$

1.

$$\dfrac{a = b \,:\, A \qquad \dfrac{A \,:\, \text{set} \quad a \,:\, A \quad x \,:\, A}{I(A,a,x) \,:\, \text{prop}} \, IF}{I(A,a,a) \,=\, I(A,a,b) \,:\, \text{prop}} \, subst.,1. \qquad \dfrac{a \,:\, A}{r(a) \,:\, I(A,a,a)} \, II$$

$$\dfrac{r(a) \,:\, I(A,a,b)}{} \, ext.$$

Figure 2.8

1.

$$\dfrac{a \,:\, A \quad b \,:\, A \quad c \,:\, I(A,a,b) \quad \dfrac{y \,:\, B(x)}{(\lambda y)y \,:\, B(x) \supset B(x)} \, \supset I,1.}{J(a,b,c,(x)(\lambda y)y) \,:\, B(a) \supset B(b)} \, IE \qquad d \,:\, B(a)$$

$$\dfrac{}{\text{ap}(J(a,b,c,(x)(\lambda y)y),d) \,:\, B(b)} \, \supset E$$

Figure 2.9

assumed, not fitting into the format of inductive proof; cf. Nordström *et al.* 1990, chapter 8, for details. In all other respects, the version of type theory presented in this chapter is the same as in Martin-Löf 1984.

Example. Using the equality proposition, one can define, for the elements of a function space, the properties of being an injection or a surjection. Thus it is possible to define explicitly quantifiers like *most, more, denumerably many,* and *almost all;* cf. Sundholm 1989.

2.26 Non-mathematical propositions

One might think that it is difficult to explain non-mathematical language type-theoretically, because there are no proofs outside mathematics, but only conjectures and plausible arguments. It is clear that we can make sense of an expectation of proof without the expectation ever getting fulfilled, but it might seem that we are not accustomed to speaking of proofs of non-mathematical propositions at all, so that we cannot even figure out what an expectation of one might be.

A part of this problem vanishes if you recall the distinction between proof objects and proof processes. A proof object is an object that makes a proposition true. The expectation is an expectation of a proof object. By the propositions as types principle, proof objects are elements of sets, and thus on a par with individuals in the sense of predicate calculus. Just as the proposition that

there is a prime number between 212 and 222

has as its proofs prime numbers between 212 and 222, so the proposition that

there is a railway from Moscow to Hong Kong

has as its proofs railways from Moscow to Hong Kong. No mental process is referred to in either case, but individual objects. The notion of a proof of an empirical proposition thus becomes as clear as the notion of an empirical object.

In the phenomenological tradition, where the conception of propositions as types originates, such a clearly non-mentalistic view of fulfilment was formulated by Heidegger in *Sein und Zeit*, §44. Heidegger examined Husserl's conception of truth, and ended up saying that what makes the proposition that

the picture on the wall is crooked

true is nothing more nor less than the crooked picture itself. But very often in the Husserlian tradition, and particularly in intuitionistic mathematics, it has been held that proofs are mental constructions. Martin-Löf's distinction between proof objects and proof processes, and its working demonstration in type theory, should free intuitionism from this type of mentalism.

Within analytic philosophy, which is usually committed to classical logic, rudiments of the propositions as types principle occur in various theories of 'truth makers' (cf. Mulligan *et al.* 1984). A well-known example is Davidson's 'ontology of events' (Davidson 1980, essays 6–10). According to Davidson, an event is an individual object that makes an event sentence true (op. cit., p. 117). For instance, the sentence

Amundsen flew over the North Pole

is made true by a flight made by Amundsen over the North Pole (ibid.). In type theory, we would say that the proposition expressed by the sentence is the set of flights by Amundsen over the North Pole.

But the ontology of events is just a rudiment of the propositions as types principle. It concerns verbs of one aspectual class only, and has not been developed for logically complex sentences. It assumes an untyped universe of all individuals, all kinds of events included. The event sentence is not understood as a type of events but as a predicate on the untyped universe. The sentence above is thus formalized by using existential quantification,

$$(\exists x)(Amundsen\ flew\ over\ the\ North\ Pole)(x).$$

In our analysis, a variable of the event type does not occur in the proposition itself, but in the assertion of the truth of it, as a proof object, if no constant proof object is given,

$$x : (Amundsen\ flew\ over\ the\ North\ Pole).$$

Given this interpretation of the ontology of events, we can make use of some of the analyses it provides; see Section 3.7 and Section 5.4.

With an untyped universe, there are certain difficulties in the individuation of events. For instance, is a war one event or millions of them? Type theory always considers different types of events, with equality definitions given as soon as the types are defined. Thus there is a type of wars and a type of shots. A war is just one event if seen within the type of wars, but there are millions of events of type shot in one war. (Cf. Davidson 1980, essay 8, for the problem of individuation.)

The most serious criticism against type-theoretical analysis of everyday language comes from intuitionistic thinking itself. That intuitionistic logic has not been used outside mathematics is because intuitionists themselves tend to think it is inappropriate. They either think that intuitionism is about mental constructions and the everyday world is non-mental; or, more seriously, that mathematical and logical reasoning is based on *fully presented objects*. A natural number is fully presented by its canonical expression. The structure of this expression determines it as a natural number. But there is no fully presenting expression for the continent of Africa, say. Even the longest encyclopedic text will leave an infinity of properties open, and it is a puzzling question what expression, if any, would determine Africa as a continent.

Another objection can be made against the formalization of common nouns as set expressions. To define a set is to give exhaustive introduction rules that generate its canonical elements. But man, or tree, does not admit of such rules. Hence man and tree are not sets, and cannot serve as domains of quantification in predicate calculus.

These criticisms concern classical logic as well, if endowed with model-theoretic semantics of the usual kind. That they have only arisen among intuitionists may be due to the fact that they are so careful about the intuitive meaning of the mathematical language they use. I see three ways to meet the criticism.

The first is to work with *types* rather than sets, in which case exhaustive introduction rules are not needed (cf. Chapter 8). It would not, however, solve the problem of full presentation. The second way is to develop the techniques of *approximating* full presentations of objects, like one approximates real numbers in the intuitionistic theory of choice sequences. (Cf. the definition of worlds in Section 7.2.)

The third way to justify everyday objects in type theory, and the most modest one, is to study delimited *models* of language use, 'language games'. Such a 'game' shows, in an isolated form, some particular aspect of the use of language, without any pretension to covering all aspects. It is a model of language in the sense in which theories are models of nature. In such a model, the term *man* is interpreted as some set like

$$\{Matthew, Mark, Luke, John\},$$

whose elements are fully presented by the canonical names *Matthew*, etc. (The set could of course be considerably larger, for example, a record of one million names, dates of birth, professions, hobbies.) The model does not fully present men in blood and flesh, with complete stories of life, but it is enough for the formalization of a fragment of language that does not appeal to any further structure of men. Such a 'model-theoretic' basis is assumed by Montague grammar, too. This becomes clear if its references to set theory are taken seriously: Montague's English is to be interpreted in a structure $< A, I, J, \leq, F >$ where A, I, and J are sets (Montague 1974, p. 258), and A is the set of all individuals the language speaks about. To give a concrete instance of this scheme of interpretation, you must really define A as a set in the strict mathematical sense.

2.27   Semantic explanations in type theory

The basic unit of expression in type theory is judgement. The semantic explanation of a judgement is given by stating the condition under which the judgement is justified. Thus the judgement A : set is justified if it is known what the canonical elements of A are, as well as its equal canonical elements. The judgement a : A is justified if a is either a canonical element of A, or computable into one.

From this, we get derivatively the semantics of set and element expressions. The semantics of a set expression is given by telling what its canonical elements are, that is, by giving its introduction rules. The semantics of a term for an element a of a set A is given by telling how it is computed into a canonical form. This will establish a definitional equality

$$a = b : A$$

where b is canonical. It is the *value* of a, to use computational terminology. If a is in a canonical form already, there is no other explanation than that it belongs to the definition of the set that a is its element.

Observe that the old verificationist principle, as stated by Waismann (1931), that the meaning of a sentence is its method of verification, matches this explanation if sentences are understood as non-canonical truth values, for the method of verification then is the computation that yields a canonical truth value.

For a functional expression,

$$f(x_1, \ldots, x_n) : A(x_1, \ldots, x_n) \ (x_1 : A_1, \ldots, x_n : A_n(x_1, \ldots, x_{n-1})),$$

semantics is given by telling how it is computed for arguments of canonical form.

Expressions for propositions and their proofs are explained in the same way as sets and their elements. No 'method of verification' is required for propositions; it may well be that the truth of a proposition is undecidable.

Someone who is accustomed to seeing model-theoretic interpretations of logical formalisms might think that what we have so far done in the presentation of type theory is purely syntactic. That is, no meaning has yet been given to the symbols, but only rules for manipulating them. But it should be observed that the information customarily provided by model-theoretic interpretations, about the domain and the truth conditions of various propositions, has here been given inside the formalism itself. Of course, the semantical understanding of a language speaking about empirical objects must at some point lead outside language, but this is not accomplished by adding a further linguistic level of metalanguage.

3

LOGICAL OPERATORS IN ENGLISH

In this chapter we shall look at some examples of English sentences that can be formalized as propositions of Σ, Π, and $+$ forms. No mechanical rules of formalization will be given, just general principles concerning various modes of expression. The formalizations are intended to be, as often as possible, *compositional* in the sense of Section 1.8; that is, the formalizations of smaller expressions are constituents of the formalizations of larger expressions of which those smaller expressions are parts.

Section 3.5 summarizes the sugaring rules of Ranta 1991a for expository purposes. A complete algorithm is not given, but only an informal description of the ways in which Σ and Π are expressed in English. Formal sugaring and parsing will be discussed in Chapter 9.

The expressions set and proposition, which are synonymous in type theory, will be used heuristically to categorize common noun phrases and sentences, respectively.

3.1 Quantifiers

Σ is the operator for existential quantification in type theory. Thus it corresponds to the English word *some* and to the indefinite article, like $\exists$ in predicate calculus. Π, like $\forall$ in predicate calculus, corresponds to *every*. *Quantifiers* are obtained by applying Π and Σ to sets. The quantifier $(\Sigma x : A)$ corresponds to the English quantifier phrases *some A, an A, a certain A*. The quantifier $(\Pi x : A)$ corresponds to *every A, any A, each A*. Thus we formalize

$$some\ man\ walks \text{ as } (\Sigma x : man)(x\ walks),$$
$$Bill\ owns\ a\ donkey \text{ as } (\Sigma x : donkey)(Bill\ owns\ x),$$
$$every\ man\ walks \text{ as } (\Pi x : man)(x\ walks),$$
$$a\ man\ owns\ a\ donkey \text{ as } (\Sigma x : man)(\Sigma y : donkey)(x\ owns\ y),$$
$$every\ man\ owns\ a\ donkey \text{ as } (\Pi x : man)(\Sigma y : donkey)(x\ owns\ y).$$

It is assumed in each formalization that the phrase A in $(\Sigma x : A)$ and in $(\Pi x : A)$ expresses a set, and that the phrase $---x---$ that follows expresses a proposition in the context $x : A$. These assumptions are either primitive, or reduced to simpler assumptions by analysing the phrases

further. Thus the sentence *every man owns a donkey* has the outermost
form

$$(\Pi x \; : \; man)(x \; owns \; a \; donkey),$$

where

> *man* : set,
> (*x owns a donkey*) : prop (*x* : *man*).

The propositional function assumed can be analysed further, as

$$(\Sigma y \; : \; donkey)(x \; owns \; y) \; : \; \text{prop} \; (x \; : \; man),$$

where

> *donkey* : set,
> (*x owns y*) : prop (*x* : *man*, *y* : *donkey*),

are left unanalysed. The unanalysed propositional functions are type-
theoretical counterparts of *verb patterns*. They tell how many as well as
what types of arguments verbs take. But they do not tell what the expressions formed by supplying the verbs with arguments mean: this is a matter
of further analysis of the verb patterns.

The syntax of type theory places the quantifier to the front of the propositional expression. In English sentences, quantifier phrases can be found
in the middle and in the end as well. Any of the argument places of a verb
pattern can be occupied by a quantifier phrase. In the type-theoretical formalization, the quantifier phrase is raised to the front. A variable is left to
represent it, the same variable as is bound by the quantifier.

3.2   Ordering principles

The usual procedure of formalization is to take the leftmost quantifier
phrase of the sentence first, and continue to the right. A sentence of the
form

$$-Q_1 A - -Q_2 B - - - Q_3 C - - - -$$

is then formalized as

$$(Q_1 x : A)(Q_2 y : B)(Q_3 z : C)(-x - -y - - - z - - - -).$$

In other words, the *scopes* of the quantifiers follow the *left to right order* of
their occurrences in the English sentence.

This procedure is not universally valid. There are certain quite definite
exceptions to it, as well as many less clear-cut ones. I shall mainly follow
the *ordering principles* formulated in game-theoretical semantics (see e.g.
Hintikka and Kulas 1985, pp. 15–21). Most of them are directly meaningful
in type theory, under the interpretation of games as propositions (cf. Section 4.13 below). In addition to the left to right rule, which is just a rule
of default, there is a special rule according to which the word *each* forms

a universal quantifier whose scope is wider than the scope of an existential quantifier formed by the indefinite article or by the word *some*, whatever is their left to right order in the sentence. Thus we formalize

a man loves each woman as $(\Pi x : woman)(\Sigma y : man)(y\ loves\ x)$.

Among existential quantifier words, *a certain* has a similar priority over *every*, so that we formalize

every man loves a certain woman as $(\Sigma x : woman)(\Pi y : man)(y\ loves\ x)$.

In formal languages, rules similar to ordering principles are known as *precedence rules*. Thus the term

$$2 + 3 * 5$$

is unambiguously parsed

$$(2 + (3 * 5)),$$

because of the higher precedence (= narrower scope) of $*$. Distinct operators with the same meaning can have different precedence. Take for instance the prefix k used with units of measurement. By definition, k is equal to 1000, so that

$$km = 1000m,$$

but the square operator x^2 has low precedence with respect to k and high precedence with respect to 1000:

$$km^2 = (km)^2 = 1000 * 1000(m^2) = 1000000m^2,$$

but

$$1000m^2 = 1000(m^2) = km^2/1000.$$

3.3 Separated subsets

To give an element of *A such that B*, in a form that makes explicit everything that is essential for the correctness of the judgement, you cannot just give a bare element $a : A$ of which B happens to be true, but you have to give a proof of $B(a)$ as well. Thus you indeed have to give what is needed to form an element of the set $(\Sigma x : A)B(x)$, which is the set of elements $a : A$ paired with proofs of $B(a)$. This consideration led Martin-Löf (1984, p. 53) to suggest the formalization of the set *A such that B* as $(\Sigma x : A)B(x)$.

We shall extend Martin-Löf's formalization of *such that* to a number of more idiomatic English structures consisting of a common noun modified by a relative clause, by an adjectival attribute, or by a participle. We can formalize, for instance,

man who runs as $(\Sigma x : man)(x\ runs)$,

man who owns a donkey as $(\Sigma x : man)(\Sigma y : donkey)(x\ owns\ y)$,

$$\textit{old man} \quad \text{as} \quad (\Sigma x : man)(x \text{ is old}),$$
$$\textit{running man} \quad \text{as} \quad (\Sigma x : man)(x \text{ is running}),$$
$$\textit{donkey owned by a man} \quad \text{as} \quad (\Sigma x : donkey)(\Sigma y : man)(y \text{ owns } x).$$

In this way, modified common noun phrases are logically treated as constituents. They often occur as set arguments in quantifier phrases, as in the sentence

$$\textit{every old man walks.}$$

The phrase *old man* is formalized as the set $(\Sigma x : man)(x \text{ is old})$. From this, *every* forms the quantifier

$$(\Pi x : (\Sigma x : man)(x \text{ is old})).$$

To formalize the rest of the sentence, we must now make sense of the propositional function

$$(z \text{ walks}) : \text{prop} \ (z : (\Sigma x : man)(x \text{ is old})).$$

As we probably also have the propositional function

$$(z \text{ walks}) : \text{prop} \ (z : man),$$

there will be two functions $(z \text{ walks})$, with different domains. Sooner or later we shall have to add $(z \text{ walks}) : \text{prop}$ for z of types young man, rich man, rich old man, man who owns a donkey, man who loves Mary, and so on.

To avoid this multiple categorization of the verb, there are at least three solutions. The first is not to treat modified common noun phrases as constituents, but to dissolve them like in predicate calculus, in the style

$$(\Pi x : man)((x \text{ is old}) \supset (x \text{ walks})).$$

The second alternative solution is to formalize modified common noun phrases as subsets in the sense of Nordström *et al.* 1990, chapter 18, that is, as sets $\{x : A \mid B(x)\}$, whose elements are bare elements of A, in accordance with the rules presented above, in Section 2.12,

$$\frac{a : A \quad B(a) \text{ true}}{a : \{x : A \mid B(x)\},} \qquad \frac{c : \{x : A \mid B(x)\}}{c : A}.$$

Consider now the formalization of *old man* as $\{x : man \mid (x \text{ is old})\}$. The second subset rule gives $z : man$ from $z : \{x : man \mid (x \text{ is old})\}$. We can then apply the function $(z \text{ walks}) : \text{prop} \ (z : man)$ to z, and form the proposition

$$(\Pi z : \{x : man \mid (x \text{ is old})\})(z \text{ walks}).$$

Thus we avoid the multiple categorization of the verb *walk*. But singular terms will in turn have multiple categorizations. For if John is a man and John is rich and old, then

> *John* : *man*,
> *John* : {*x* : *man* | (*x is rich*)},
> *John* : {*x* : *man* | (*x is old*)},
> *John* : {*z* : {*x* : *man* | (*x is old*)} | (*z is old*)}.

The third alternative solution preserves both modified common noun phrases as constituents, and unique types. It makes use of the possibility of restricting any function of $x : A$ into a function of the left projection $p(z) : A$ where $z : (\Sigma x : A)B(x)$. In particular, if

$$C(x) : \text{prop} \quad (x : A),$$

then

$$C(p(z)) : \text{prop} \quad (z : (\Sigma x : A)B(x)).$$

Using $(z \ walks) : \text{prop} \quad (z : man)$, we can now formalize *every old man walks* as

$$(\Pi z : (\Sigma x : man)(x \ is \ old))(p(z) \ walks).$$

This way of restricting functions can be systematized by introducing the notation

$$C_{(x)B(x)}(z) : \text{prop} \quad (z : (\Sigma x : A)B(x)), \quad \text{if } B(x) : \text{prop} \quad (x : A).$$

The new predicate is defined

$$C_{(x)B(x)}(z) = C(p(z)) : \text{prop} \quad (z : (\Sigma x : A)B(x)),$$

and the subindex $(x)B(x)$ is dropped in sugaring.

The formalization by dissolution, in the style of predicate calculus, is not compositional with respect to the modified common noun phrase *old man*, as there is no constituent of the quantified proposition that formalizes it. This style is very unnatural for such complicated sentences as

> *every man who hurts every man who hurts him hurts himself*

(Cf. Geach 1972, p. 494). It reads

$$(\Pi x : man)((\Pi y : man)((y \ hurts \ x) \supset (x \ hurts \ y)) \supset (x \ hurts \ x)).$$

By using Σ and projections, we formalize

$$(\Pi u : (\Sigma x : man)(\Pi y : \overbrace{(\Sigma z : man)(z \ hurts \ x)})(x \ hurts \ p(y)))$$
$$(p(u) \ hurts \ p(u)),$$

in which the underlined constituent formalizes the phrase *man who hurts every man who hurts him*, and the constituent with a brace above formalizes the phrase *man who hurts him*.

An element of $\{x : A \mid B(x)\}$, if understood as a bare element a of A, does not contain the information that $B(a)$ is true. An element of $(\Sigma x : A)B(x)$ yields this information as its right projection. $\{x : A \mid B(x)\}$ can thus replace $(\Sigma x : A)B(x)$ only if right projections do not matter. In the following example they do. Consider the sentence

every man who owns a donkey beats it

(cf. Geach 1962, p. 117). First take the common noun phrase *man who owns a donkey*, and formalize it as the set

$$(\Sigma x : man)(\Sigma y : donkey)(x \; owns \; y).$$

For the rest of the sentence, assume the propositional function

$$(x \; beats \; y) : prop \quad (x : man, \; y : donkey).$$

To form the universally quantified proposition with the domain

$$(\Sigma x : man)(\Sigma y : donkey)(x \; owns \; y),$$

derive a proposition from the hypothesis

$$z : (\Sigma x : man)(\Sigma y : donkey)(x \; owns \; y).$$

In virtue of the projection rules, we have

$p(z) : man,$
$q(z) : (\Sigma y : donkey)(p(z) \; owns \; y),$
$p(q(z)) : donkey,$
$q(q(z)) : (p(z) \; owns \; p(q(z))).$

The context thus provides arguments of types *man* and *donkey* for the propositional function $(x \; beats \; y)$, and Geach's sentence receives the formalization

$$(\Pi z : (\Sigma x : man)(\Sigma y : donkey)(x \; owns \; y))(p(z) \; beats \; p(q(z))).$$

Note. There is a well-known problem with *most* quantification over separated subsets. If separation is understood in the way just described, and *most* quantification in the way described in the Example of Section 2.25, the proposition

most men who own a donkey are happy

comes out true if there are ten unhappy men who own one donkey each and one happy man who owns twenty donkeys. The solution proposed by Sundholm (1989) is to define another type of *most* quantification over $(\Sigma x : A)B(x)$ in terms of the existence of an A injection, that is, an injection forgetting about the second component of the pair.

3.4 Conjunction and implication

Besides existential quantifier and subset separator, Σ functions as conjunction. Besides universal quantifier, Π functions as implication. Thus we formalize

John walks and Mary runs as $(\Sigma x : (John\ walks))(Mary\ runs)$,

if John walks Mary runs as $(\Pi x : (John\ walks))(Mary\ runs)$.

These formalizations can also be written by using the defined operators & and $\supset$, as

$(John\ walks)\&(Mary\ runs)$,
$(John\ walks) \supset (Mary\ runs)$,

respectively.

The operators & and $\supset$ do not, however, exploit the whole strength of Σ and Π. In $A\&B$, both A and B must be propositions categorically, whereas in $(\Sigma x : A)B(x)$, $B(x)$: prop may depend on $x : A$. Such a dependence results in what we shall call the *progressive conjunction*. It is abundantly manifested in natural languages.

Groenendijk and Stokhof (1991) provide a good list of examples of progressive, or, as they call them, *dynamic* structures in English. Their simplest example of progressive conjunction is the text

A man walks in the park. He whistles.

As we shall formalize texts in a different way (see Section 6.2), we replace the first example of Groenendijk and Stokhof by a sentence that has the same structure in their theory,

a man walks and he whistles.

The pronoun *he* in the latter conjunct makes a reference to what is introduced by the phrase *a man* in the former conjunct. Type-theoretically, the former conjunct is the existential proposition

$$(\Sigma x : man)(x\ walks).$$

Given a proof $z : (\Sigma x : man)(x\ walks)$, we have $p(z) : man$, to which we can apply the propositional function

$$(x\ whistles) : \text{prop} \quad (x : man)$$

and form the proposition $(p(z)\ whistles)$ to formalize the latter conjunct in the context of a proof z of the former conjunct. By combining the conjuncts with Σ, we obtain the proposition

$$(\Sigma z : (\Sigma x : man)(x\ walks))(p(z)\ whistles)$$

to formalize the sentence.

$$\frac{\dfrac{\dfrac{(x \ : \ man)}{(x \ wa.) \ : \ prop} \quad \begin{array}{c} 1. \\ x \ : \ man \end{array}}{(x \ wa.) \ : \ prop} \ s. }{(\Sigma x \ : \ man)(x \ wa.) \ : \ prop} \ \Sigma F, 1. \qquad \frac{\dfrac{(x \ : \ man)}{(x \ whi.) \ : \ prop} \qquad \dfrac{\dfrac{2.}{z \ : \ (\Sigma x \ : \ man)(x \ wa.)}}{p(z) \ : \ man} \ \Sigma E}{(p(z) \ whi.) \ : \ prop} \ s.}{(\Pi z \ : \ (\Sigma x \ : \ man)(x \ walks))(p(z) \ whistles) \ : \ prop}} \ \Pi F, 2.$$

Figure 3.1

In analogy with the progressive conjunction, we have the *progressive implication*, which uses the full strength of Π. To formalize

if a man walks he whistles,

we form the implicatum $(p(z) \ whistles)$ in the context of a variable proof of the implicans, $z \ : \ (\Sigma x \ : \ man)(x \ walks)$, and combine the two by Π formation into

$$(\Pi z \ : \ (\Sigma x \ : \ man)(x \ walks))(p(z) \ whistles).$$

Figure 3.1 shows the formation process in tree form.

Both the conjunction and the implication are composed of the propositions $(\Sigma x \ : \ man)(x \ walks)$ and $(p(z) \ whistles)$, which formalize the two sentences *a man walks* and *he whistles*, respectively. The formalizations are thus compositional with respect to the subclauses of these *if* and *and* sentences. In predicate calculus, we would have to formalize *a man walks and he whistles* as

$$(\exists x)((x \ is \ a \ man)\&(x \ walks)\&(x \ whistles)),$$

and *if a man walks he whistles* as

$$(\forall x)((x \ is \ a \ man)\&(x \ walks) \supset (x \ whistles)),$$

Neither of these propositions has a constituent formalizing the sentence *a man walks*. Nor is there any logical operator that uniformly corresponds to the indefinite article. The indefinite phrase *a man* is formalized with an existential quantifier in the former sentence, and with a universal quantifier in the latter sentence. In type theory, it is formalized as the quantifier $(\Sigma x \ : \ man)$ in both cases.

Note. Given the ordering principle

if has wider scope than *a* and *every* in the implicans, but narrower scope than *any*,

suggested by Hintikka (1979, p. 98), the sentences

if a man owns a donkey he beats it,
if any man owns a donkey he beats it,
if a man owns any donkey he beats it,
if any man owns any donkey he beats it,

are formalized

$$(\Pi z : (\Sigma x : man)(\Sigma y : donkey)(x \; owns \; y))(p(z) \; beats \; p(q(z))),$$
$$(\Pi x : man)(\Pi z : (\Sigma y : donkey)(x \; owns \; y))(x \; beats \; p(z)),$$
$$(\Pi y : donkey)(\Pi z : (\Sigma x : man)(x \; owns \; y))(p(z) \; beats \; y),$$
$$(\Pi x : man)(\Pi y : donkey) \; (\Pi z : (x \; owns \; y))(x \; beats \; y),$$

respectively. These propositions are easily proved equivalent, but they are of course distinct propositions. The compositional structure of every sentence is different, depending on whether *man* and *donkey* are existentially or universally quantified.

3.5   Sugarings of Σ and Π

English makes a distinction between sentences and common nouns roughly corresponding to the distinction between propositions and sets in classical logic. Connective words, like *if*, connect pairs of sentences, whereas quantifier words, like *every*, combine common nouns with sentences. As type theory identifies the categories of propositions and sets, the distinction between sentences and common nouns is only relevant in sugaring (cf. Section 8.11).

When the proposition $(\Pi x : A)B(x)$ is sugared into the conditional of A and $B(x)$, both A and $B(x)$ must be sugared into sentences. When it is sugared into the sentence $B(every \; A)$, in which the quantifier phrase *every A* is substituted for x in $B(x)$, A must be sugared into a common noun. In the following description of sugaring alternatives, we shall use the operators S and N to indicate sugaring into sentences and common nouns, respectively.

To propositions of Π form, only S applies, but in two alternative ways,

$$S((\Pi x : A)B(x)) \;\triangleright\; \begin{cases} if \; S(A), \; S(B(x)), & (C) \\ S(B(every \; N(A))). & (Q) \end{cases}$$

The labels C and Q stand for *connective* and *quantifier*, respectively.

Propositions of Σ form can be sugared into sentences, both in the connective and in the quantifier style, but also into common nouns modified by *relative clauses*. There are thus three possibilities, (C), (Q), and (R).

$$S((\Sigma x : A)B(x)) \;\triangleright\; \begin{cases} S(A) \; and \; S(B(x)), & (C) \\ S(B(\mathrm{INDEF}(N(A)))), & (Q) \end{cases}$$
$$N((\Sigma x : A)B(x)) \;\triangleright\; N(A) \; \mathrm{REL}(x : A, B(x)) \; S(B(\varnothing)). \quad (R)$$

Any common noun can be turned into a sentence,

$$S(A) \;\triangleright\; there \; is \; \mathrm{INDEF}(N(A)).$$

The principles (C), (Q), and (R) for sugaring Σ and Π produce a great many English readings of complex type-theoretical propositions. For instance, to see how to sugar

$$(\Pi z : (\Sigma x : man)(\Sigma y : donkey)(x \ owns \ y))(p(z) \ beats \ p(q(z))),$$

start with Π and get the two alternatives

if $S((\Sigma x : man)(\Sigma y : donkey)(x \ owns \ y))$, $S((p(z) \ beats \ p(q(z))))$,
beat$(p(every \ N((\Sigma x : man)(\Sigma y : donkey)(x \ owns \ y))), p(q(z)))$,

by (C) and (Q), respectively. The C alternative leads to 3×3 different sugarings of the sentence, resulting from the alternative ways of sugaring the two Σ's of the implicans. The notation $(P, \dots, P')$ indicates the sugaring principles applied to the quantifiers from left to right.

there is a man and there is a donkey and he owns it (C, C),
there is a man and he owns a donkey (C, Q),
there is a man and there is a donkey that he owns (C, R),
there is a donkey and a man owns it (Q, C),
a man owns a donkey (Q, Q),
there is a donkey that a man owns (Q, R),
there is a man such that there is a donkey and he owns it (R, C),
there is a man who owns a donkey (R, Q),
there is a man such that there is a donkey that he owns (R, R).

One of the resulting sentences has been paid explicit attention to, the (C, Q, Q) one,

if a man owns a donkey he beats it,

in Groenendijk and Stokhof 1991, section 2.1.

Starting with (Q) gives as many sugarings as there are common nouns resulting from $(\Sigma x : man)(\Sigma y : donkey)(x \ owns \ y)$. The principle (R) is the only one that produces common nouns from Σ propositions. It requires *man* to be sugared into a noun. The rest can be sugared into a sentence in three ways. Thus we get three complex common nouns,

man such that there is a donkey and he owns it (R, C),
man who owns a donkey (R, Q),
man such that there is a donkey that he owns (R, R).

Of the resulting sentences, the (Q, R, Q) one

every man who owns a donkey beats it,

has been discussed in literature, with minor variations since Geach (1962), for example, by Hintikka and Carlson (1979), and by Kamp (1981).

We have now generated $3 \times 3 + 3 = 12$ English sentences not only equivalent but propositionally equal to the original donkey sentence. The number can be multiplied in at least two ways. One can use other quantifier words than *every* and *a*, for example, *any*, *each*, *some*, *a certain*. And one can choose definite noun phrases or modified definite phrases instead of pronouns, for example, *the man* instead of *he*, *the donkey* or *the donkey that he owns* instead of *it* (cf. Section 4.7). An early Prolog implementation of sugaring (earlier than the one reported in Mäenpää and Ranta 1990) produced 1128 alternatives.

The sugaring procedure of Mäenpää and Ranta 1990 and of Ranta 1991a is very much like the declarative statement of sugaring possibilities just presented. Various English quantifier and connective words are given as alternative sugarings of Σ and Π. Similarly, various anaphoric expressions are given as alternative sugarings of singular terms. The procedure to be investigated in Chapter 8 and Chapter 9 introduces these words directly in type theory, by explicit definitions like

$(every\, x\, :\, A)B(x)\, =\, (\Pi x\, :\, A)B(x)\, :\, \text{prop},$
if $A\, :\, \text{set},\, B(x)\, :\, \text{prop}\,\, (x\, :\, A),$
$(\text{Indef}\, x\, :\, A)B(x)\, =\, (\Sigma x\, :\, A)B(x)\, :\, \text{prop},$
if $A\, :\, \text{set},\, B(x)\, :\, \text{prop}\,\, (x\, :\, A),$
$(and\, x\, :\, A)B(x)\, =\, (\Sigma x\, :\, A)B(x)\, :\, \text{prop},$
if $A\, :\, \text{prop},\, B(x)\, :\, \text{prop}\,\, (x\, :\, A),$
$There(A)\, =\, A\, :\, \text{prop},\quad \text{if } A\, :\, \text{set},$
$\text{Pron}(A, a)\, =\, a\, :\, A,\quad \text{if } A\, :\, \text{set},\, a\, :\, A,$
$the(A, a)\, =\, a\, :\, A,\quad \text{if } A\, :\, \text{set},\, a\, :\, A.$

Sugaring then becomes deterministic. Different English expressions for the same proposition are obtained from different type-theoretical expressions for that proposition.

3.6 Nominalization

In the previous section, we employed the operation of prefixing *there is* and the indefinite article to a common noun to obtain a sentence. In the other direction, one would need a *nominalization* procedure that takes sentences into common nouns, but there does not seem to be any such procedure as general as *there is*. Sometimes the gerund can be used,

$N((\Sigma x\, :\, donkey)(John\ owns\ x))\ \triangleright\ owning\ of\ a\ donkey\ by\ John,$

sometimes a verbal noun,

$N(train\ 55\ departs)\ \triangleright\ departure\ of\ train\ 55,$
$N(John\ criticizes\ the\ book)\ \triangleright\ criticism\ of\ the\ book\ by\ John,$
$N(John\ refuses\ the\ job)\ \triangleright\ refusal\ of\ the\ job\ by\ John.$

Observe that the simpler nominal phrases

John's owning a donkey,
John's refusal of the job,

etc., cannot be combined with quantifier words like the indefinite article. They behave like singular terms, and will be analysed as anaphoric expressions in Section 4.5. (Chomsky 1970, pp. 187–188, points out that even the simple gerund form cannot always be formed.)

It is always possible to express a type-theoretical proposition by using a sentence. If the simplest sugaring is a common noun phrase, the prefix *there is* can be used to turn it into a sentence. But if there is no effective nominalization procedure, it is not always possible to express a proposition by a common noun. For the sugaring of Σ and Π, this means that the connectives (C) can always be used, but the quantifiers (Q) cannot.

3.7   Reference to proofs of Π propositions

Groenendijk and Stokhof (1991) use the term *internally dynamic* for what we have been calling progressive connectives. Just like here, conjunction and implication are internally dynamic for them. They explain the internal dynamicity of conjunction in their *dynamic predicate logic* by giving it a 'power to pass on variable bindings' from the former conjunct to the latter. Implication exercises this power from the implicans to the implicatum (op. cit., section 2.3). Thus the variable x is bound in $(x \; whistles)$ in the following propositions of dynamic logic.

$(\exists x)((x \; is \; a \; man)\&(x \; walks))\&(x \; whistles)$,
$(\exists x)((x \; is \; a \; man)\&(x \; walks)) \supset (x \; whistles)$.

In this way, they provide compositional formalizations to the two sentences discussed in Section 3.4.

In the dynamic logic of Groenendijk and Stokhof, conjunction and existential quantification are, moreover, *externally dynamic*, which means that bindings can be passed on from them to further propositions. This power of theirs is needed in the two examples just cited, in addition to the internal dynamicity of conjunction and implication. Implication and universal quantification are not, however, externally dynamic. Thus the variable x is not bound in the subformula $(x \; whistles)$ in

$(\forall x)((x \; is \; a \; man) \supset (x \; walks))\&(x \; whistles)$,
$(\forall x)((x \; is \; a \; man) \supset (x \; walks)) \supset (x \; whistles)$,

despite the internal dynamicity of & and $\supset$ in them. By this stipulation, Groenendijk and Stokhof explain why the pronoun *he* in the sentences

every man walks and he whistles,
if every man walks he whistles,

does not refer to anything introduced earlier in the sentences (cf. op. cit., section 2.5). An analogous explanation is given to the failure of reference by *it* in

if Pedro owns every donkey he beats it,

as contrasted to the unsuccessful reference in

if Pedro owns a donkey he beats it.

Groenendijk and Stokhof inherit their analysis from Kamp (1981, pp. 296–297), who observes the same contrast and implements it in his discourse representation rules: *a donkey* introduces a discourse referent but *every donkey* does not.

Type-theoretically, the implicans of the former sentence is

$$(\Pi x\ :\ donkey)(Pedro\ owns\ x),$$

whose proof does not yield any donkey, but just a function on the set of donkeys. Hence our analysis, too, results in the failure of anaphoric reference in this sentence.

The type-theoretical explanation of anaphora does not introduce internal and external dynamicity as independent notions, but they can be explained as follows. A two-place connective is *internally dynamic* if the second argument may depend on the proof of the first, that is, if the arguments are not just

$$A\ :\ \text{prop},\ B\ :\ \text{prop}$$

but

$$A\ :\ \text{prop},\ B(x)\ :\ \text{prop}\ (x\ :\ A).$$

We have been calling such connectives progressive, instead of internally dynamic. An operator is *externally dynamic* if it 'introduces a discourse referent', that is, if it makes sense to consider the proofs of the propositions formed by it. In virtue of the propositions as types principle,

all proposition-forming operators are externally dynamic.

In particular, the quantifier $(\Pi z\ :\ (\Pi x\ :\ donkey)(Pedro\ owns\ x))$ exists, even if it cannot be prefixed to *Pedro beats it* in such a way that *it* is interpreted as a function of z. But in the sentence

if Pedro owns every donkey he likes it,

it is natural to understand *it* as referring to the proof of the proposition that Pedro owns every donkey, that is, to what makes it true that Pedro owns every donkey, to his owning every donkey. We can then formalize the sentence as the proposition

$$(\Pi z\ :\ (\Pi x\ :\ donkey)(Pedro\ owns\ x))(Pedro\ likes\ z),$$

which employs the propositional function

$$(x\ likes_A\ y)\ :\ \text{prop}\ (x\ :\ man,\ y\ :\ A),$$

where A can be any proposition of suitable kind. The subindex A is omitted by the sugaring convention explained in Section 2.5.

A better-known example, of the kind studied by Barwise (1981), is

John broke every bottle and Bill saw it,

formalized

$$(\Sigma z : (\Pi x : bottle)(John\ broke\ x))(Bill\ saw\ z).$$

The formalization employs the propositional function

$$(x\ saw_A\ y) : prop\ (x : man,\ y : A),$$

where A is any set whose elements, in other words, any proposition whose proof objects, can be seen. Such proofs are *scenes* in Barwise's terminology (see Barwise 1981, p. 390).

But the most natural instances of the 'external dynamicity' of the universal quantifier are those in which the function $f : (\Pi x : A)B(x)$ is provided with an argument $a : A$, and reference is made to $\mathrm{ap}(f, a) : B(a)$. In the sentence

if you give every child a present some child will open it,

the phrase *a present* occurs in the scope of the universal quantifier *every child*, and thus fails to bind any variable in the implicans, according to the dynamic logic of Groenendijk and Stokhof. But the English sentence does have an interpretation in which the pronoun *it* refers to the present given to the child introduced by the phrase *some child*.

In type-theoretical formalization, we find the implicans introducing

$$z : (\Pi x : child)(\Sigma y : present)(you\ give\ x\ y).$$

The implicatum opens with the existential quantifier $(\Sigma u : child)$. Applying the function z to the argument u, we get, by Π elimination,

$$\mathrm{ap}(z, u) : (\Sigma y : present)(you\ give\ u\ y),$$

whence by left projection,

$$p(\mathrm{ap}(z, u)) : present.$$

Of this present, it is also known that you give it to the child u, because by right projection,

$$q(\mathrm{ap}(z, u)) : (you\ give\ u\ p(\mathrm{ap}(z, u))).$$

Thus it provides the searched-for interpretation for *it* in the latter conjunct. The whole sentence gets formalized

$$(\Pi z : (\Pi x : child)(\Sigma y : present)(you\ give\ x\ y))$$
$$(\Sigma u : child)(u\ will\ open\ p(\mathrm{ap}(z, u))).$$

Sentences of this type have been studied in game-theoretical semantics (see Hintikka and Carlson 1979, p. 71). The dynamic predicate calculus of Groenendijk and Stokhof is not able to deal with them, fundamentally because universal quantification is not treated as externally dynamic. The discourse representation theory of Kamp (1981) fails as well, for analogous reasons (cf. Section 4.13).

Example. The only way to interpret the text

> *Every player chooses a pawn. He puts it on square one.*

mentioned as problematic by Groenendijk and Stokhof is by treating the pronoun *he* as an abbreviation of *every player*. The pronoun *it* can then be interpreted as the pawn chosen by the player, so that the second sentence is paraphrased

> *Every player puts the pawn he has chosen on square one.*

The pawn is given as the application of the function introduced by the first sentence to the variable bound by the quantifier *every player* that opens the second sentence.

3.8 Disjunction

There is no progressive strengthening of disjunction in type theory. Nor does there seem to be in English, at least if tested by the familiar pattern,

> *Pedro owns a donkey and he beats it,*
> *if Pedro owns a donkey he beats it,*
> *Pedro owns a donkey or he beats it.*

The pronoun *it* in the third sentence, unlike in the first two sentences, cannot be understood as making reference to a donkey introduced in *Pedro owns a donkey*. The sentence can at most be formalized as

$$(\Sigma x : donkey)((Pedro\ owns\ x) \vee (Pedro\ beats\ x)),$$

which does not treat *Pedro owns a donkey* as a constituent, and maybe as

$$(\Sigma x : donkey)(Pedro\ owns\ x) \vee (\Sigma x : donkey)(Pedro\ beats\ x),$$

according to which *it* does not refer to anything introduced by the first disjunct.

We here agree with Groenendijk and Stokhof (1991, section 2.5), who do not see disjunction as internally dynamic. They also conclude that it is not externally dynamic. But later on, in section 4.3, they introduce another disjunction, called program disjunction, which is externally dynamic, to account for the sentence

> *if a professor or an assistant professor attends the meeting of the university board, then he reports to the faculty.*

To show that the ordinary type-theoretical disjunction works here as well, consider a simpler sentence having the same structure,

> *if Pedro owns a donkey or Bill owns a donkey, John takes care of it.*

The implicans is of the form

$$(\Sigma x \; : \; donkey)(Pedro \; owns \; x) \vee (\Sigma x \; : \; donkey)(Bill \; owns \; x),$$

and the implicatum employs the propositional function

$$(x \; takes \; care \; of \; y) \; : \; prop \; (x \; : \; man, \; y \; : \; donkey).$$

Given a proof z of the implicans, a donkey can be derived as follows, by making use of $\vee$ elimination. Assume

$$u \; : \; (\Sigma x \; : \; donkey)(Pedro \; owns \; x).$$

Then $p(u) \; : \; donkey$. Next assume

$$v \; : \; (\Sigma x \; : \; donkey)(Bill \; owns \; x).$$

Then $p(v) \; : \; donkey$. Discharge the assumptions by forming

$$D(z, (u)p(u), (v)p(v)) \; : \; donkey.$$

The sentence can now be formalized

$$(\Pi z : (\Sigma x : donkey)(Pedro \; owns \; x) \vee (\Sigma x : donkey)(Bill \; owns \; x))$$
$$(John \; takes \; care \; of \; D(z, (u)p(u), (v)p(v))).$$

Note. Of the donkey $D(z, (x)p(x), (y)p(y))$, it can be proved that Pedro owns it or Bill owns it. But this fact is much easier to prove if a donkey is derived in an alternative way, by first proving

$$(\Sigma x \; : \; donkey)((Pedro \; owns \; x) \vee (Bill \; owns \; x)).$$

3.9   Negation

Negation is defined as the implication of the absurdity, so that $\sim A$ is equal to $A \supset \bot$, which in turn is equal to $(\Pi x \; : \; A)\bot$. There is no room for internal dynamicity in negation, as $\bot$ is a constant proposition. External dynamicity is found in sentences like

if you don't salute the colonel will see it,

which is formalized

$$(\Pi z \; : \; \sim (you \; salute))(the \; colonel \; will \; see \; z).$$

Groenendijk and Stokhof (1991, section 5.1) would like to find external dynamicity in the double-negated sentence

it is not true that John doesn't own a car; it is in front of his house.

Type-theoretically, it is possible to interpret *it* as the car introduced in the first sentence, if the double-negated proposition is *decidable*, that is, if there is a proof of the corresponding instance of the excluded middle,

$$c \; : \; ((\Sigma x \; : \; car)(John \; owns \; x) \vee \sim (\Sigma x \; : \; car)(John \; owns \; x)).$$

For together with

$$z : \sim \sim (\Sigma x : car)(John\ owns\ x),$$

c yields a proof of $(\Sigma x : car)(John\ owns\ x)$, whence a car as the left projection. To see this, assume

$$y : \sim (\Sigma x : car)(John\ owns\ x).$$

Then $\mathrm{ap}(z, y) : \bot$, whence by $\bot$ elimination,

$$\mathrm{case}_\bot (\mathrm{ap}(z, y)) : (\Sigma x : car)(John\ owns\ x).$$

Disjunction elimination gives

$$D(c, (x)x, (y)\mathrm{case}_\bot (\mathrm{ap}(z, y))) : (\Sigma x : car)(John\ owns\ x).$$

From this, you get a car by left projection,

$$p(D(c, (x)x, (y)\mathrm{case}_\bot (\mathrm{ap}(z, y)))) : car.$$

The whole sentence can now be formalized as the progressive conjunction

$$(\Sigma z : \sim \sim (\Sigma x : car)(John\ owns\ x))$$
$$(p(D(c, (x)x, (y)\mathrm{case}_\bot (\mathrm{ap}(z, y))))) \text{ is in front of John's house}),$$

which depends on the proof c of the proposition that either John owns a car or he does not own one.

4

ANAPHORIC EXPRESSIONS

Many of the sentences formalized in the previous chapter contain pronouns, like *he* and *it*. This chapter will focus on the formalization of pronouns and, more generally, of *anaphoric expressions*, expressions interpreted in the context created by the foregoing text. They include, in addition to pronouns, definite noun phrases, like *the man*, and modified definite phrases, like *the rich man*, but also the zero sign, that is, ellipsis. All these expressions are introduced by type-theoretical rules followed by sugaring procedures. Thus we follow the new strategy of sugaring discussed at the end of Section 3.6, deriving different anaphoric expressions with the same interpretation from different but definitionally equal type-theoretical expressions.

Anaphoric expressions also function as *indexical expressions* in the general sense, that is, as expressions that are understood in a context. The context need not be created by text alone, but also by information acquired otherwise.

4.1 A pronoun may refer to any object of appropriate type

In the sentence

if John walks he talks,

it is easy to make sense of *he*, provided we have made sense of *John*. For *he* occurs here as a singular term equal to *John* in meaning. But if we simultaneously consider the sentence

if Bill walks he talks,

we must admit that *he* functions, after all, in a way different from *John*. In the latter sentence, *he* is used as equal to *Bill*, which would be quite unnatural for the word *John*. *John* would normally be used for John only, and *Bill* for Bill, but

he can be used for referring to any man.

This principle is our first observation about the functioning of the word *he*. Analogous observations can be made about a variety of expressions, for example,

> *she* can be used for any woman,
> *the man* can be used for any man,
> *the rich man* can be used for any rich man,
> *the man who owns a donkey* can be used for any man who owns a donkey,
> *it* can be used for any donkey, city, natural number, etc.

The precise reference of each of these expressions varies from context to context. Just like *he* is used now for John and now for Bill, so *the rich man* is used now for Croesus, now for Rockefeller. When they are interpreted in the light of the previous text, they are called *anaphoric expressions*. As a rule,

> an anaphoric expression can be used for referring to any individual of appropriate type.

In the model-theoretic approach we have chosen to take (cf. Section 2.26), types of individuals are sets. The type of a singular term is the set whose element the term denotes. As *John* : *man*, the type of the term *John* is *man*. As $0 : N$, the type of the term 0 is N. The type of the term $(0,0)$ is $(\Sigma x : N)N$. This terminology is also used for variables in the context in which they have been introduced, so that in the context

$$x : N, \; y : I(N, x, x * x)$$

the type of x is N, and the type of y is $I(N, x, x * x)$.

4.2   The pronominalization rule

If a fixed interpretation is given to an anaphoric expression, it can be categorized as a singular term, for example,

> $he : man$,
> $he = John : man$.

But if we want to give anaphoric expressions the generality over contexts that they obviously have, we must make their dependence on context explicit. For instance, *he* can be used for any man given in context. Put differently, given any man a, *he* can be used for a. But the use of *he* then depends on the man a, in two ways. First, *that* it can be used is only because the man a is given. Second, *what* it is used for is the man a. Hence the pronoun *he* is governed by a pair of rules, which we shall call *pronominalization rules*. They introduce the pronoun *he* as the identity mapping on the set *man*.

$$\frac{a \; : \; man}{\begin{cases} he(a) \; : \; man, \\ he(a) \; = \; a \; : \; man \end{cases}}.$$

We shall follow the convention of compressing a rule that introduces a new constant and the rule that defines the constant into one rule with two conclusions from the same premises. The rule above thus abbreviates the rule pair

$$\frac{a \,:\, man}{he(a) \,:\, man}, \qquad \frac{a \,:\, man}{he(a) \,=\, a \,:\, man}.$$

The pronominalization rules do not yet tell how, in the English text, the argument a can be dropped and the bare pronoun he can be used. They just state a minimal condition of the use of the pronoun: there must be a man given to which the pronoun refers. They correspond to what is called the *condition of existence* in game-theoretical semantics, and distinguished from the *condition of uniqueness*, which says that there must not be more that one man given; cf. Hintikka and Kulas 1985, p. 90. We shall separate the two conditions even more, not treating uniqueness as a type-theoretical rule at all.

The pronominalization rules are type-theoretical rules used in the formation of type-theoretical expressions. In sugaring, the term $he(a)$ produces the pronoun he. In formalization, one tries to find, conversely, a man given in context to provide the pronoun he with the necessary argument; in other words, to provide an *interpretation* for the pronoun.

For instance, when we formalize the sentence

if a man walks he talks,

we first formalize the sentence *a man walks* as

$$(\Sigma x \,:\, man)(x \,\, walks),$$

and then consider the sentence *he talks* in the context

$$z \,:\, (\Sigma x \,:\, man)(x \,\, walks).$$

In this context, we derive $p(z) \,:\, man$. Now we have found an argument for the function he; in other words, an interpretation of the pronoun he. We can form the term $he(p(z)) \,:\, man$, and then the proposition

$$(\Pi z \,:\, (\Sigma x \,:\, man)(x \,\, walks))(he(p(z)) \,\, talks)$$

to formalize the sentence. As he is the identity mapping, this proposition is equal to the proposition

$$(\Pi z \,:\, (\Sigma x \,:\, man)(x \,\, walks))(p(z) \,\, talks).$$

In effect, the principle that he can be used for any man has now been generalized to the principle that

he can be used for any man given in context,

where the word context is used in the technical sense of type theory. Just like any rules of type theory, the pronominalization rules can be used in an arbitrary context. To make explicit the relativization of the rules above to context, we may write

$$\frac{a(x_1,\ldots,x_n) \,:\, man \;\; (x_1 \,:\, A_1, \;\ldots, \; x_n \,:\, A_n(x_1,\ldots,x_{n-1}))}{\begin{cases} he(a(x_1,\ldots,x_n)) \,:\, man \;\; (x_1 \,:\, A_1, \;\ldots, \; x_n \,:\, A_n(x_1,\ldots,x_{n-1})), \\ he(a(x_1,\ldots,x_n)) \,=\, a(x_1,\ldots,x_n) \,:\, man \end{cases}}.$$
$$(x_1 \,:\, A_1, \;\ldots, \; x_n \,:\, A_n(x_1,\ldots,x_{n-1}))$$

But this rule need not be formulated separately, as it follows from the general principles concerning type-theoretical rules.

In the formalization of English, the context relevant for a pronoun is revealed by the type-theoretical analysis of the foregoing text. For an individual given in context, there need not be any constant English expression like *John*. In the sentence just discussed, there indeed was no constant expression that could have been used instead of *he*. The interpretation was constructed from the variable z.

Generalizing from the pronoun *he*, we can now formulate the pronominalization rules for an arbitrary set A,

$$\frac{A \,:\, set \;\; a \,:\, A}{\begin{cases} \mathrm{Pron}(A,a) \,:\, A, \\ \mathrm{Pron}(A,a) \,=\, a \,:\, A \end{cases}}.$$

How $\mathrm{Pron}(A,a)$ is written in English depends on A. We introduce the morphological operator $\mathrm{PRO}(A)$ for turning the common noun A into a pronoun. Thus we get sugarings like

$\mathrm{Pron}(man,a) \;\triangleright\; \mathrm{PRO}(man) \;\triangleright\; he$,
$\mathrm{Pron}(woman,a) \;\triangleright\; \mathrm{PRO}(woman) \;\triangleright\; she$,
$\mathrm{Pron}(donkey,a) \;\triangleright\; \mathrm{PRO}(donkey) \;\triangleright\; it$,
$\mathrm{Pron}(city,a) \;\triangleright\; \mathrm{PRO}(city) \;\triangleright\; it$.

Our above use of $he(a)$ instead of $\mathrm{Pron}(man,a)$ does not, strictly speaking, conform to this general pattern, because *he* also results from $\mathrm{Pron}(boy,a)$, $\mathrm{Pron}(king,a)$, etc. The sugaring of $\mathrm{Pron}(A,a)$ does not only delete the individual argument a, but the set argument A, too. To interpret a pronoun you generally have to find out the exact type of the individual referred to.

The principle that a pronoun may be used for any individual of appropriate type, and the corresponding treatment of pronouns as identity mappings whose arguments are sugared away, is a very simple and naive explanation of pronouns. It can hardly be found in contemporary linguistic theories, and it would hardly be very powerful without the type-theoretical notion of context and the propositions as types principle. But in the programming language ML, we find a similar use of the identifier *it*, governed by the principle that

it denotes the value of the latest value declaration, of whatever type.

The pronoun *it* thus functions as a polymorphic identity mapping with the argument sugared away. (Cf. Wikström 1987.) Observe that ML has been designed for mathematics, so that *it* is the pronoun of every type considered. The interpretation of *it* is the value of the latest value declaration; no conditions of uniqueness are needed.

4.3 Definite noun phrases

In analogy with the pronominalization rule, we formulate a pair of rules for the formation of *definite noun phrases*,

$$\frac{A : set \quad a : A}{\left\{ \begin{array}{l} the(A,a) \; : \; A, \\ the(A,a) \; = \; a \; : \; A \end{array} \right.}.$$

The following sugaring rule is valid for the cases to be discussed here, in which A can always be sugared into a common noun.

$$the(A,a) \; \triangleright \; the \; A.$$

As far as the condition of existence is concerned, pronouns and definite noun phrases function in the same way, as expressions for individuals given in context. The difference between them, due to sugaring, is that pronouns are less specific. The pronoun *it* gives less information than any of the definite noun phrases *the city, the village, the donkey, the cat.* The specifications made by the latter so to say neutralize in the pronoun *it*, which matches the types of them all. The use of a pronoun is thus more likely to violate the *principle of uniqueness*, which says that

an anaphoric expression must have a unique interpretation in the context in which it is used.

The principle of uniqueness rules out, for instance, the use of the pronoun *it* in a context where both a donkey and a cat are given, because both $\text{Pron}(donkey, a) \; \triangleright \; it$ and $\text{Pron}(cat, b) \; \triangleright \; it$. The interpretation of *it* is then not unique. But *the donkey* and *the cat* are distinct expressions, and their use does not violate uniqueness, as far as only one donkey and one cat are given.

For instance, the sentence

if Pedro owns a donkey and a cat he beats it

violates the principle of uniqueness, because both a donkey and a cat are given in the context of the implicans. But the sentence

if Pedro owns a donkey and a cat he beats the donkey

is all right.

4.4 Modified definite phrases

The sentence

> *Pedro owns a donkey and Bill owns a donkey*

creates the context

$$z \,:\, (\Sigma x \,:\, donkey)(Pedro\ owns\ x)\&(\Sigma y \,:\, donkey)(Bill\ owns\ y).$$

In this context, two donkeys, $p(p(z))$ and $p(q(z))$, are given. Even the use of the definite noun phrase *the donkey* thus violates the principle of uniqueness. But it is possible to refer uniquely to either of the donkeys by making use of further information given about it. The context of the previous sentence does not only give the two donkeys, but also the proofs

$q(p(z)) \,:\, (Pedro\ owns\ p(p(z)))$,
$q(q(z)) \,:\, (Bill\ owns\ p(q(z)))$.

As only one donkey is given together with the information that Pedro owns it, it is possible to refer uniquely to it by the phrase

> *the donkey that Pedro owns.*

The general structure we shall employ to make use of pieces of further information is the *modified definite phrase* formed in accordance with the rule

$$\frac{(x \,:\, A) \qquad\qquad\qquad\qquad\qquad}{A \,:\, \mathrm{set} \quad B(x) \,:\, \mathrm{prop} \quad a \,:\, A \quad b \,:\, B(a)}{\begin{cases} \mathrm{Mod}(A, (x)B(x), a, b) \,:\, A, \\ \mathrm{Mod}(A, (x)B(x), a, b) = a \,:\, A \end{cases}}.$$

The variable x gets bound in $B(x)$. To provide the arguments of the Mod phrase, the context has to give not only an element $a \,:\, A$, but also a piece of further information, a proof $b \,:\, B(a)$, although the interpretation of the Mod term is a alone.

The uniformly applicable way of sugaring Mod terms into modified definite phrases is

$$\mathrm{Mod}(A, (x)B(x), a, b) \;\triangleright\; the\ A\ such\ that\ B(x).$$

But there are as many other ways as in the sugaring of $(\Sigma x \,:\, A)B(x)$ into modified common nouns. The modifier $B(x)$ can be a relative clause, a participle, or an adjective. For instance,

$\mathrm{Mod}(man, (x)(x\ is\ old), a, b) \;\triangleright\; the\ old\ man$,
$\mathrm{Mod}(donkey, (x)(Pedro\ owns\ x), a, b)$
$\qquad \triangleright\; \begin{cases} the\ donkey\ that\ Pedro\ owns, \\ the\ donkey\ owned\ by\ Pedro. \end{cases}$

To make sugaring deterministic in the formal grammar, we can introduce variants of Mod, like AdjMod, RelMod, PartMod; cf. Section 8.9.

In the context created by our example sentence, the term *the donkey that Pedro owns* results uniquely from

$$\text{Mod}(donkey, (x)(Pedro\ owns\ x), p(p(z)), q(p(z))),$$

and refers *a fortiori* uniquely to $p(p(z))$.

For unique reference by $\text{Mod}(A, (x)B(x), a, b)$, it is not required that b must be unique. In a context in which Pedro owns two donkeys and John only owns a cat, *the man who owns a donkey* refers uniquely to Pedro.

Notice that $\text{Mod}(A, (x)B(x), a, b)$ is not equal to

$$the((\Sigma x\ :\ A)B(x), (a, b)),$$

despite their homonymous sugarings. The former term is of type A, the latter of type $(\Sigma x\ :\ A)B(x)$.

4.5   Some uses of the genitive

There is one more natural reading for the modified phrase

$$\text{Mod}(donkey, (x)(Pedro\ owns\ x), a, b),$$

the genitival phrase

Pedro's donkey.

In general, a genitival construction of the form *a's B* may function as a phrase referring to an element b of B, given some appropriate relation between a and b. Such a relation obtains whenever a *has* b. This is not only the case when a owns b; as Aristotle observed,

> 'To have' has a good many meanings. We use it of habits, dispositions and also of all other qualities. Thus we are said to 'have' virtue, to 'have' this or that piece of knowledge. And then it is used of a quantity, such as the height a man has. So it is that we say that a man 'has' a stature of three or four cubits. Again, it is used of apparel; a man 'has' a cloak or a tunic. Moreover, we use it of things that we 'have' on some part of the body, a ring on the finger, for instance. We employ it of parts of the body; a man 'has' a hand or a foot. ... Once more, we use 'have' of a property, men 'having' houses or fields.
> People say that a man 'has' a wife and a wife, in like manner, a husband. This meaning is very far-fetched. (*Cat.* 15b18–33).

There are at least as many meanings of the genitive. Thus we can use

John's virtue for a virtue that John has,
John's knowledge for anything that John knows,
John's height for the height of John,
John's tunic for a tunic John is wearing,
John's hand for either of the two hands of John,

John's house for a house John owns, or lives in,
John's wife for a woman John is married to.

We introduce the *anaphoric genitive* by the following rule.

$$\frac{(x\,:\,A,\ y\,:\,B)}{A\,:\,\text{set}\quad B\,:\,\text{set}\quad C(x,y)\,:\,\text{prop}\quad a\,:\,A\quad b\,:\,B\quad c\,:\,C(a,b)}$$
$$\left\{\begin{array}{l} \text{Gen}(A,B,(x,y)C(x,y),a,b,c)\,:\,B, \\ \text{Gen}(A,B,(x,y)C(x,y),a,b,c)\,=\,b\,:\,B \end{array}\right.$$

The variables x and y get bound in $C(x,y)$. The sugaring of the Gen phrase deletes all arguments except a and B, and forms the morphological genitive of the two,

$$\text{Gen}(A,B,(x,y)C(x,y),a,b,c)\ \triangleright\ \text{GEN}(a,B),$$

which is either *a's B* or *the B of a*, depending on a. For instance,

Gen(*man, donkey,* $(x,y)(x$ *owns* $y), Pedro, b, c)$
  $\triangleright$ *Pedro's donkey,*
Gen(*castle, ghost,* $(x,y)(y$ *haunts* $x), Canterville, b, c)$
  $\triangleright$ *the ghost of Canterville.*

The genitive rule says that

the phrase *a's B* may be used for any individual b of type B standing in some appropriate relation C to the individual a of type A.

An appropriate relation C is a propositional function

$$C(x,y)\,:\,\text{prop}\quad (x\,:\,A,\ y\,:\,B).$$

Typically, $C(a,b)$ may be expressed *a has b*. The explicit grammatical representation of the genitival phrase must indicate this relation, as well as a proof that it holds, even if they are not visible in the genitival phrase itself. This means, furthermore, that Gen phrases are less specific than Mod phrases. Thus *John's donkey* is ambiguous between *the donkey that John owns* and *the donkey that John is riding on*.

The uses of the genitive are not exhausted by what arises from uses of *have*. Phrases like *Bill's jump* and *the departure of train 55* do not involve any relation of the subject to anything, but just an action, which is introduced by an intransitive verb. The general structure here is the *subjective genitive*, for which we have the rule

$$\frac{(x\,:\,A)}{A\,:\,\text{set}\quad B(x)\,:\,\text{prop}\quad a\,:\,A\quad b\,:\,B(a)}$$
$$\left\{\begin{array}{l} \text{Gensubj}(A,(x)B(x),a,b)\,:\,B(a), \\ \text{Gensubj}(A,(x)B(x),a,b)\,=\,b\,:\,B(a) \end{array}\right.$$

Sugaring produces the morphological genitive of a and a suitable verbal noun corresponding to $B(x)$. For instance,

Gensubj($man, (x)(x\ jumps), Bill, b$) ▷ *Bill's jump.*

The sentence

if Bill jumps John will see Bill's jump

gets formalized

($\Pi z\ :\ (Bill\ jumps))(John\ will\ see$ Gensubj($man, (x)(x\ jumps), Bill, z$)).

Observe that this explanation of the subjective genitive relies on the propositions as types principle. The subjective genitive phrase *Bill's jump* refers to a proof of the proposition that Bill jumps.

The phrase

the refusal of the job by John

can be derived as the definite form of the verbal noun *refusal of the job by John*. But the phrase

John's refusal of the job

must be formed as the subjective genitive outright, as there is no corresponding common noun; cf. Section 3.7.

Traditional grammar also recognizes the *objective genitive*, and some other genitives. In many of these uses, genitival phrases have the anaphoric character of referring to something given in context. Thus the phrase *Pedro's donkey* does not presuppose that Pedro really owns a donkey, nor that he only owns one donkey. All that is needed is that in the context of the discourse, there is a unique donkey to which Pedro bears some appropriate relation, for example, of owning or of riding on.

An example of a genitival construction that is not anaphoric is the expression of an application instance $f(a)$ of a function

$$f(x)\ :\ B\ \ (x\ :\ A)$$

to an argument $a\ :\ A$. Consider

$s(0)$ ▷ *the successor of zero,*
$capital(Denmark)$ ▷ *the capital of Denmark,*
$father(John)$ ▷ *John's father.*

The apparent common nouns *successor, capital, father* are really functors here, not set expressions. The existence and uniqueness of the successor of n, etc., is guaranteed as soon as $n\ :\ N$, etc., is given.

But even here we cannot be sure about the English genitival phrase, for it can be the result of sugaring from a different construction. Thus *father* may function as a set term, for the set of men that have children,

$$(\Sigma x\ :\ man)(\Sigma y\ :\ child)I(man, x, father(y)).$$

Suppose John is a teacher, and teachers contact their pupils' fathers, each teacher one father a day. The sentence

John's father was not at home

may then refer, anaphorically, to the father whom John was supposed to contact on the day in question.

Note. To formalize the sentence *John's father was not at home* in the context of the sentence

every teacher went to meet a father,

we do obtain *John's father* as an application of a function to *John*, but the function is given in the context, as the 'discourse referent' introduced by the universal quantifier.

4.6   Nested anaphoric expressions

Nested anaphoric expressions are formed by iterating the operators Pron, *the*, Mod, and Gen. For instance, the phrase

his donkey

can be used in a context where a man and a donkey that he owns are given. To form the phrase in the context of the sentence

Pedro owns a donkey and Mary owns a donkey,

formalized as

$$z \,:\, (\Sigma x \,:\, donkey)(Pedro \ owns \ x)\&(\Sigma x \,:\, donkey)(Mary \ owns \ x),$$

first form Pron(*man, Pedro*) from *Pedro* : *man*. Now $p(p(z))$: *donkey* and $q(p(z))$: $(Pedro \ owns \ p(p(z)))$, whence by substitution of equals,

$$q(p(z)) \,:\, (\mathrm{Pron}(man, Pedro) \ owns \ p(p(z))).$$

Now we may form

Mod(*donkey*, (x)(Pron(*man, Pedro*) *owns* x), $p(p(z)), q(p(z))$)
$\triangleright$ $\begin{cases} \textit{the donkey that he owns,} \\ \textit{the donkey owned by him,} \end{cases}$
Gen(*man, donkey*, $(x, y)(x$ *owns* y), Pron(*man, Pedro*), $p(p(z)), q(p(z))$)
$\triangleright$ *his donkey.*

In the context of the sentence in which *Bill* occurs instead of *Mary*, *his donkey* would of course violate the principle of uniqueness, unlike *Pedro's donkey*.

4.7   The spectrum of anaphoric expressions

The pronoun, the definite noun phrase, and the variety of modified definite phrases, including genitives, form a partial ordering of more and less specific anaphoric expressions. The system of expressions usable for an object given in context, ordered according to specificity, will be called the *spectrum* of the object. For instance, the spectrum of the donkey $p(p(z))$ given in the context

$$z : (\Sigma x : donkey)(Pedro\ owns\ x)\&(\Sigma x : donkey)(Mary\ owns\ x)$$

comprises at least the following expressions.

Pron($donkey, p(p(z))$) $\triangleright$ *it*,
the($donkey, p(p(z))$) $\triangleright$ *the donkey*,
Mod($donkey, (x)$(Pron($man, Pedro$) *owns* x), $p(p(z)), q(p(z))$)
  $\triangleright$ *the donkey that he owns*,
Mod($donkey, (x)(Pedro\ owns\ x), p(p(z)), q(p(z))$)
  $\triangleright$ *the donkey that Pedro owns*,
Gen($man, donkey, (x, y)(x\ owns\ y), Pedro, p(p(z)), q(p(z))$)
  $\triangleright$ *Pedro's donkey*,
Gen($man, donkey, (x, y)(x\ owns\ y),$ Pron($man, Pedro$)$, p(p(z)), q(p(z))$)
  $\triangleright$ *his donkey*.

The following *comparison procedure* ensures unique interpretation of anaphoric expressions created in sugaring.

Form the spectra of all objects given in context. Erase the common parts of the spectra of distinct objects. The expressions that remain can be interpreted uniquely in the context.

In our example context, the donkeys $p(p(z))$ and $p(q(z))$ are given. A part of the spectrum of $p(p(z))$ was listed above. The spectrum of the donkey $p(q(z))$ contains, for example,

Pron($donkey, p(q(z))$) $\triangleright$ *it*,
the($donkey, p(q(z))$) $\triangleright$ *the donkey*,
Mod($donkey, (x)$(Pron($woman, Mary$) *owns* x), $p(q(z)), q(q(z))$)
  $\triangleright$ *the donkey that she owns*,
Mod($donkey, (x)(Mary\ owns\ x), p(q(z)), q(q(z))$)
  $\triangleright$ *the donkey that Mary owns*,
Gen($man, donkey, (x, y)(x\ owns\ y), Mary, p(q(z)), q(q(z))$)
  $\triangleright$ *Mary's donkey*,
Gen($man, donkey, (x, y)(x\ owns\ y),$

$$\text{Pron}(woman, Mary), p(p(z)), q(p(z)))$$

  $\triangleright$ *her donkey*.

The comparison procedure rules out the expressions *it* and *the donkey*, which belong to both spectra. The remaining expressions are usable without violation of uniqueness. In a context where *Bill* occurs instead of *Mary*, we would also have to rule out the expressions *the donkey that he owns* and *his donkey* from both spectra.

As a consequence of the rules for forming modified definite phrases, the information that counts in the comparison procedure is information that is given in the context. Thus the phrase

the tuberculous young man

in the beginning of Thomas Mann's *Magic Mountain* refers uniquely to Joachim, although it turns out later that Hans, too, was tuberculous all the time.

Example. The spectrum of the present in the sentence

if you give every child a present some child will open it

discussed in Section 3.7 contains, in addition to *it*, the expressions *the present, the present you give him, the present you give the child,* and *his present.*

4.8   The type matching of an interpretation

The comparison procedure, which erases the common parts of spectra, is more restrictive than the informal principle of uniqueness. An anaphoric expression may have a unique interpretation even if it belongs to the spectra of several objects given in context. Consider the following text.

Donald was handed a gold medal and a glass of champagne. He drank it up immediately.

The pronoun *it* is uniquely interpreted as the glass of champagne, although it also belongs to the spectrum of the gold medal. The type-theoretical explanation of this is that the interpretation of *it* as the gold medal would produce a *type mismatch* in the second sentence, which employs the propositional function

$$(x \, drank_A \, y \, up) : \text{prop} \ (x : man, \ y : A).$$

The type A of the second argument can be glass of champagne, cup of coffee, etc., but not gold medal.

The comparison procedure must be completed by the principle of *type matching,*

An anaphoric expression E has a unique interpretation in the passage $---E---$, if E belongs to the spectrum of only one object c given in context such that $---c---$ makes sense.

The phrase $---E---$ need not be a whole sentence. The interpretation of *her* in

her husband

is unique in a context in which many women are given, if only one of them is given as married.

As another example of the principle of type matching, consider a case in which what decides is not the type of the individual itself, but the additional information given about the individual. In the text

John hit Pedro. He hit him back.

the interpretations of the two occurrences of the pronoun *he* are unique, because the latter sentence employs the propositional function

$$(x \text{ hits } y \text{ back}(z)) : \text{prop} \ (x : man, \ y : man, \ z : (y \text{ has hit } \text{ACC}(x))).$$

Only the substitutions of *Pedro* for x and of *John* for y make it possible to find a substitute for z in the context created by the sentence *John hit Pedro.*

To interpret an anaphoric expression in a context, one sometimes makes considerations that resemble the type matching principle, but are not quite as definitive. There are several interpretations that make sense, but one of them makes *more sense* than the others. In the text

John found a coin in a hollow tree. He put it in his pocket.

we interpret *it* as the coin, if we do not think that hollow trees can be put into pockets. In the text

John found a coin in a cupboard. He wanted to take it along.

both the coin and the cupboard make sense as interpretations of *it*. But there are many situations in which it makes more sense to take along the coin.

It is difficult to give formal rules to deal with the last two examples. For the decisions are not stable with respect to the further information that can be given in the context. If John is an enthusiast for old furniture? If he has very large pockets? One would need formal rules that capture the intelligence involved in the actual interpretation of anaphoric expressions. Here we have a fundamental difficulty for automatic translation. To translate the former text into German, one has to find out whether *it* should be translated *ihn* (*den Baum*) or *sie* (*die Münze*). If this cannot be decided algorithmically, there is no algorithm translating the whole sentence either.

4.9 What is given in context

A context, in the technical sense of type theory, is a sequence of hypotheses of the form

$$x_1 : A_1, \ x_2 : A_2(x_1), \ldots, x_n : A_n(x_1, \ldots, x_{n-1}).$$

We shall use capital Greek letters Γ, Δ, Θ, etc., to abbreviate contexts.

A context is created whenever a quantified proposition is formed. According to the rule of Σ formation,

$$\frac{A \,:\, \text{set} \quad B(x) \,:\, \text{prop}}{(\Sigma x \,:\, A)B(x) \,:\, \text{prop}}\,,\quad \overset{\textstyle (x \,:\, A)}{}$$

to form $(\Sigma x \,:\, A)B(x)$ one first forms the set A, and then the proposition $B(x)$ in the context $x \,:\, A$. Π formation is similar. When Σ and Π formation are iterated, longer contexts are assumed. To form

$$(\Pi x \,:\, A)(\Sigma y \,:\, B(x))C(x,y),$$

the set A is first formed in the empty context, then $B(x)$ in the context $x \,:\, A$, then $C(x,y)$ in the context $x \,:\, A$, $y \,:\, B(x)$. A derivation in tree form is made in Section 2.13.

What is *given in the context*

$$\Gamma \;=\; x_1 \,:\, A_1, \;\ldots,\; x_n \,:\, A_n(x_1,\ldots,x_{n-1})$$

are hypothetical judgements of the form

$$J(x_1,\ldots,x_n) \;\; (\Gamma),$$

that is,

$$J(x_1,\ldots,x_n) \;\; (x_1 \,:\, A_1, \;\ldots,\; x_n \,:\, A_n(x_1,\ldots,x_{n-1})).$$

Derivatively of judgements given in context, we speak of objects and equal objects, of any types, as given in context. In particular, we say $A(x_1,\ldots,x_n)$ is a *proposition given in the context* Γ, when we have made the judgement

$$A(x_1,\ldots,x_n) \,:\, \text{prop} \;\; (\Gamma).$$

We say that $a(x_1,\ldots,x_n)$ is an *element of A given in* Γ, when

$$a(x_1,\ldots,x_n) \,:\, A \;\; (\Gamma).$$

This generalizes immediately to elements $a(x_1,\ldots,x_n)$ of a set $A(x_1,\ldots,x_n)$ itself given in the context Γ,

$$a(x_1,\ldots,x_n) \,:\, A(x_1,\ldots,x_n) \;\; (\Gamma).$$

In the alternative terminology of propositions instead of sets, we say that $a(x_1,\ldots,x_n)$ is a *proof of the proposition* $A(x_1,\ldots,x_n)$ *given in the context* Γ. Suppressing the proof yields

$$A(x_1,\ldots,x_n) \;\text{true} \;\; (\Gamma),$$

that is, the judgement that the proposition $A(x_1,\ldots,x_n)$ is *true in the context* Γ.

Finally, we have *equal sets in* Γ and *equal elements of a set in* Γ, that is, judgements of the forms

$$A(x_1, \ldots, x_n) = B(x_1, \ldots, x_n) : \text{set } (\Gamma),$$
$$a(x_1, \ldots, x_n) = b(x_1, \ldots, x_n) : A(x_1, \ldots, x_n) \ (\Gamma),$$

respectively.

4.10 Actual and potential in context

To summarize the definitions of the previous section, what is given in the context $\Gamma = x_1 : A_1, \ldots, x_n : A_n(x_1, \ldots, x_{n-1})$ is whatever can be derived from the hypotheses $x_1 : A_1$ to $x_n : A_n(x_1, \ldots, x_{n-1})$. Derivations make use of the rules of type theory. In the examples of this and the previous chapter, we have mainly made use of the Σ and Π elimination rules.

We can distinguish between what is *actually given* in the context Γ, namely the variables $x_1 : A_1$ to $x_n : A_n(x_1, \ldots, x_{n-1})$ themselves, and what is *potentially given*, namely what can be derived by the rules of type theory from what is actually given. This distinction is in accordance with the distinction between actual and potential judgements made by Martin-Löf in 1991, p. 142. Actual judgements are those that *have been made already*. Judgements that *can be made* by applying iteratively the rules of type theory, but have not been made, are only potential, and there is no reason why all of them should ever be actually made by anyone.

Actual and potential admit of comparison. The general principle of comparison is that each of the arguments to which a functor is applied is more actual than the application instance,

$F(a(x_1, \ldots, x_n), \ldots, b(x_1, \ldots, x_n))$ is less actually given in the context $x_1 : A_1, \ldots, x_n : A_n(x_1, \ldots, x_{n-1})$ than any of $a(x_1, \ldots, x_n), \ldots, b(x_1, \ldots, x_n)$.

For instance, if

$$c(x_1, \ldots, x_n) : (\Sigma x : A(x_1, \ldots, x_n))B(x_1, \ldots, x_n, x)$$

is given, actually or potentially, then

$$p(c(x_1, \ldots, x_n)) : A(x_1, \ldots, x_n)$$

is also given, but less actually.

The objects given in a context form a *universe of discourse*, on which comparative actuality imposes a partial ordering. One of the uses that can be made of this ordering is that when the uniqueness of interpretation of an anaphoric expression is considered no attention need be paid to objects below a certain level of actuality.

In the examples of this chapter, we only consider the finite part of the universe of discourse that is generated from the explicit context by p, q, and ap. This practice has a more general motivation in the view that selectors, that is, operators introduced in elimination rules, are used for *analysing* the objects to which they are applied, whereas constructors, operators given in introduction rules, *synthesize* new objects. (A more elaborate view of analysis and synthesis in type theory, presented in Mäenpää 1993, might be used for obtaining a more sophisticated principle of actuality.)

Application of constructors can have curious effects on the universe of discourse. For instance, by the second NI rule

$$\frac{a \,:\, N}{s(a) \,:\, N},$$

$s(a) : N$ is given in any context in which $a : N$ is. There are two numbers (indeed, an infinity of numbers) given in the context, provided one number is. Yet it should be possible to say

if a number is prime it is not divisible by four,

without violating the principle of uniqueness.

The simplest example of this kind is provided by atomic constants that are constructors of enumerated sets. If we have made the categorical judgement

John : man

in the definition of the set *man*, *John : man* is vacuously given in any context. Hence the term Pron(*man*, *John*) can be formed in any context. But in English, the pronoun *he* cannot be used for John in all contexts. Nor is John relevant for uniqueness considerations in all contexts.

We need an account of how primitive constants, and other elements in constructor forms, are made actual. One way in which a text can make a constant object actual is by explicitly *mentioning* it. Thus *John : man* is actual in the context created by the sentence

John walks.

The pronoun *he* can be used for John in this context. But it cannot be used for John's father, who has not been explicitly mentioned.

Both John and John's father are mentioned in the sentence

John's father walks.

The pronoun *he* can thus be used both for John and for John's father in the context created by this sentence.

Actuality, like uniqueness, is a principle foreign to pure type-theoretical analysis. In type theory, the term Pron(*man*, *John*) can be used anywhere, as definitionally equal to *John*. In English, the term *he* can be used for John only if certain conditions of uniqueness and actuality are satisfied. We have isolated some of these conditions, like the comparison of spectra, type matching, explicit mentioning, and the exclusion of introduction rules. These conditions do not belong to type theory itself, even though their precise expression uses type-theoretical concepts.

4.11 The zero sign

Transitive verbs are often used with one argument only. You say

John is eating

without specifying any object of eating. Yet you think that *eat* is a transitive verb; semantically speaking, to eat is to eat something. From this, it is sometimes concluded that *John is eating* means the same as

John is eating something.

This suggests the general procedure of reducing the number of argument places by defining

$C'(x) = (\exists y : B)C(x,y) : \text{prop} \ (x : A),$
where $C(x,y) : \text{prop} \ (x : A, \ y : B).$

A rule having this effect is called *unspecified object deletion* by Dowty (1982, p. 91). There is an analogous rule of subject deletion, by which agentless passives are formed. For instance,

John is loved

gets formalized as

$(\exists x : woman)(x \ loves \ John).$

From the point of view of generation of English sentences, what we have here is the sugaring of an existential quantifier into the *zero sign*. We shall use $\emptyset$ as the zero sign. The whole procedure of sugaring an existential quantifier into the zero sign will be called *existential ellipsis*. (Ellipsis is an ancient Greek term. The term *signe zéro* appears in Saussure, *Cours de linguistique générale*, p. 124.)

Even though you cannot just eat, without eating something, it does not follow that *John is eating* means the same as *John is eating something*. The latter sentence contains an existential quantifier bringing in a new object of eating, but the object involved in the former sentence may well be previously given in context, so that reference is made to it in a definite way. This is clear in the text

I gave him a dried cod. Now he is eating.

The latter sentence can be paraphrased by either of

now he is eating it,
now he is eating the dried cod,

rather than by *now he is eating something*. To take an example from Bally (1944, §129), in

Voici votre soupe, mangez!

it is the soup that is to be eaten, not just something. Bally uses the terms *contextual ellipsis*, *situational ellipsis*, and *anaphoric ellipsis*. He makes distinctions between each of them, but we shall bypass the distinctions. They have to do with how the object referred to is made actual in the context, which we have left outside discussion anyway.

Bally relies on the structuralistic view of language as a system of oppositions between distinguishable elements. In such a system, there can be an opposition between positive signs, but also an opposition of something to nothing: 'la langue peut se contenter de l'opposition de quelque chose avec rien' ('language can content itself with the opposition of something to nothing', Saussure, *Cours*, p. 124). Thus when an object is to be picked out, 'la représentation peut se faire soit par un signe positif, soit par un signe zéro, dont le sens se déduit du contexte' ('the representation can be made either by a positive sign or by a zero sign, whose sense is deduced from the context', Bally 1944, §127).

We shall here speak of the zero sign as one of the possible anaphoric expressions, and of the mechanism producing it as *anaphoric ellipsis*. Anaphoric ellipsis generalizes to *indexical ellipsis*, in which the interpretation is found in the nonlinguistic context. You are just given the soup, without any other instruction than 'Eat!'

The type-theoretical rule for the anaphoric zero sign, analogous to the other anaphoric rules, is

$$\frac{A \,:\, \text{set} \quad a \,:\, A}{\begin{cases} \text{Zero}(A, a) \,:\, A, \\ \text{Zero}(A, a) \,=\, a \,:\, A \end{cases}}.$$

In sugaring, $\text{Zero}(A, a)$ produces $\emptyset$, without dependence on A. $\text{MOR}(\emptyset)$, where MOR is any morphological operation, sugars into $\emptyset$.

There is hence no unique logical form corresponding to the zero sign, but at least two alternative mechanisms for producing it. We write

$$B(\emptyset) \;\lhd\; \begin{cases} (\Sigma x \,:\, A)B(x), \\ B(a), \text{ where } a \,:\, A \text{ is given in context} \end{cases}$$

to express schematically the idea that ellipsis occurring in an English sentence can be existential as well as anaphoric. It is often the case that only one of the interpretations is possible, and this can be tested by means of paraphrases making the alternatives explicit. Thus Bally gives the paraphrases *mangez-la* and *mangez votre soupe* for the imperative in his example. The paraphrase *mangez quelque chose* is inadequate in this situation, but quite possible in some other situations.

The use of ellipsis is more heavily restricted than the use of pronouns and definite noun phrases. In English, it seems to be delimited to certain argument positions of the verb, so that, for example, the subject can never be omitted. The solution of Dowty (1982) is, indeed, to explain it in terms of the reduction of the number of argument places, rather than as an independent mode of expression. Whatever alternative is chosen, one should recognize the different semantic functions of the ellipsis, the existential and the indexical function.

4.12   Presupposition

Type-theoretical judgements have presuppositions, so that a judgement can only be meaningfully made provided certain other judgements have been made. The presuppositions of judgements of each of the four forms are laid down in a table in Section 2.17.

Most of the discussion under the title of presupposition in linguistic literature (see e.g. the recent survey in Soames 1989) is not about presupposition in the sense of type theory. It is rather about anaphoric reference, about something depending on variables provided by context. In the simplest case, we have a proposition depending on the proof of another proposition,

$$B(x) \; : \; \text{prop} \; (x \; : \; A).$$

If we suppress the proof x, we obtain

$$B \; : \; \text{prop} \; (A \; \text{true}),$$

that is, B is a proposition under the assumption that A is true. For instance, to express that *John stops smoking* presupposes that John smokes, we write

$$(\textit{John stops smoking}) \; : \; \text{prop} \; ((\textit{John smokes}) \; \text{true}).$$

This will of course follow from the more general categorization of *stop smoking* as a two-argument verb,

$$(x \; \textit{stops} \; (y) \; \textit{smoking}) \; : \; \text{prop} \; (x \; : \; \textit{man}, \; y \; : \; (x \; \textit{smokes})).$$

The verb *stop smoking* can be used in a context that gives a man and a proof of the proposition that he smokes. In sugaring, the second argument is deleted. (Cf. Section 8.7 for a general treatment of the verb *stop*.)

The hypothetical judgement $B \; : \; \text{prop} \; (A \; \text{true})$ expresses a relation between A and B that cannot be understood as any kind of logical entailment. It simply cannot be expressed unless the forms of judgement $A \; : \; \text{prop}$ and A true are available. In ordinary predicate calculus, these forms are used in the metalanguage only. In Chapter 2, we found independent reasons to make them explicit in the formalism. Type theory adds to this the further analysis of truth in terms of proofs. At the same time, presupposition becomes an instance of the same pattern as anaphoric reference.

There is indeed no clear classification of modes of expression into anaphora and presupposition. Does the sentence

John saw the departure of train 55

presuppose that train 55 departed, or refer anaphorically to a departure of train 55? In the context created by the sentence *train 55 departed*, we can both say that the presupposition is satisfied, and form the anaphoric term *the departure of train 55*, the subjective genitive referring to the proof of the proposition that train 55 departed.

We conclude that presupposing, in the sense of expressing a proposition under the assumption that some other proposition is true, is not a logically independent phenomenon. Presuppositions between forms of judgement is another matter. So will be presuppositions between questions and answers, discussed in Sections 6.11–6.14.

4.13   Discourse referents

Anaphoric expressions are formed by means of the operators Pron, the, Mod, Gen, and Zero, which operate on arguments of appropriate types. Just like the arguments of any operators, these arguments may depend on variables given in context. The interpretation of an anaphoric expression need not be a constant object; correlatively, there need not be any constant expression substitutible for the anaphoric expression.

As an example of a process in which a context is created, we have considered the formation of quantified propositions, of the form $(Qx : A)B(x)$, where A : prop is formed independently, and $B(x)$: prop is formed in the context $x : A$. The general type-theoretical form of a context is

$$x_1 : A_1, \ x_2 : A_2(x_1), \ldots, x_n : A_n(x_1, \ldots, x_{n-1}),$$

where the k'th proposition is formed in the context of the $k - 1$ variables introduced by the foregoing hypotheses,

$$A_k(x_1, \ldots, x_{k-1}) : \text{prop} \ (x_1 : A_1, \ \ldots, x_{k-1} : A_{k-1}(x_1, \ldots, x_{k-2})).$$

The variables could now be compared with the device of *discourse referents* employed in the *discourse representation theory* of Kamp (1981). They both play a role in an account of how discourse proceeds by introducing new objects and by later referring to objects introduced earlier.

One clear difference is that variables belong to type theory from the beginning, whereas the discourse referents of Kamp's theory constitute a new category, distinct from both constants and variables. This new category has been devised for the very purpose of representing progression in text. At the final stage of the semantic analysis of the text, in the model-theoretic interpretation of the discourse representations, discourse referents vanish. For the interpretation is made in standard predicate calculus, which only countenances constants and variables.

Another difference is in the *typing* of the discourse referents. Variables introduced in a context can have any sets as their types. But discourse referents are *individuals* without any inner structure. For instance, there are no discourse referents of function types, and hence no application of one discourse referent to another. Such things are needed for the interpretation of pronouns in sentences like

> *if you give every child a present, some child will open it*
> $\vartriangleleft\ (\Pi z\ :\ (\Pi x\ :\ child)(\Sigma y\ :\ present)(you\ give\ x\ y))$
> $\quad\quad\quad\quad (\Sigma u\ :\ child)(u\ will\ open\ \mathrm{Pron}(present, p(\mathrm{ap}(z, u)))).$

Examples requiring application of functions given in context were first discussed in game-theoretical semantics, by Hintikka and Carlson (1979). Game-theoretical analyses can often be carried over to type theory by virtue of a general interpretation of

> *games* as propositions,
> *Myself's winning strategies* as proofs.

Game-theoretical semantics analyses sentences of English by assigning games to them, games between Myself and Nature. In the type-theoretical interpretation, propositions of Σ form correspond to games starting with Myself's moves. Π corresponds to Nature's moves. Thus, for example, the game rule

> to play $- - -every\ A - --$, Nature chooses an element $a\ :\ A$, and the game continues from $- - -a - --$

gives the type theoretical formalization rule

> $- - -every\ A - --$ is formalized $(\Pi x\ :\ A)(- - -x - --).$

The *truth* of a sentence means, game-theoretically, that

> Myself has a winning strategy in the game.

A context formalizes the game-theoretical notion of

> the series of strategies chosen in earlier subgames.

The series of strategies generates a *choice set*, from which the interpretations of pronouns are chosen. The choice set is closed under operations like functional application. (For the correspondence between game-theoretical semantics and type theory, see Ranta 1988, 1990a.)

Both type theory and game-theoretical semantics go beyond the level of propositions endowed with an unanalysed notion of truth. They give an analysis of truth in terms of proofs or strategies. In the absence of this dimension of *strategic meaning* (to use the term of Hintikka and Kulas 1985, p. 147), one must try to capture the anaphoric relations on the level of propositions and with an unanalysed notion of truth. Dynamic predicate logic does this in terms of variable binding (cf. Section 3.7), discourse representation theory in terms of rules telling how each connective and quantifier contributes to discourse representations.

Attempts to explain anaphora on the level of propositions and unanalysed truth are analogous to the Hilbertian theory of ϵ terms (cf. Hilbert and Bernays 1939, §1.2). Hilbert wanted to derive individuals from true existential propositions, but this is not possible in predicate calculus. He thus postulated new rules, introducing a new class of singular terms to serve as names of such individuals. In the explicit predicate calculus, these rules read

$$\frac{(\exists x \, : \, A)B(x) \text{ true}}{(\epsilon x \, : \, A)B(x) \, : \, A} \, , \qquad \frac{(\exists x \, : \, A)B(x) \text{ true}}{B((\epsilon x \, : \, A)B(x)) \text{ true}} \, .$$

But these rules cannot be justified by constructive standards. The element $(\epsilon x \, : \, A)B(x) \, : \, A$ is of a non-canonical form, but there is no rule for computing it into canonical form (cf. Section 2.14).

Martin-Löf's (1984, pp. 45–46) analysis of the situation is that the ϵ term should not be construed as a function of the domain A and the propositional function $B(x)$, but as a function of the proof of the existential proposition. Understood in this way, ϵ terms are left projections. The desired rules are precisely the projection rules,

$$\frac{c \, : \, (\exists x \, : \, A)B(x)}{p(c) \, : \, A} \, , \qquad \frac{c \, : \, (\exists x \, : \, A)B(x)}{q(c) \, : \, B(p(c))} \, .$$

Thus the comparison of anaphoric expressions to Hilbertian ϵ terms by Hintikka and Kulas (1985, p. 94), is adequate as concerns what ϵ terms were designed to do, but inadequate as concerns how they were introduced by Hilbert.

4.14 Indexical expressions

When pronouns, definite noun phrases, and the like, are interpreted anaphorically, objects of appropriate types are sought in the context created by the foregoing text. But a context, in the sense of type theory, formalizes other situations as well. As such, a context is just a specification of a sequence of objects, a *frame of reference*.

Recognizing ways of creating contexts other than use of language, we also generalize the above discussion of anaphoric expressions to *indexical expressions*. The pronoun *he* can be used for a man entering the room, and if he is old, the phrase *the old man* can be used. Uniqueness fails if two old men are around. It also fails if you are talking about some other old man while this one is entering. Then you can exploit the visually given information and use the modified phrase *the man who is entering*. To make an object actual, you can, besides mentioning it by name, point it out by finger. An object pointed out is decisively more actual than objects that just happen to be around. Thus you can point out a man among one thousand and say, *look, he is asleep*.

There are indexical expressions that are more naturally used in non-linguistic contexts than anaphorically. Thus *this man*, *that man* are preferred in concrete situations, *the man, he* in texts. The pronouns *I* and *you* are used in dialogues, but not in a text to refer to persons originally given in the third person. However, what we can say about these expressions in type theory are the conditions of existence, the pronominalization rules

$$\frac{A \,:\, \text{set} \quad a \,:\, A}{\begin{cases} this(A,a) \,:\, A, \\ this(A,a) \,=\, a \,:\, A \end{cases}},\qquad \frac{A \,:\, \text{set} \quad a \,:\, A}{\begin{cases} that(A,a) \,:\, A, \\ that(A,a) \,=\, a \,:\, A \end{cases}},$$

$$\frac{a \,:\, person}{\begin{cases} I(a) \,:\, person, \\ I(a) \,=\, a \,:\, person \end{cases}},\qquad \frac{a \,:\, person}{\begin{cases} you(a) \,:\, person, \\ you(a) \,=\, a \,:\, person \end{cases}}.$$

Any further conditions there are for the use of these expressions, have, like the conditions of uniqueness and actuality, definite type-theoretical approximations, plus a residue of informal intelligence.

There is another use of the personal pronouns *I* and *you*, in the semantic explanations of linguistic acts; see Sections 6.11– 6.14. In this 'transcendental' use, *I* and *you* are not singular terms used in the argument places of propositional functions, but dialogue partners performing acts, like assertions, in which propositions figure.

Example. Suppose the wind blows a piece of paper to you, with the writing

I am here now, waiting for you to bring back my coat.

No other information is available. To make sense of the message, you can only reconstruct a context in which it is meaningful,

$t \,:\, time, s \,:\, place, x \,:\, person, y \,:\, person, z \,:\, coat,$

$Z \,:\, (person)(coat)\text{prop}, u \,:\, Z(x,z),$

$v \,:\, (y \text{ has taken } z \text{ away from } x),$

and formalize the sentence as a proposition given in this context. (Observe that we need a higher-level context, in the sense of Chapter 8, to introduce a propositional function variable.)

5

TEMPORAL REFERENCE

Temporal reference can be studied formally by introducing a *time scale*, a set of points of time. Various verbs can be categorized as propositional functions over the time scale. In English sentences in which those verbs are used, the time argument is sometimes made explicit by means of an *adverbial of time*, sometimes omitted. Certain time adverbials are close to canonical names of time points, indicating them explicitly (*on September 9, 1992, at 8.22*). Certain adverbials are indexical (*then, at the same time, five minutes later*). Ellipsis is sometimes existential, sometimes indexical. Moreover, the time argument affects the *tense* of the verb, which remains as a trace left of the time argument even if it is omitted itself.

The logical study of temporal reference using singular terms for time points and quantification over time is in contrast with *tense logic* as formulated by Prior (1957), in which the tenses Past, Present, and Future are treated as proposition-forming operators without any further structure. Such structure, with explicit reference to points of time, is only used in the semantics given in a metalanguage. Making it explicit in the object language is in harmony with our explicit approach to predicate calculus (cf. Chapter 2). But the need to make it explicit in the formalization of natural language was observed quite early, by Partee (1973) and Needham (1975). Our view comes particularly close to Dowty (1979, p. 323), who writes,

> tenses in English are primarily parasitic on time adverbials ... and cannot be properly understood without an understanding of their interaction with time adverbials.

Dowty does not, however, distinguish between canonical and non-canonical, constant and indexical expressions of time, nor between indexical and existential ellipsis of the time argument.

Aspect constitutes another dimension of temporal reference in natural language. In our analysis, it is best understood in terms of *aspectual systems*, systems involving several interrelated verbs, rather than in terms of aspectual features of individual verbs.

5.1   Time scales

If you say,

> *Estonia was a part of Sweden,*

I may ask, *when?*, and the answer will make a difference. The sentences

> *Estonia was a part of Sweden in 1685,*
> *Estonia was a part of Sweden in 1770,*

express different propositions, which even differ in truth value. The proposition expressed by the original sentence depends on time. The simplest way to represent such a sentence both in predicate calculus and in type theory is as a propositional function with an argument place for time,

$$A(t) : \text{prop} \ (t : \textit{time}).$$

To complete this formalization, we must, of course, justify the judgement

$$\textit{time} : \text{set}$$

by telling what the elements of the set *time* are.

We shall not define the set *time* uniformly but introduce several *time scales*, such as

> *year* : set,
> *day* : set,
> *minute* : set.

The canonical elements of the set *year* are numbers, for example,

$$1917 : \text{year}.$$

To define the set *day*, we need the set of the twelve months,

$$\textit{month} = \{\textit{January}, \textit{February}, \ldots, \textit{December}\} : \text{set},$$

as well as the family of sets

$$\textit{day\_of}(x, y) : \text{set} \ (x : \textit{year}, \ y : \textit{month}),$$

such that each set of the family comprises the numerals from 1 to 28 or 29 or 30 or 31, depending on x and y. Now we can give the introduction rule of the set *day*,

$$\frac{a : \textit{year} \quad b : \textit{month} \quad c : \textit{day\_of}(a, b)}{(a, b, c) : \textit{day}}$$

producing canonical elements like

$$(1917, \textit{December}, 6) : \textit{day}.$$

The family

$$\textit{minute\_of}(x, y, z) : \text{set} \ (x : \textit{year}, \ y : \textit{month}, \ z : \textit{day\_of}(x, y))$$

has its dependences due to changes between winter and summer time. Normally, it comprises pairs of numerals of the form $h.m$ where $h = 0, 1, \ldots, 23$ and $m = 0, 1, \ldots, 59$, for example,

$$9.14 : minute(1917, December, 6).$$

The introduction rule

$$\frac{a : year \quad b : month \quad c : day\_of(a, b) \quad d : minute\_of(a, b, c)}{(a, b, c, d) : minute}$$

produces canonical elements like

$$(1917, December, 6, 9.14) : minute.$$

In the scales *year*, *day*, and *minute*, time is divided by increasing accuracy, but they are all sets of discrete points of time. One could think of further scales of seconds, hundredths of seconds, etc., and of a structure isomorphic to the real line as the *limit* of this sequence of scales of increasing accuracy. Time points, as points of the real line, are *approximated* by points of the discrete scales. But for the constructive mathematician, only approximations are ever actual. Points of the real line are unattainable (cf. Brouwer 1907, chapter 1). In language, we have a series of expressions,

1917,
December 6, 1917,
December 6, 1917, at 9.14,
December 6, 1917, at 9.14.56,
December 6, 1917, at 9.14.56.87,

but no expression of this explicit form ever reaches a point on the real line.

Expressions for points on the time scales usually occur in *adverbials of time*, which are formed, for example, by means of prepositions. In the logical literature, the form *at t* is customarily used, but it is inadequate for years and days, as well as for the zero sign Ø. I shall use the morphological operator AT for forming adverbials of time from names of points of time. Thus

AT(1917) $\triangleright$ *in 1917,*
AT((1917, December, 6)) $\triangleright$ *on December 6, 1917,*
AT((1917, December, 6, 9.14)) $\triangleright$ *on December 6, 1917, at 9.14,*
AT(Ø) $\triangleright$ Ø.

Note. It would be possible to define the time scales in terms of Σ, for example,

minute $=$
$(\Sigma x : year)(\Sigma y : month)(\Sigma z : day\_of(x, y))minute\_of(x, y, z) :$ set.

This is equivalent to the direct definition given in the text. In both cases it is easy to define projections, which for a point on the scale of minutes give a year, a month, a day, and a minute.

5.2   Appropriate accuracy

A time-dependent proposition employed in everyday life often has a fixed level of accuracy, beyond which it is not meaningful to go. In a discussion of historical events on the basis of a chronicle that only indicates years, there is no basis for a greater accuracy than years. One then employs propositional functions like

$$(x \; is \; enthroned \; \mathrm{AT}(y)) \; : \; \mathrm{prop} \; (x \; : \; king, \; y \; : \; year).$$

The year 1509 is the *exactly right answer* to the question *When was Henry VIII enthroned?* in this situation.

   In a discussion about births and deaths on the basis of works of reference of the ordinary kind, the appropriate scale is the set of days,

$$(x \; is \; born \; \mathrm{AT}(y)) \; : \; \mathrm{prop} \; (x \; : \; person, \; y \; : \; day).$$

In a discussion about departures and arrivals of trains on the basis of a timetable, the appropriate scale is the set of minutes. To say,

$$train \; 55 \; arrives \; in \; Oslo \; at \; 14.37.12$$

in such a discussion is nonsense. The propositional function employed is

$$(x \; arrives \; \mathrm{IN}(y) \; \mathrm{AT}(z)) \; : \; \mathrm{prop} \; (x \; : \; train, \; y \; : \; station, \; z \; : \; minute).$$

   The accuracy is not a once and for all property of the English verb, like *arrive*, but relative to the situation in which the verb is used. Standing at the station of Oslo, equipped with a chronometer, you can make perfectly good use of the scale of seconds in talking about arrivals. But if you lose your chronometer and have to rely on the old-fashioned clock on the wall, which shows minutes only, you are again in a situation in which seconds make no sense.

   Schematically, you have two distinct propositional functions,

$arrive_1(t) \; : \; \mathrm{prop} \; (t \; : \; minute),$
$arrive_2(t,s) \; : \; \mathrm{prop} \; (t \; : \; minute, \; s \; : \; second).$

There are, however, interpretations in both directions. If you have grounds for indicating seconds, and employ the function $arrive_2(t,s)$, you can make sense of $arrive_1(t)$ as

$$(\exists s \; : \; second) \, arrive_2(t,s).$$

On the other hand, even if you only have grounds for indicating minutes, you can still make sense of $arrive_2(t,s)$, as

$$arrive_1(t),$$

which suppresses the unwarranted second.

Recall that we are all the time interested in meaningful words, that is, words in use, rather than words divested of meaning. It may well be that the verb *arrive* does not carry with it a time scale, but any proposition expressed by using it does. The relation between the definite propositional functions *arrive₁* and *arrive₂* and the verb *arrive* is sugaring, schematically

$$\left.\begin{array}{l} arrive_1 \\ arrive_2 \end{array}\right\} \ \triangleright \ arrive.$$

5.3 Existential and indexical ellipsis of time

Consider, again, the discussion about dates of birth, which employs the propositional function

$$(x \text{ is born } \mathrm{AT}(y)) : \mathrm{prop} \ (x : person, \ y : day).$$

It makes no sense to speak of the minute in this connection. But it is quite meaningful to use the coarser scale of years, to say things like

Beethoven was born in 1770.

This sentence is then usually understood as paraphrasable by

Beethoven was born on some day of 1770,

that is, in terms of existential ellipsis of the month and the day,

$$(\exists x : month)(\exists y : day\_of(1770, x))(Beethoven \text{ was born } \mathrm{AT}((1770, x, y))).$$

But if the year is omitted,

Beethoven was born on December 16,

the ellipsis is usually indexical, so that the year is given in the context. We already know that Beethoven was born in 1770, and we are discussing the exact date. It is less typical to understand the ellipsis existentially, making the sentence mean that Beethoven was born on December 16 of some year. This is only relevant in marginal topics like horoscopes.

The natural direction of approximation is from coarser to finer. When the year is known, that is, given in context, the month comes into question, then the day, etc. In everyday life, we share the knowledge of the larger scales, and safely leave it unexpressed by using indexical ellipsis and making only the finer-scale components explicit. I say

I'll finish the job by Christmas,

meaning the same year, and

see you at half past eight,

meaning the same day.

To sum up, a sentence employing the propositional function

$$C(t, u) : \text{prop} \quad (t : A, \; u : B(t))$$

where $u : B(t)$ adds accuracy to the time $t : A$, can omit the time in all possible modes of ellipsis,

$$C(\varnothing, \varnothing) \; \lhd \; \begin{cases} (\exists x : A)(\exists y : B(x))C(x, y), \\ (\exists x : A)C(x, u), \text{ where } u : B(x) \text{ is given in context, } (*) \\ (\exists y : B(t))C(t, y), \text{ where } t : A \text{ is given in context,} \\ C(t, u), \text{ where } t : A, \quad u : B(x) \text{ are given in context,} \end{cases}$$

$$C(t, \varnothing) \; \lhd \; \begin{cases} (\exists y : B(t))C(t, y), \\ C(t, u), \text{ where } u : B(t) \text{ is given in context, } (*) \end{cases}$$

$$C(\varnothing, u) \; \lhd \; \begin{cases} (\exists x : A)C(x, u), \; (*) \\ C(t, u), \text{where } t : A \text{ is given in context.} \end{cases}$$

The readings marked by stars belong to situations like those in which the minute is already known but the date is in question. They are less natural than their alternatives. If $B(x)$: set effectively depends on $x : A$, it is not possible to know $u : B(t)$ prior to knowing $t : A$. For instance, *on February 29* is safely used only in a context in which the year is known.

5.4   Complementary and adjunctive time adverbials

There are two extreme ways to understand the total ellipsis of the time argument,

$$A(\varnothing) \; \lhd \; \begin{cases} (\exists x : time)A(x), \\ A(t), \text{ where } t : time \text{ is given in context.} \end{cases}$$

Individual cases can be tested by paraphrases construed with *at some time* and *then*, respectively. One can also try to see what the sense of the question *when?* is. If I say,

Napoleon conquered Spain,

you pose the question *when?* in order to get some more information about the event that I have already managed to communicate to you. Type-theoretically, you are asking the identity of the time $p(c)$, which is given in the context of my assertion

$$c : (\exists y : year)(Napoleon\ conquered\ Spain\ \text{AT}(y)).$$

The time adverbial that the sentence is sometimes endowed with is optional, an *adjunct* in traditional grammatical terminology. In the traditional sense, an adjunct is a phrase added to a sentence to form another sentence. In the logical sense, an adjunct is an operator turning a proposition into another proposition, F in the scheme

$$\frac{A : \text{prop}}{F(A) : \text{prop}}.$$

But if I say, out of the blue,

the sun was shining,

I must mean some specific time. If you do not know the time I mean, I fail
to communicate anything to you. You then ask *when?* in order to know
what I mean to say, what proposition I am asserting. My assertion is of the
form

$c : (\textit{the sun was shining } \mathrm{AT}(t)),$

where t should be given in context. But as it is given in my context only, not
in yours, you do not know it. A time adverbial is needed as a *complement*
in the sentence, not only as an adjunct. It may well not be a complement
in the traditional sense, that is, necessary for the verb *be shining* to form a
sentence, but it is certainly a complement in the logical sense: it completes
the expression with a time variable into a propositional expression. In the
scheme

$$\frac{a \,:\, A}{B(a) \,:\, \mathrm{prop}},$$

a is a complement in the logical sense.

The preferred understanding of the ellipsis of time depends on the verb
and on the form of the verb. The sentence with *conquered* is understood as
existential over time, but if the verb is put into the progressive form,

Napoleon was conquering Spain,

the hearer feels he would have to know when, in order to understand what
is being said.

Many authors have suggested that the status of the time argument
depends on whether the verb is a *state verb* or an *event verb*. Dowty (1979),
who interprets state verbs as propositional functions over times, does not
want to extend this treatment to event verbs, as 'events ... are not literally
true or false *for* a period of time or even at a point in time. Rather, events
somehow "take place" *in* time.' (op. cit., p. 74). Davidson (1981, p. 166)
does not want event verbs to have argument places for times, but analyses
the time adverbial in an event sentence as an optional modifier of the *event*
which is introduced by the bare event sentence.

In type theory, one can make a distinction between complementary
and adjunctive temporal reference as follows. A verb requiring a temporal
complement is a propositional function on a time scale *time*, of the general
form (other arguments ignored)

$A(t) : \mathrm{prop} \ (t : \textit{time}).$

A verb for which temporal modification makes sense but is not necessary,
forms a proposition whose proofs (e.g. events) can be timed by using a

timing function,

$$\begin{cases} A : \text{prop}, \\ t(x) : time \ (x : A). \end{cases}$$

These modes of temporal reference are translatable into each other. Given
a verb of the first kind, we have the variant

$$\begin{cases} (\exists t : time)A(t) : \text{prop} \\ p(x) : time \ (x : (\exists t : time)A(t)) \end{cases}$$

of the second kind. Given a verb of the second kind, we have the variant

$$(\Sigma x : A)I(time, t(x), t) : \text{prop} \ (t : time)$$

of the first kind. A temporally modified event sentence, like

Napoleon conquered Spain in 1808

can then be analysed as the progressive conjunction of the event proposition
that Napoleon conquered Spain and the proposition that the year of the
event is 1808

$$(\Sigma x : (Napoleon \ conquered \ Spain))I(year, t(x), 1808),$$

which resembles the analysis in the style of Davidson in terms of existential
quantification over events (ibid.),

$$(\exists x)((Napoleon \ conquered \ Spain)(x)\&(x \ was \ in \ 1808)).$$

We have now shown one possible way of giving a type-theoretical status
to the distinction between state and event verbs. State verbs are propositional functions over times. They take time complements. Event verbs are
independent of time. But they can be temporally modified by means of
adjuncts defined in terms of timing functions and equality.

However, the informal distinction between state and event verbs seems
to me too weak to be identified with the formal distinction between the
two kinds of time reference. Even in an informal consideration of aspect
in an extremely simple situation, the classification of verbs into state and
event verbs will appear to be superficial; cf. Section 5.8 below.

In what follows, I shall treat all verbs for which time adverbials make
sense as propositional functions over times. A distinction can still be made,
on the level of sentences, between indexical and existential ellipsis as the
right way to understand the omission of the time argument. Event *sentences*, then, are typically formalized as existential propositions, which have
no free time variables, and to which left projections give timing functions.
But as will be seen in Section 6.3, a sequence of event sentences in a text
has a different structure.

5.5   Anaphoric expressions of time

Besides the anaphoric zero sign, Chapter 4 presents the operators Pron, *the*, Mod, Gen, *that*, and *this* for the formation of anaphoric expressions. For a time scale, schematically *time*, they have, for example, the following instantiations.

$$\frac{t \,:\, time}{\begin{cases} \mathrm{Pron}(time,t) \,:\, time, \\ \mathrm{Pron}(time,t) \,=\, t \,:\, time \end{cases}}, \qquad \frac{t \,:\, time}{\begin{cases} the(time,t) \,:\, time, \\ the(time,t) \,=\, t \,:\, time \end{cases}},$$

$$\frac{\begin{array}{c}(x \,:\, time)\\ A(x) \,:\, \mathrm{prop} \quad t \,:\, time \quad a \,:\, A(t)\end{array}}{\begin{cases} \mathrm{Mod}(time,(x)A(x),t,a) \,:\, time, \\ \mathrm{Mod}(time,(x)A(x),t,a) \,=\, t \,:\, time \end{cases}}.$$

Anaphoric time expressions are sugared in accordance with the principles laid down in Sections 4.2–4.4. Anaphoric time adverbials are then formed by applying AT to the time expressions, for instance

$\mathrm{AT}(\mathrm{Pron}(time,t)) \,\triangleright\, \mathrm{AT}(it) \,\triangleright\, then,$

$\mathrm{AT}(the(minute,t)) \,\triangleright\, \mathrm{AT}(the\ minute) \,\triangleright\, at\ the\ minute,$

$\mathrm{AT}(\mathrm{Mod}(day,(x)(Beethoven\ was\ born\ \mathrm{AT}(x)),t,a))$
   $\triangleright\, \mathrm{AT}(the\ day\ on\ which\ Beethoven\ was\ born)$
   $\triangleright\, on\ the\ day\ on\ which\ Beethoven\ was\ born.$

Modified definite phrases for times can also be formed idiomatically, by the operator *when*,

$$\frac{\begin{array}{c}(x \,:\, time)\\ A(x) \,:\, \mathrm{prop} \quad t \,:\, time \quad a \,:\, A(t)\end{array}}{\begin{cases} when(time,(x)A(x),t,a) \,:\, time, \\ when(time,(x)A(x),t,a) \,=\, t \,:\, time \end{cases}}.$$

We sugar

$when(day,(x)(Beethoven\ was\ born\ \mathrm{AT}(x)),t,a)$
   $\triangleright\, when\ Beethoven\ was\ born.$

(The past tense is not analysed further here, but only in Section 5.9.) The application of AT does not change the *when* clause: the same clause is used both as a singular term and as an adverbial.

Since the same *when* clause results from

$$when(year,(x)(Beethoven\ was\ born\ \mathrm{AT}(x)),t,a)$$

as well, it may refer both to the day and to the year. To avoid this ambiguity, the less idiomatic modified phrases *on the day Beethoven was born* and *in the year Beethoven was born* can be used.

The anaphoric *when* is not a proposition-forming connective, but an operator that forms singular terms. As its individual arguments, it takes a time and a proof of a proposition about that time. The anaphoric use of the clause *when A* thus presupposes the truth of the proposition *A* at some time, in the anaphoric sense of presupposition discussed in Section 4.12. The presupposition of the clause

$$when\ Estonia\ became\ independent$$

is fulfilled in the context

$$z\ :\ (\exists x\ :\ year)(Estonia\ became\ independent\ \mathrm{AT}(x))$$

created, for example, by the assertion

$$Estonia\ became\ independent.$$

The type-theoretical *when* term formed in this context is

$$when(year, (x)(Estonia\ became\ independent\ \mathrm{AT}(x)), p(z), q(z))\ :\ year.$$

The presupposition need not be fulfilled outside the context, in the actual world. A text saying that Scotland has become independent creates a context in which the presupposition of the clause *when Scotland became independent* is fulfilled.

The anaphoric use of *when* can be contrasted with the use of *when* as a connective synonymous to *whenever*. The sentence

$$the\ virus\ attacks\ when\ the\ computer\ is\ switched\ on$$

is paraphrasable by both of the sentences

the virus attacks whenever the computer is switched on,
the virus attacks every time the computer is switched on.

There is no presupposition that the computer is ever switched on, but universal quantification over times at which the computer is switched on,

$$(\Pi z\ :\ (\Sigma t\ :\ time)(the\ computer\ is\ switched\ on\ \mathrm{AT}(t)))$$
$$(the\ virus\ attacks\ \mathrm{AT}(p(z))).$$

There is another sugaring for this proposition, following the principle (C) of Section 3.5 for sugaring Π into a conditional sentence. First sugar the implicans

$$(\Sigma t\ :\ time)(the\ computer\ is\ switched\ on\ \mathrm{AT}(t))$$

into a sentence. Using existential ellipsis to omit the time, as is typical of event propositions, you obtain

$$the\ computer\ is\ switched\ on.$$

Now there is a time indication $p(z)$ given in the context in which the implicatum is formed. Indexical ellipsis is therefore usable,

$$(\text{the virus attacks } \text{AT}(\text{Zero}(\text{time}, p(z)))) \ \triangleright \ \text{the virus attacks}.$$

(Indeed, if several event sentences are combined into a complex sentence, it is unnatural to understand each of them as making an existential reference to time.) It remains to combine the two sentences into a conditional,

$$\text{the virus attacks if the computer is switched on.}$$

In this sentence, *when* and *if* produce the same formalization. It is the anaphoric use of *when* that makes the well-known difference between the two words.

5.6 Examples of time anaphora

Now that we have made time explicit in type theory by introducing time scales, anaphoric reference to time has become a special case of anaphoric reference in general. It is easy to find examples of time anaphora analogous to any other example of anaphora. To begin with the first example of anaphora in Section 3.4, consider the text

Estonia was occupied by Sweden. Reformation was over then.

The first sentence, analysed in terms of existential ellipsis of time, creates the context

$$z \ : \ (\Sigma y \ : \ year)(\textit{Estonia was occupied by Sweden } \text{AT}(y)).$$

In this context, we can form the time adverbial

$$\text{AT}(\text{Pron}(year, p(z))) \ \triangleright \ \textit{then},$$

as well as many variants, all substitutible for *then* to express the same proposition.

$\text{AT}(\textit{that}(year, p(z))) \ \triangleright \ \textit{in that year},$

$\text{AT}(\text{Mod}(year, (y)(\textit{Estonia was occupied by Sweden } \text{AT}(y)), p(z), q(z)))$
$\quad \triangleright \ \textit{in the year in which Estonia was occupied by Sweden},$

$\text{AT}(\textit{when}(year, (y)(\textit{Estonia was occupied by Sweden } \text{AT}(y)), p(z), q(z)))$
$\quad \triangleright \ \textit{when Estonia was occupied by Sweden}.$

As an example with the same structure as the sentence

if John owns a donkey he beats it,

consider the following sentence of Partee (1973, p. 606).

When you eat Chinese food, you're always hungry an hour later.

The intended reading finds in this sentence an implication expressed jointly by the words *when* and *always*. The problem is thus to formalize the sentence *you're hungry an hour later* in the context created by the sentence *you eat Chinese food.* The latter, understood in terms of existential ellipsis of time, creates the context

$$z : (\Sigma x : time)(you \ eat \ Chinese \ food \ \mathrm{AT}(t)).$$

The time scale must be at least as fine as hour. Then it makes sense to form the term

$$(an \ hour \ later \ \mathrm{THAN}(p(z))) : time,$$

from which *an hour later* is obtained if $p(z)$ is sugared into $\emptyset$. The whole sentence is formalized

$$(\Pi z : (\Sigma x : time)(you \ eat \ Chinese \ food \ \mathrm{AT}(t)))$$
$$(you're \ hungry \ (an \ hour \ later \ \mathrm{THAN}(p(z))))).$$

The original version of the Hintikka-Carlson sentence discussed in Sections 5.5 and 6.13 reads

if you give every child a present for Christmas, some child will open it the same day.

The phrase *the same day*, which was ignored in the previous considerations (nor is it explained by Hintikka and Carlson themselves), makes a reference to the time at which you give the child the present. To make the implicans temporally explicit, we use a time scale at least as fine as day. The phrase *for Christmas* is construed as referring to that time, too, indicating the Christmas that follows. The sentence creates the context

$$z : (\Pi x : child)(\Sigma t : time)(\Sigma y : present)$$
$$(you \ give \ \mathrm{ACC}(x) \ \mathrm{ACC}(y) \ \mathrm{AT}(t) \ for \ Christmas(t)),$$

in which the implicatum can be formed as

$$(\Sigma u : child)(u \ will \ open \ \mathrm{Pron}(present, p(q(\mathrm{ap}(z, u)))))$$
$$\mathrm{AT}(\ the \ same \ day \ \mathrm{AS}(p(\mathrm{ap}(z, u)))))).$$

5.7   The perfect

Quantification over time, such as that involved in the existential ellipsis of the time argument, is often restricted to time anterior or posterior to a given time t_0. For a discrete time scale, such quantification can be defined as quantification over numbers of units to be subtracted from or added to t_0,

$$(\exists t < t_0)A(t) = (\exists n : N)A(t_0 - s(n)) : \mathrm{prop},$$
$$(\exists t > t_0)A(t) = (\exists n : N)A(t_0 + s(n)) : \mathrm{prop}.$$

There are systematic English expressions for these operations,

$$(n \ \mathrm{UNITS}(time) \ before \ t) = t - n : time \ (n : N, \ t : time),$$
$$(n \ \mathrm{UNITS}(time) \ after \ t) = t + n : time \ (n : N, \ t : time),$$

where

(5 UNITS($year$)) ▷ *five years,*
(1 UNITS($minute$)) ▷ *one minute,*

etc. So we have phrases like *five minutes before noon*, *76 years after 1917*.

According to Montague (1974, p. 259) and many others, the *perfect* form of a verb expresses existential quantification over anterior times. *55 has arrived in Oslo* means that there is a time anterior to the time of speech such that 55 arrives in Oslo at that time. The following rule defines the perfect of a time-dependent proposition in this way. In the rule, *time* may be replaced by any time scale.

$$\frac{(t \,:\, time)}{A(t) \,:\, \text{prop} \quad t_0 \,:\, time}$$

$$\begin{cases} \text{Perfect}((t)A(t), t_0) \,:\, \text{prop}, \\ \text{Perfect}((t)A(t), t_0) \,=\, (\exists t < t_0)A(t) \,:\, \text{prop} \end{cases}$$

Observe the binding of the variable t in $A(t)$. Sugaring turns the main verb of $A(t)$ into the perfect form and deletes the bound time argument t. The result is prefixed by BY(t_0), sometimes by AT(t_0).

$$\text{Perfect}((t)A(t), t_0) \,\triangleright\, \text{BY}(t_0), \text{PERF}(A(\emptyset)).$$

Thus we form

Perfect((t)(55 *arrives in Oslo* AT(t)), 15.00)
  ▷ *by 15.00, 55 has arrived in Oslo,*
Perfect((t)(55 *arrives in Oslo* AT(t)), Zero($minute$, 15.00))
  ▷ *55 has arrived in Oslo.*

The time t_0 is typically omitted by indexical ellipsis, especially when it is the now point of the utterance.

The perfect form *have arrived* of the event verb *arrive* is a kind of a state verb. It predicates of the subject the state of having arrived at the time t_0. It does not have an argument place for the time of arrival, since the time argument of the verb *arrive* is bound by an existential quantifier.

It is often observed that the English perfect does not admit of time adverbials in the past, indicating the time at which the event occurs (see e.g. Comrie 1985, p. 32, and Kuhn 1989, p. 537). Thus it is ungrammatical to say, at 15.00,

55 has arrived in Oslo at 14.37.

The Montague-style formalization provides a simple explanation of this observation: in the existential proposition there is no argument place free for such a time specification. There is a similar reduction of argument places in existential sentences in general. The sentence *there is a man in the garden* has no argument place free for a man.

But we can form the proposition

$$(\Sigma z : (\Sigma x : man)(x \text{ is in the garden}))I(man, p(z), John)$$

and sugar it into the sentence

there is a man in the garden; he is John.

Likewise, we can make sense of the sentence

55 has arrived in Oslo; it was at 14.37

uttered at 15.00, as the proposition

$$(\Sigma z : (\Sigma t < \text{Zero}(minute, 15.00))(55 \text{ arrives in Oslo AT}(t)))$$
$$I(minute, p'(z), 14.37),$$

where $p'(z)$ indicates the time of arrival as a function of the event z,

$$p'(c) = t_0 - p(c) : time, \text{ for } c : (\Sigma t < t_0)A(t) = (\Sigma n : N)A(t_0 - s(n)).$$

The same proposition can be expressed by saying

55 has arrived in Oslo, namely at 14.37,

or even

55 has arrived in Oslo, at 14.37.

The comma that separates the time adverbial from the main clause indicates that the adverbial is a clause of its own, an adjunctive modifier.

Example. Given

> u : *(train 55 arrives in Oslo at 14.37)*,
> v : *(train 57 departs from Stockholm at 15.36)*,

it is straightforward to prove

> *train 55 has arrived in Oslo when train 57 departs from Stockholm,*
> *train 57 departs from Stockholm when train 55 has arrived in Oslo.*

Note. In analogy with the anaphoric *when A*, one can define anaphoric *n units before A* and *n units after A*. Using them, one can go on and define *A before B* and *A after B*, to formalize sentences like

> *John left before Mary came,*
> *train 57 departs from Stockholm after train 55 arrives in Oslo.*

5.8   Aspectual systems

State and event verbs, and simple and progressive verb forms, create a cluster of problems that have been studied under the title of *aspect*. To get a grip of these problems, let us build a simple model in which these concepts are instantiated in a clear-cut way, an *aspectual system*. The model will give us, first, the possibility of saying something definite about a number of expressions, and second, a basis of comparison for cases that cannot be treated in such a simple way.

		55
Stockholm	dep.	8.22
Hallsberg	arr.	10.02
Hallsberg	dep.	10.07
Oslo	arr.	14.37

Table 5.1

Our model is based on a *timetable* (Table 5.1) that describes the journey of one single train, train 55, which used to run daily from Stockholm to Oslo. The timetable justifies, for example, the following assertions.

Train 55 departs from Stockholm at 8.22.
Train 55 arrives in Oslo at 14.37.
At noon, train 55 is running from Hallsberg to Oslo.
At 10.05, train 55 is standing at Hallsberg.
Train 55 runs from Stockholm to Oslo in six hours and a quarter.

If you want to use the words *state* and *event* to classify verbs, the timetable model gives a basis for the following classifications.

Depart and *arrive* are *event verbs*, and events that prove propositions formed by means of them are *momentary*, that is, their timings are points on the minute scale.
Be running and *be standing* are *state verbs*, that is, propositional functions true at some points of time and false at other points.
Run is an event verb, but one that calls for *extended events*, whose timings are *spans* of time, with a *beginning* and an *end*.

Observe, in particular, the class of extended event verbs, which is distinct from both momentary event verbs and state verbs. On a coarser time scale, many extended events collapse into momentary events. Thus *Wittgenstein travelled from Vienna to Amsterdam* expresses an extended event on the minute scale but a momentary event on the year scale.

Spans, or *intervals*, as they are often called, can be defined as pairs of points and numbers of units to be added, on each scale T,

$$\mathrm{span}(T) = T \times N : \mathrm{set},$$

whence the notions of beginning and end and the conventional square bracket notation can be defined as follows.

$\mathrm{begin}(d) = p(d) : T$ for $d : \mathrm{span}(T)$,
$\mathrm{end}(d) = p(d) + q(d) : T$ for $d : \mathrm{span}(T)$,
$[t_0, t_1] = d : \mathrm{span}(T)$
for $d : \mathrm{span}(T)$, $t_0 = \mathrm{begin}(d) : T$, $t_1 = \mathrm{end}(d) : T$.

The above classifications concern verbs one by one. But in an aspectual system, there are also things to be said about how the verbs relate to each other.

> *Depart* is *ingressive* with respect to *be running*, that is,
> (a *is running* AT(t)) begins to be true at the time t such that
> (a *departs* AT(t)) is true.
> *Arrive* is *terminative* with respect to *be running*, that is,
> (a *is running* AT(t)) ceases to be true at the time t such that
> (a *arrives* AT(t)) is true.
> *Arrive* is ingressive and *depart* is terminative with respect to *be standing*.
> An event of type (a *runs* FROM(b) TO(c)) occupies the span that
> begins when a departs from b and ends when a arrives at c.

The terms ingressive and terminative are from Bally's discussion about the 'quantification of processes' (see Bally 1944, §115 IIb). The diagram in Figure 5.1, in which time proceeds upwards, summarizes these relations in the timetable model. The thick line is the time axis, on which momentary events are marked by short horizontal lines. The left braces enclose the points at which the indicated state propositions are true. The right square brackets mark the spans that the indicated extended events occupy. The diagram is *deterministic*, in the sense that the time axis does not branch. This is how these verbs function in connection with scheduled time. Factual train traffic is of course *non-deterministic*. Neither the times nor the results of the running processes are determined in advance. The verb *be running* has other terminatives besides *arrive*, such as *crash*. (Cf. the discussion about 'imperfection' in Dowty 1979, pp. 134–135.)

There is nothing particularly type-theoretical in aspectual systems as presented above. They belong to our modes of speaking about actions, events, and states on a level that is external to propositional content. Martin-Löf's analysis of the two verbs *prove* and *know* (Martin-Löf 1985, pp. 231–233) indicates that they are even external to the forms of judgement. His discussion can be summarized in an aspectual system (Figure 5.2), in which *prove* is ingressive with respect to *know*. He points out, moreover, that the perfect *have proved* is equivalent to *know* in this system.

Likewise, we could equate any state verb with the perfect of its ingressive, for example, *be running* with *have departed*. The problem is that state verbs have terminatives whereas a perfect form proposition, by the definition in Section 5.7, is uniformly true from a certain point onwards.

We can now reconsider the perfect by locating it in the timetable model. When considered as a state verb, *has departed* belongs to the structure of a journey, as a propositional function true of points of time after departure. But now we can also make sense of the state of having departed as having an end. When sitting in the train, we use the sentence

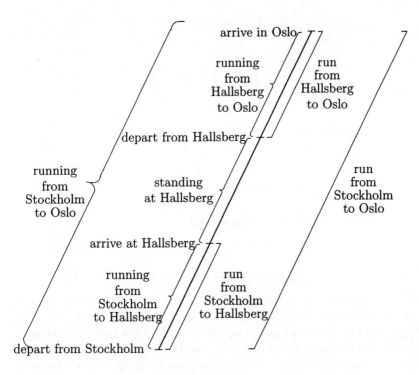

Figure 5.1

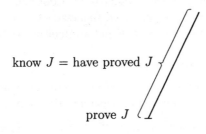

Figure 5.2

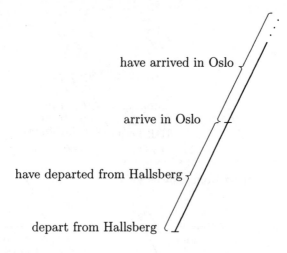

have arrived in Oslo

arrive in Oslo

have departed from Hallsberg

depart from Hallsberg

Figure 5.3

55 has departed from Hallsberg,

after the departure from Hallsberg, but not so willingly after the arrival in Oslo. The relevant aspectual system for us sitting in the train is shown in Figure 5.3. On the other hand, if we are standing at the station of Hallsberg, observing the coming and going of trains, the relevant system is shown in Figure 5.4. In this system, the departure from Hallsberg starts a period for which there is no end like in the former structure. The arrival of the train in Oslo does not matter at Hallsberg.

Locating the perfect in the aspectual system explains what Comrie (1985, p. 25) calls its *present relevance*. Comrie appeals to present relevance also when explaining why the present perfect does not admit of past time adverbials, whereas we have explained this restriction in another way, namely by formalizing the perfect as existential quantification.

5.9   Past, present, and future

When speaking about scheduled time, like in timetables, you can use the present tense of the verb in combination with any time adverbial.

Train 55 departs from Stockholm at 8.22.
Train 55 arrives in Oslo at 14.37.
Train 57 departs from Stockholm only after train 55 has already arrived in Oslo.
Train 57 also runs on Sunday.

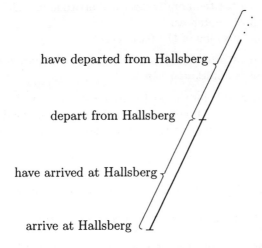

Figure 5.4

You, so to say, see all of time at once, in the way you see all places at once on a map. But when situated in time yourself, you have different positions with respect to different times. A transition from the timetable model to such a situation is involved when you read the timetable in relation to a *now*. You are in Stockholm and suddenly get something urgent to do in Oslo. You call the Central Station of Stockholm and ask questions like whether 55 has already departed, whether there are any more trains to depart for Oslo, and whether there will be a departure after 17.00.

Following the definitions of indexical expressions in Section 4.14, we could introduce *now* as an identity mapping,

$$\frac{t \; : \; time}{\left\{ \begin{array}{l} now(t) \; : \; time, \\ now(t) \; = \; t \; : \; time \end{array} \right.}.$$

But instead, we shall simply write *now* as a variable for the chosen *now* point,

$$now \; : \; time.$$

In temporally situated discourse, a *now* point is given in context. If something is said about a time t prior to *now*, a sentence in the past tense is used. For t posterior to *now*, the future tense is used. If you are making plans for a journey on the same day, and it is eleven o'clock, you will say

train 55 departed at 8.22,
train 57 will depart at 15.36,

instead of assuming the temporally detached attitude in which you use the present tense in both sentences.

To sum up the meaning of the past tense,

a time-dependent proposition can be put into the past tense when its time argument is anterior to *now*.

The type-theoretical rule for the past tense must thus have four arguments: a time scale *time*, a *now* point on the scale, a propositional function on the scale, and a point anterior to *now* on the scale. To express that t is anterior to *now*, we write

$$t < now,$$

which is really an abbreviation of a sequence of three judgements,

$$t : time, \; n : N, \; t = now - s(n) : time.$$

For simplicity, we leave out the premise *time* : set and the corresponding argument of the operator Past.

$$\frac{now : time \quad A(x) : \text{prop} \quad t < now}{\begin{cases} \text{Past}(now, (x)A(x), t) : \text{prop}, \\ \text{Past}(now, (x)A(x), t) = A(t) : \text{prop} \end{cases}}.$$
$$(x : time)$$

In sugaring, Past affects the verb or verbs of the sentence. If there is one main verb, it turns it into the past tense. (Cf. the INFL feature in the formal grammar presented in the appendix.) The *now* argument is always omitted.

$$\text{Past}(now, (x)A(x), t) \; \triangleright \; \text{PAST}(A(t)).$$

If the main verb is in the perfect form, the auxiliary verb *have* is turned into *had*. This gives rise to the *past perfect*.

Given $now = 11.00$, we can form

Past(11.00, (x)(55 *departs from Stockholm* AT(x)), 8.22)
▷ *55 departed from Stockholm at 8.22.*

Using ellipsis of the time 8.22, we would sugar

train 55 departed from Stockholm.

Although the time of departure is omitted, the sentence gives the information that the time is anterior to *now*. This information is not given by the detached present sentence *train 55 departs from Stockholm*. Nor is it given by the detached present sentence *train 55 departs from Stockholm at 8.22*. If you do not know what time it is now, you do not necessarily know whether 8.22 has gone.

Rules analogous to the Past rule can be stated for the present and the future as well.

$$\frac{\begin{array}{cc} (x \,:\, time) \\ now \,:\, time \quad A(x) \,:\, \text{prop} \end{array}}{\left\{\begin{array}{l} \text{Present}(now, (x)A(x)) \,:\, \text{prop}, \\ \text{Present}(now, (x)A(x)) = A(now) \,:\, \text{prop} \end{array}\right.},$$

$$\frac{\begin{array}{cc} (x \,:\, time) \\ now \,:\, time \quad A(x) \,:\, \text{prop} \quad t > now \end{array}}{\left\{\begin{array}{l} \text{Future}(now, (x)A(x), t) \,:\, \text{prop}, \\ \text{Future}(now, (x)A(x), t) = A(t) \,:\, \text{prop} \end{array}\right.}.$$

The information value of the tense is obvious when the time argument is omitted. The tense of the verb is the trace that the time argument leaves to the sentence, so that the time is not completely unspecified. This partial specification of the omitted time by the tense can be compared to the partial specification of the person by the gender of a pronoun. *Train 55 will arrive in Oslo* makes it clear that the arrival is in the future, even though it does not tell when. *John left with her* makes it clear that John left with a woman, even though it does not tell with whom. (Cf. Comrie 1985, p. 4, for an amusing comparison between tense and gender.)

The informational value of the tense is often spelt out by saying that tenses are *indexical*. Thus for Lyons (1977, section 15.4), tense is a 'deictic category'. One might even see here a distinction between the simple past and the present perfect. Sentences in the simple past make indexical reference to a time before *now*, whereas sentences in the present perfect make existential reference. This principle is put into question by examples like

Columbus discovered America,

which, in the terminology used by Kuhn (1989, pp. 533), makes an indefinite rather than a definite time reference. And it does not follow from our rules, either, that the ellipsis of the time argument in simple past sentences is always indexical, because the simple past may also combine with existential ellipsis, as in

$(\exists y < 1993)\text{Past}(1993,$
$\qquad (t)(Columbus\ discovered\ America\ \text{AT}(t)), \text{Zero}(year, y))$
$\rhd\ Columbus\ discovered\ America.$

Example. Consider once again the sentence

if you give every child a present, some child will open it the same day

(cf. Sections 3.7, 4.7, 5.6). The future tense of the implicatum can be formalized using existential ellipsis of time later than the time at which the present is given. The spectrum of the present also contains *the present that you have given him.*

5.10   A synoptic table of tenses

Let us summarize the type-theoretical formalizations we have given to the tenses of traditional grammar.

simple past: $\text{Past}(now, (x)A(x), t)$
    $= A(t)$, where $t < now$,
past perfect: $\text{Past}(now, (x)\text{Perfect}((t)A(t), x), t_0)$
    $= (\exists t < t_0)A(t)$, where $t_0 < now$,
simple present: $\text{Present}(now, (x)A(x))$
    $= A(now)$,
present perfect: $\text{Present}(now, (x)\text{Perfect}((t)A(t), x))$
    $= (\exists t < now)A(t)$,
simple future: $Future(now, (x)A(x), t)$
    $= A(t)$, where $t > now$,
future perfect: $\text{Future}(now, (x)\text{Perfect}((t)A(t), x), t_0)$
    $= (\exists t < t_0)A(t)$, where $t_0 > now$.

A well-known analysis of tenses was given by Reichenbach (1948, §51), in terms of a *point of speech* S, a *point of reference* R, and a *point of event* E. What Reichenbach tells us about the six tenses is the relative order of these three points.

simple past: $R = E < S$,
past perfect: $E < R < S$,
simple present: $S = R = E$,
present perfect: $E < S = R$,
simple future: $S = R < E$,
future perfect: $S < E < R$.

Dowty (1979, p. 331) observes that Reichenbach's analysis does not really give the semantics of the tenses: it does not result in a formalization of the tenses in predicate calculus, in the way the other investigations in his op. cit., chapter VII do. Thus he does not even distinguish between existential and indexical time reference.

To interpret Reichenbach's results in terms of our definitions, we make the following identifications.

The point of speech S is *now*.
The point of event E is the time argument t in $A(t)$.
The point of reference R is the time of comparison t_0 in the perfect tenses, which are formalized $(\exists t < t_0)A(t)$.

It is easy to see that Reichenbach's orderings of S, E, and R are satisfied in our definitions, with two exceptions. First, we do not introduce a separate point R in the simple tenses. Reichenbach, too, identifies it with either S

or E in them, but, without any motivation, $R = E$ in the simple past and $R = S$ in the simple future. Second, and more substantially, Reichenbach's future perfect requires E to be between S and R. That is, when I say,

the train will have arrived by midnight,

I should also mean it has not yet arrived. Our definition does not relate E and S at all. One explanation for Reichenbach's analysis is that when you order the three points S, E, R on a line, you cannot avoid relating all of them to each other. Thus the kind of analysis our definition implies is impossible to represent by Reichenbach's graphical machinery. On the other hand, it would be possible to modify our definition to correspond to Reichenbach's,

future perfect:
$(\Sigma z \; : \; \text{Future}(now, (x)\text{Perfect}((t)A(t), x), t_0))(p'(z) > now)$
$\quad = (\Sigma z \; : \; (\exists t < t_0)(t > now \& A(t)))(p'(z) > now),$
where $t_0 > now$.

But this definition is no longer directly obtained by composing the future and the perfect. Compositionality thus favours our analysis. Pieces of linguistic evidence have been gathered for both analyses; cf., for example, the discussion in Comrie 1985, pp. 69–74, which results in the same solution as ours.

The end results of our analysis are more or less familiar from other logical treatments. Some of the problems arising in them are solved by taking into account the twofold origin of ellipsis. Some problems are solved by locating verbs in aspectual systems. These things have nothing special to do with type theory or any other system of logic. But if they are not recognized, any logical formalization will almost immediately appear to be inadequate. The major import of type theory itself in this area is the general theory of anaphoric reference, which extends to temporal reference as well.

Example. Strawson (1952, p. 194, footnote 1) discussed the following piece of dialogue.

—*A man has just drunk a whole bottle of methylated spirits.*
—*No one who takes a dose like that ever survives it.*
—*So he'll die.*

He noted that the interesting structure is in the alteration of tense and in the use of the pronoun *he* in the conclusion. This structure is preserved in the following variant, which can be formalized compositionally so that the fourth sentence comes out as a consequence of the first three.

—*A man has just drunk a bottle of methylated spirits; it was an hour ago.*
—*Anyone who drinks a bottle of methylated spirits dies within two*

hours.
—*So he will die within an hour.*

Notice that the original example is problematic, since it somehow assumes that the man is still alive. The addition of time specifications makes the consequence clearer. But there are other ways of accomplishing this, of course, also ones that do not specify the time.

TEXT AND DISCOURSE

6.1 Text as a progressive conjunction

Under the titles of anaphora, presupposition, and temporal reference, we have been discussing progression within complex sentences. Progression of all these forms is found in texts as well, between distinct sentences. If the sentences

$$S_1, S_2, \ldots, S_n$$

of a text are formalized as one proposition each, the reference made in each sentence to earlier sentences is captured by means of variable proofs of the earlier propositions. The whole text could then be represented, for instance, as the progressive conjunction

$$(\Sigma x_1 : A_1) \ldots (\Sigma x_{n-1} : A_{n-1}(x_1, \ldots, x_{n-2})) A_n(x_1, \ldots, x_{n-1}),$$

where $A_k(x_1, \ldots, x_{k-1})$ formalizes S_k in the way described by the type-theoretical sentence grammar. The resulting text grammar would be *compositional with respect to the sentence grammar*, in the sense that the formalization of each sentence is retained as a constituent of the formalization of the text.

Compositionality with respect to sentence grammar is an obvious requirement for a text grammar. But we can also require compositionality with respect to initial segments of the text. That is, if the text $S_1, \ldots, S_n$ is completed by adding a new sentence S_{n+1}, the formalization of the resulting text should have the formalization of the initial text as its constituent. This requirement does justice to *sequential reading*, in which a text is taken in sentence by sentence, without adjustments in the parts of the text already read.

But sequential reading fails in the progressive conjunction form suggested above. For, the formalization

$$(\Sigma x_1 : A_1) \ldots (\Sigma x_{n-1} : A_{n-1}(x_1, \ldots, x_{n-2})) A_n(x_1, \ldots, x_{n-1}),$$

of the text $S_1, \ldots, S_n$ is not a constituent of

$$(\Sigma x_1 : A_1) \ldots (\Sigma x_n : A_n(x_1, \ldots, x_{n-1})) A_{n+1}(x_1, \ldots, x_n),$$

which is the formalization of the text $S_1, \ldots, S_n, S_{n+1}$.

To satisfy the principle of sequential reading, one could use the conjunction form

$$(\Sigma x_{n-1} : \ldots (\Sigma x_1 : A_1) A_2(x_1) \ldots)$$
$$A_n(p^{n-2}(x_{n-1}), q(p^{n-3}(x_{n-1})), \ldots, q(x_{n-1})).$$

Each addition of a sentence yields the conjunction of the foregoing text and the new sentence. It is easy to see that a conjunction of this form is logically equivalent to a conjunction of the form first considered, in the sense that their implication is true in both directions.

6.2   Text as a context

In type-theoretical grammar, we are of course not satisfied with formalizations correct up to logical equivalence only. We make the much stronger demand of compositional formalization. As regards a text, in contrast with a long complex sentence, we must also pay attention to the fact that it consists of indicative sentences, each by itself properly formalized as an assertion, and not as a proposition (cf. Section 2.7). Neither of the conjunction forms does justice to this. A text is a sequence of assertions, but a conjunction is not. The context form

$$x_1 : A_1, \; x_2 : A_2(x_1), \; \ldots, \; , x_n : A_n(x_1, \ldots, x_{n-1})$$

is therefore to be preferred to both of the conjunction forms. In it, each sentence S_k is represented as the hypothesis

$$x_k : A_k(x_1, \ldots, x_{k-1}),$$

where $A_k(x_1, \ldots, x_{k-1})$ formalizes the propositional content of S_k in accordance with the sentence grammar. The hypothesis introduces to the context a proof x_k of this proposition. The proposition itself depends on the proofs $x_1, \ldots, x_{k-1}$ introduced by earlier sentences of the text. In other words, each sentence adds to the context, and is itself interpreted in the context created by the foregoing sentences.

The proofs introduced in each assertion are variables. We do not require of a text that it give constant proofs of the propositions asserted; very few texts do. But given a context

$$\Gamma = x_1 : A_1, \; \ldots, \; x_n : A_n(x_1, \ldots, x_{n-1}),$$

we can speak of a sequence of elements

$$a_1, \ldots, a_n,$$

one for each of the variables $x_1, \ldots, x_n$, as an *instance* of Γ. The sequence of assignments of these values to the variables,

$$x_1 = a_1 : A_1, \; \ldots, \; x_n = a_n : A_n(a_1, \ldots, a_{n-1}),$$

is called an *instantiation* of Γ. The context Γ is *equivalent* to both of the conjunctions of $A_1, \ldots, A_n(x_1, \ldots, x_{n-1})$ presented in the previous section in the sense that an instance of Γ can be transformed into a proof of the conjunction, and conversely.

A context Γ is said to be *equivalent* to another context Δ, if any instance of Γ can be transformed into an instance of Δ and conversely. This gives us a definition of logical equivalence between texts.

6.3 Pure text

A text is adequately formalized as a context if it consists of indicative sentences each of which only makes references to the foregoing sentences. Such a text will be called *pure*. We shall later consider deviations from pure text, but let us start with some examples of pure text.

The three-sentence text

> *Peter owns a donkey.*
> *It wears a hat.*
> *The hat is green.*

is formalized, sentence by sentence, and in accordance with Chapters 3 and 4, as the three-hypothesis context

$x_1 \; : \; (\Sigma x \; : \; donkey)(Peter \; owns \; x),$
$x_2 \; : \; (\Sigma x \; : \; hat)(\text{Pron}(donkey, p(x_1)) \; wears \; x),$
$x_3 \; : \; (the(hat, p(x_2)) \; is \; green).$

The anaphoric expressions *it* and *the hat* are interpreted in the context created by the foregoing sentences.

In the following text, the first sentence provides the fulfilment of the presupposition (in the sense of Section 4.12) of the second sentence.

> *One window is broken.*
> *John will repair it.*

The verb *repair* requires, in addition to a subject and an object, a proof of the proposition that the object is broken.

$(x \; will \; repair(z) \; y) \; : \; \text{prop} \; (x \; : \; man, \; y \; : \; window, \; z \; : \; (y \; is \; broken)).$

The formalization of the text makes explicit the reference of the second sentence to the fact that the window is broken.

$x_1 \; : \; (\Sigma x \; : \; window)(x \; is \; broken),$
$x_2 \; : \; (John \; will \; repair \; (q(x_1)) \; \text{Pron}(window, p(x_1))).$

In addition to anaphoric temporal reference, texts often show events *proceeding in time*. The normal reading of the text

> *John fell ill.*
> *He took medicine.*

differs from the normal reading of the text

> *John took medicine.*
> *He fell ill.*

Taken one by one, the two sentences express mutually independent existential quantification over time,

> $(\Sigma t : time)(John\ fell\ ill\ \mathrm{AT}(t)),$
> $(\Sigma t : time)(John\ took\ medicine\ \mathrm{AT}(t)).$

But a temporal sentence in a text is normally read as making a reference to the times of foregoing sentences, so that

> the event introduced by each sentence is later than the events introduced by foregoing sentences.

Following this principle, the first example text is formalized

> $x_1 : (\Sigma t : time)(John\ fell\ ill\ \mathrm{AT}(t)),$
> $x_2 : (\Sigma t > p(x_1))(John\ took\ medicine\ \mathrm{AT}(t)).$

(As for the definition of $(\Sigma x > t)A(x)$, cf. Section 5.7.)

Temporal proceeding in text is, moreover, often forced by a presupposition. Assuming the propositional function

> $(x\ hit\ \mathrm{ACC}(y)\ back(z)\ \mathrm{AT}(t)) : prop$
> $\qquad (x : man,\ y : man,\ t : time,\ z : (\Sigma u < t)(y\ hit\ \mathrm{ACC}(x)\ \mathrm{AT}(u))),$

the way to understand the text

> *John hit Pedro.*
> *He hit him back.*

as a pure text is by reading temporal order into it,

> $x_1 : (\Sigma t : time)(John\ hit\ Pedro\ \mathrm{AT}(t)),$
> $x_2 : (\Sigma t > p(x_1))(\mathrm{Pron}(man, Pedro)\ hit$
> $\qquad\qquad\qquad \mathrm{ACC}(\mathrm{Pron}(man, John))\ back(f(q(x_1)))\ \mathrm{AT}(t)).$

Note. In the last example, $f(q(x_1))$ is a certain function of $q(x_1)$, which can be found by first replacing the proposition asserted in the second sentence by its definiens; see Section 5.7.

6.4   Forward reference

An often observed deviation from the pure text is reference to later sentences in the text, by the use of anaphoric expressions or by other means. The pronouns *he* and *it* occurring in the first sentence of the following text are interpreted in the light of the second sentence.

> *He gave it an immense kick.*
> *John was trying to open a cupboard.*

It is only after reading the whole text that we can interpret *he* as John and *it* as the cupboard John was trying to open. It is hard to give the text a compositional formalization. At least, the text seems to require a violation of sequential reading; the first sentence is only understood when the second sentence has been read. The information that *he* refers to John and *it* to the cupbord is only gained at the reading of the second sentence. Moreover, a cupboard is only introduced in the second sentence.

But looking closer at our actual reading of the text, we realize that it still proceeds sequentially, as follows. We read the first sentence with a partial understanding: we recognize the form *x gave y an immense kick*, but we do not know how to interpret the pronouns *he* and *it*. Reading the second sentence, we gain the information needed for interpreting the pronouns. Then we know how to complete the first sentence, but now after the second sentence has been read. To be faithful to sequential reading, formalization should treat this process in this very order.

The first question we must pose in order to understand forward reference is how we can understand incompletely interpreted passages. For, any text that makes a 'forward reference', like the example above, also has an initial segment not making forward reference, but just containing uninterpreted expressions. It is a further question whether these expressions ever get interpreted later in the text; we must first know how to go on with the incompletely interpreted passage.

Not only does every case of forward reference involve an incompletely interpreted initial passage, but in practice, there is a lot of successful reading of incompletely interpreted passages that never gets resolved as forward reference. Just think of starting a novel from page 187, or reading the second volume of a novel set before reading the first. There will be a lot of reference to the foregoing text that you have not read. It would turn into forward reference if you read that text later; but quite independently of this, you can make sense of what you read without making the interpretations fully specified.

6.5   Background hypotheses

You can find incompletely interpreted passages of text by producing them yourself, by starting in the middle of a pure text. But even in orderly reading, they are ubiquitous in modern prose. Suppose you are testing a theory of discourse representation. You start to read a story from the very beginning, Hemingway's short story 'Big Two-Hearted River' for instance. The story opens

> *The train went up the track out of sight, around one of the hills of burnt timber.*

(*The Nick Adams Stories*, Charles Scribner's Sons, New York, 1972, p. 177.)
You have not been told what train, what track, what hills of burnt timber,
neither will you be.

Hemingway, so to say, places his reader in the middle of a context, without having prepared the context for him. The reader can just *reconstruct*
the context on the basis of indications he finds in the text. The definite
phrase *the train* in the text indicates that a train must be given in the
context, *the track* indicates that a track must be given, *the hills of burnt
timber* indicates that (a group of) hills of burnt timber are given in the context. These indications lead the reader to reconstructing three *background
hypotheses*,

$$y_1 : train, \; y_2 : track, \; y_3 : (hills \; of \; burnt \; timber).$$

In this context, he can then formalize the opening sentence of the story as
the assertion

$$x_1 : (y_1 \; went \; up \; y_2 \; out \; of \; sight, \; around \; one \; of \; y_3).$$

A more explicit style would use indefinite articles instead of definite
ones,

> *A train went up a track out of sight, around one of a group of hills of
> burnt timber.*

But this does not seem to make any difference at all in the reader's understanding. Here we have a challenge to what Heim (1983) calls the *familiarity
theory of definiteness*, also implicit in our formulation of *the* rules, to the
effect that

> A definite is used to refer to something that is already *familiar* at the
> current stage of the conversation. An indefinite is used to introduce a
> *new* referent.

(Quote from Heim, 1983, p. 164.) Our solution in terms of background hypotheses preserves compositionality with respect to the sentence grammar,
which assumes the familiarity theory.

If Hemingway had used indefinite articles, the compositional formalization of the first sentence would contain three existential quantifiers, and no
background hypotheses would be needed,

$$x_1 : (\Sigma x : train)(\Sigma y : track)(\Sigma z : (hills \; of \; burnt \; timber))$$
$$(x \; went \; up \; y \; out \; of \; sight, \; around \; one \; of \; z).$$

This one-hypothesis context is logically equivalent to the context

$$y_1 : train, \; y_2 : track, \; y_3 : (hills \; of \; burnt \; timber),$$
$$x_1 : (y_1 \; went \; up \; y_2 \; out \; of \; sight, \; around \; one \; of \; y_3),$$

consisting of the three background hypotheses and the compositional formalization of the sentence using definite articles. In this very sense, the two

sentences are equivalent openings of the text. But we are, again, aiming at more than logical equivalence, and it is clear that the two sentences employ different modes of expression.

Example. That definite articles can be used equivalently with indefinite articles is further illustrated by the variation found between two editions of Hemingway's short story 'The Battler'. In *The Nick Adams Stories*, the text opens

> *Nick stood up.*
> *He was all right.*
> *He looked up the track at the lights of the caboose going out of sight around a curve.*

In *The Snows of Kilimanjaro and Other Stories* (Penguin Books, Harmondsworth), the third sentence reads

> *He looked up the track at the lights of the caboose going out of sight around the curve.*

The reader hardly notices that it says *the curve* instead of *a curve*. (Cf. Ranta 1991b for a detailed exposition of this example.)

6.6 The general form of a text

We cannot generally make sense of a text

$$S_1, S_2, \ldots, S_n$$

as the mere sequence of hypotheses of the form $x_k : A_k(x_1, \ldots, x_{k-1})$, one for each S_k. We have to insert a sequence H_k of background hypotheses to precede the formalization of S_k proper. Each of the background hypotheses belonging to H_k may depend on

the background hypotheses of earlier sentences of the text,
the earlier sentences themselves,
the earlier hypotheses of the sequence H_k.

The general form of H_k is thus no less complicated than

$$y_{k1} : B_{k1}(y_{11}, \ldots, y_{1m_1}, x_1, \ldots, y_{(k-1)1}, \ldots, y_{(k-1)m_{k-1}}, x_{k-1}),$$
$$\ldots,$$
$$y_{km_k} : B_{km_k}(y_{11}, \ldots, x_{k-1}, y_{k1}, \ldots, y_{k(m_k-1)}).$$

The asserted proposition A_k itself can depend on

the background hypotheses of the earlier sentences,
the earlier sentences themselves,
the hypotheses of the sequence H_k.

The formalization of the k'th sentence is thus

$$x_k : A_k(y_{11}, \ldots, y_{1m_1}, x_1, \ldots, x_{k-1}, y_{k1}, \ldots, y_{km_k}).$$

A simple example in which a background hypothesis refers to the foregoing text is

> *I read a book.*
> *The preface was long.*

The first sentence introduces a book. The second sentence uses the background hypothesis that the book has a preface. If there were a function that for any book gives a preface, no background hypothesis would be needed. But of course there is no such function.

We cannot speak of a *background context*, as the background hypotheses only form a whole context when filled in by the assertions of the explicit story. If we mark the sequence of background hypotheses of S_k by H_k, and the assertion representing S_k itself by J_k, we can say that, logically speaking, *the whole of the story* told by the text $S_1, S_2, \ldots, S_n$ is

$$H_1, J_1, H_2, J_2, \ldots, H_n, J_n.$$

The *explicit story*

$$J_1, J_2, \ldots, J_n$$

is only the 'tip of an iceberg'.

Note. Yet another kind of difficulty is revealed by a careful study of the following passage (from 'Big Two-Hearted River', p. 187 of the *Nick Adams Stories.*)

> *Nick stretched under the blanket comfortably.*
> *A mosquito hummed close to his ear.*
> *Nick sat up and lit a match.*
> *The mosquito was on the canvas, over his head.*
> *Nick moved the match quickly up to it.*
> *The mosquito made a satisfactory hiss in the flame.*
> *The match went out.*
> *Nick lay down again under the blankets.*

This can be neatly formalized, even without background hypotheses, if the blankets and the tent are taken from the foregoing text. A match is introduced by the indefinite article and then lit, which gives a flame and something that can go out.

But as soon as time is made explicit, difficulties arise. For the presupposition for a match going out at t is that the match is in flame at t. The text gives that a match has been lit at a time prior to t, but this is not enough, since that match may have gone out in the meantime. Yet it seems cumbersome to provide for the presupposition in a background hypothesis; we feel that the third sentence does suffice for the seventh sentence to make sense. One way to satisfy this feeling would be to define the time scale of a narrative text as consisting of the events that are explicitly stated, so that nothing can happen but what is stated. Quite independently of the problem discussed, this seems better than any of the conventional time scales of hours, minutes, or seconds. But this idea still needs to be worked out.

6.7 Background hypotheses and style

Different styles of writing use background hypotheses to different degrees. Careful scientific writing tries to avoid them totally, at least in books that are 'self-contained'. Sometimes fiction, too, makes very little use of them. See, for example, the opening of *The Prince and the Pauper* by Mark Twain (University of California Press, Berkeley, Los Angeles, and London, 1979):

> *In the ancient city of London, on a certain autumn day in the second quarter of the sixteenth century, a boy was born to a poor family of the name of Canty, who did not want him. On the same day another English child was born to a rich family of the name of Tudor, who did want him. All England wanted him, too.*

Every place and person is carefully introduced by a proper name or by an indefinite phrase. The fictional proper name *Canty* is not used out of the blue, but in the phrase *a poor family of the name of Canty*. This is a pure text in the sense of Section 6.3.

Newspapers are rich in references to current background of world news, using expressions like *the war, the strike* out of the blue. A part of these expressions can be interpreted in the context created by the earlier issues of the paper. But many of them just refer to something 'in the air'. They may therefore be difficult to read for later generations.

Modern prose, most famously Hemingway's, makes frequent reference to a context the reader just has to build up for himself. Such reference is easily recognized in the use of anaphoric expressions like *the train* out of the blue, but it reaches, through presuppositions of a conventional kind (*Nick stood up* presupposes Nick was sitting or lying down), to subtle allusions to the personage's untold earlier life. The sentence

> *'I've got a right to eat this kind of stuff, if I'm willing to carry it,' Nick said.*

in the 'Big Two-Hearted River' (p. 184) may make one reader reconstruct a hypothesis about Nick's past, while some other reader is not so sensitive as to find any allusion in it.

A simple stylistic device involving background hypotheses is the *epithetic* use of modified definite phrases. In the text

> *Pedro owns a donkey.*
> *The young Texan beats it.*

the first sentence does not give Pedro as a young Texan, and the phrase *the young Texan* is thus only justified by an intervening background hypothesis. Particularly frequent is the use of anaphoric *when* clauses out of the blue,

I was listening to Brahms when the phone rang.

The information that the phone rang is not given directly but by an indication leading the reader to construct a background hypothesis. That the sentence does convey this information may suggest that *when* functions like the conjunction. But such a formalization would be analogous to the formalization of definite noun phrases as existential quantifiers in situations that really require background hypotheses.

6.8   Contexts with definitions

In accordance with sequential reading, we can now explain 'forward reference' as consisting of two parts. First there is a passage with uninterpreted variables, then a passage providing interpretations for them. Consider the example in Section 6.4. To make sense of the first sentence, we need three background hypotheses,

$$y_1 : man, \ Y_1 : set, \ y_2 : Y_1.$$

(This is really a higher-level context, because it introduces a set variable; see Chapter 8.) The text itself is formalized

$$x_1 : (\text{Pron}(man, y_1) \ gave \ \text{Pron}(Y_1, y_2) \ an \ immense \ kick),$$
$$x_2 : (\Sigma x : cupboard)(John \ was \ trying \ to \ open \ x).$$

These background hypotheses can be cancelled in the light of the second sentence. That is, the variables can be assigned values,

$$y_1 = John : man, \ Y_1 = cupboard : set, \ y_2 = p(x_2) : cupboard.$$

In the sequential formalization of the text, the proper place of these definitions is after the formalization of the second sentence, which is where the reader comes to know them.

In type theory, we can extend a context

$$\Gamma = x_1 : A_1, \ \ldots, \ x_n : A_n(x_1, \ldots, x_{n-1})$$

into a *context with a definition*

$$\Gamma, \ x_k = f(x_1, \ldots, x_n) : A_k(x_1, \ldots, x_{k-1}),$$

where k is one of $1, \ldots, n$. In order for the addition of the definition

$$x_k = f(x_1, \ldots, x_n) : A_k(x_1, \ldots, x_{k-1}),$$

to the context Γ, possibly itself containing definitions, to make sense, certain obvious requirements must be met. The variable x_k must not have been defined already; the definiens $f(x_1, \ldots, x_n)$ may not depend on x_k; the type of any of the variables on which $f(x_1, \ldots, x_n)$ depends may not depend on x_k.

6.9 Proper names in fiction

It is of no logical significance whether the author endows his characters with names or only uses anaphoric expressions for them. The sentence

Nick stood up.

which opens 'The Battler' calls for the background hypothesis

Nick : *man*,

as *Nick* does not belong to our vocabulary of constant expressions. We do not know who is meant by *Nick*, only that it is to be a man. *Nick* can thus only be understood as a *variable* of type *man*. This means that *Nick* can be instantiated by any man. The story is *universal* in the sense of applying to all men without distinction.

That the universal significance of a piece of literature is in its variability is an idea discussed by Kundera. According to Kundera, a personage in a fictional text is not a 'simulation of a living person', but an 'experimental ego', not fixed to any particular person. It is up to the reader to make an interpretation of the personage, or give further specifications of it (*L'art du roman*, p. 51). For instance, Kundera himself at the age of fourteen used to endow Kafka's K with the characteristics of a famous ice-hockey player living in the neighbourhood (p. 52).

The same variability concerns places and times. A novel is not about history, but about a 'possible situation of man' (*op. cit.*, p. 61), and this means free variation over places, times, and persons. Not even Prague 1968 in Kundera's novels is intended to be fixed to what we know as the city of Prague in the year 1968 (p. 63). The real significance of *The Unbearable Lightness of Being* comes, according to Kundera, from the insight that it could be about *any* city and *any* year.

6.10 The interpretations of a text

We have been discussing the formalization of a text as a context

$$\Gamma = x_1 : A_1, \ldots, x_n : A_n(x_1,\ldots,x_{n-1})$$

in which some hypotheses are formalizations of the sentences of the text, and the others are background hypotheses. The context is the logical form of the text, its *literal meaning* so to say. Such a formalization leaves the values of the variables $x_1,\ldots,x_n$ unspecified. Some of these variables are proofs of propositions asserted in the text, the others are introduced by background hypotheses.

An instantiation of the context,

$$x_1 = a_1 : A_1, \ldots, x_n = a_n : A_n(a_1,\ldots,a_{n-1}),$$

assigns values to all variables, and gives what we can call an *interpretation* of the text. An interpretation of Hemingway's short story 'The Battler' might start with the definition

$$Nick\ Adams\ =\ Ernest\ Hemingway\ :\ man,$$

and go on by assigning events from the young Hemingway's life to the variable proofs of event propositions asserted in the story. An interpretation goes beyond the literal meaning of the story, which is open to many different interpretations. Instead of looking for a *key* in the author's life, the interpreter may assign himself and events from his own life to the variables of the story, thus giving a kind of an *existential* interpretation. Sometimes there is an interpretation *intended* by the author. Such is certainly the case with history writing, where names of persons, places, and times are not open to assignments of new values, and propositions asserted are meant to have definite proofs in the stream of historical events. But in true fiction, in Kundera's sense, the intended interpretation is precisely that there is no intended interpretation. As for Hemingway, the critic Philip Young writes:

> Exploring the connections between actuality and fiction in Hemingway can be an absorbing activity, and readers who wish to pursue it are referred to the biographical studies listed at the end of this preface. But Hemingway naturally intended his stories to be understood and enjoyed without regard for such considerations—as they have been for a long time. (Preface to the *Nick Adams Stories*, p. 6.)

Our choice of the word interpretation is not only motivated by its usage in the theory of literature. It is in accordance with the mathematical usage, in which an *abstract theory* is formalized as a context, and an instantiation of the context gives an *interpretation of the theory*. Thus group theory is the higher-level context (cf. Chapter 8)

G : set,
$\circ$: $(G)(G)G,$
e : $G,$
$-$: $(G)G,$
$ax1$: $(\forall x : G)(\forall y : G)(\forall z : G)I(G, x \circ (y \circ z), (x \circ y) \circ z),$
$ax2$: $(\forall x : G)(I(G, e \circ x, x)\&I(G, x \circ e, x)),$
$ax3$: $(\forall x : G)(I(G, -x \circ x, e)\&I(G, x \circ -x, e)).$

It has various interpretations, for example,

$G = Z$: set,
$\circ = +$: $(Z)(Z)Z,$
$e = 0$: $Z,$
$- = (x)(0 - x)$: $(Z)Z,$
$ax1 = c1$: $(\forall x : Z)(\forall y : Z)(\forall z : Z)I(Z, x + (y + z), (x + y) + z),$

$$ax2 = c2 : (\forall x : Z)(I(Z, 0 + x, x)\&I(Z, x + 0, x)),$$
$$ax3 = c3 : (\forall x : Z)(I(Z, (0 - x) + x, 0)\&I(Z, x + (0 - x), 0)),$$

where $c1, c2, c3$ are constant proofs of the axioms for $Z, +, 0$, and the function $(x)(0 - x)$. Another interpretation begins

$$G = Q' : \text{set}, \circ = * : (Q')(Q')Q', e = 1 : Q', - = (x)(1/x) : (Q')Q',$$

where Q' is the set of rational numbers without zero.

Being freely interpretable, abstract mathematics is thus like fiction in Kundera's sense, whereas concrete mathematics, such as arithmetic, is like history.

In abstract mathematics, there are also interpretations of one abstract theory in another, for example, the interpretation of group theory in axiomatic set theory using the set-theoretical definition of integers. Type-theoretically, an interpretation of the context

$$\Gamma = x_1 : A_1, \ldots, x_n : A_n(x_1, \ldots, x_{n-1})$$

in the context

$$\Delta = y_1 : B_1, \ldots, y_m : B_m(y_1, \ldots, y_{m-1})$$

is a sequence of definitions

$$x_1 = f_1(y_1, \ldots, y_m) : A_1,$$
$$\ldots,$$
$$x_n = f_n(y_1, \ldots, y_m) : A_n(f_1(y_1, \ldots, y_m), \ldots, f_n(y_1, \ldots, y_m)).$$

The values of $y_1, \ldots, y_m$ are left unspecified. In the terminology of the theory of literature, this amounts to an *intertextual* interpretation of fiction.

6.11   Propositional questions

Unlike predicate calculus, type theory makes explicit the level of judgements, which is beyond the level of propositions. The level of judgements is a part of the level of *linguistic acts*, and of *acts* in general. If you look at the forms of acts that have so far been codified in various formalisms, you realize that they are very few. Frege had one form of assertion, $\vdash A$, and type theory has four. According to Wittgenstein, there are innumerably many kinds of sentences, not only assertion, question, and command (*Philosophical Investigations*, §23).

To codify a form of linguistic act in a formalism, you must give its *syntax*, a syntactic form with something rigid and something schematic; the syntax must also tell what can fill in the schematic. Take for instance the syntactic form of assertion

$$\vdash A$$

where A is schematic; A may be any proposition.

To make a syntactic form into a form of linguistic act, you must also give its *semantics*. That is, you must explain what act is performed by means of an expression of that form. This explanation is often given in terms of a *condition of correct performance* of an act of that form. Thus assertion is governed by the condition

($\vdash$) You may make the assertion $\vdash A$ if you know that A is true.

Constructively, this rule is further analysed in terms of proofs,

($\vdash C$) You may make the assertion $\vdash A$ if you know a proof of A.

Now let us introduce the form of *propositional question*

$$A \mid B$$

where A and B may be any propositions. The most straightforward semantic explanation is not a condition for making the question, but a rule stating how the hearer must react to it.

($\mid$) Answer the question $A \mid B$ by asserting either $\vdash A$ or $\vdash B$.

This form of question is manifested by English questions like

Was the train late or did you sleep too long?
Is 367 prime or composite?

The form of question

$$?A$$

where A is a proposition can be explained as an abbreviation of

$$A \mid {\sim} A$$

That is, it must be answered either $\vdash A$ or $\vdash {\sim} A$. (Cf. Stenius 1967 for an explanation of a 'game' in which assertions and questions are 'moves' interrelated in a similar way. Our discussion can be seen as a type-theoretical development of Stenius's ideas. All propositions Stenius considers are decidable, which makes the situation considerably simpler.)

When introducing the form of question $A \mid B$, as when introducing the forms of judgement $A = B$: prop, $a : A$, and $a = b : A$, we must reject the view that all forms of linguistic act are like $\vdash A$, in which there is just one argument place, which is for a proposition, that is, the view that every linguistic act has a *propositional kernel*. Such a view is assumed in many theories, for example, in Bally's theory of modus and dictum (Bally 1944, §28), in Stenius's theory of mood and descriptive content (Stenius 1967), and in Dummett's theory of sense and force (Dummett 1973, chapter 10).

6.12 Fairness in a dialogue

In a *fair* dialogue, there is a certain *harmony* between the conditions of correct performance and the consequences for the hearer. Assuming fairness, we can derive from the rule (|) concerning the hearer a rule concerning the speaker,

(|′) You may ask the question $A \mid B$ if the hearer knows $A \vee B$ is true.

In a fair dialogue, the hearer does not come to the situation in which the rule (|) forces him to assert either $\vdash A$ or $\vdash B$, but the rule ($\vdash$) does not allow him either. Such a fairness condition is sometimes called a *presupposition* of the question (see e.g. Hintikka 1976, p. 27); this is the third use of that word encountered in this book.

Observe that *I don't know* is not one of the possible answers to the question $A \mid B$, but an objection to the question, to the effect that it is not fair to oblige the hearer to answer.

For the form $?A$, the rule (|′) is vacuous if classical logic is assumed, since anybody knows $A \vee \sim A$ is true provided he knows A is a proposition. But constructively, the hearer knows $A \vee \sim A$ is true only if he knows a proof of $A \vee \sim A$, that is, something he can compute into a proof of either A or $\sim A$. Provided he knows a proof of the disjunction, he is in the position of being eventually able to assert one of the disjuncts. (In Stenius 1967, the question of knowing $A \vee \sim A$ true never arises, because only decidable propositions are considered.)

In a 'dialogue' with a computer, what the computer *knows* is what is *given in the database* it uses. Type-theoretically, a database is a sequence of objects, each of some datatype. As datatypes are sets in type theory, databases can be represented as contexts. (A context, as a series of variables and not of constants, corresponds to an abstract database rather than an ordinary database, but the structure that is relevant here is the same.) What is given in a database is what is given in a context. To pose the question $?A$ without a proof of $A \vee \sim A$ being given in the database leads to a futile search never terminating.

But even the rule (|′) does not prevent the infinite search of an answer. The hearer might know $A \vee B$ is true *potentially* only; a proof of $A \vee B$ is given in his context, but not *actually*, and there is no algorithmic search procedure. We may strengthen the rule (|′) into

(|″) You may ask the question $A \mid B$ if the hearer knows actually that $A \vee B$ is true,

where actual knowledge, in the database model, is actual givenness in the context. (Cf. Section 4.10 for actuality in context, and Section 7.4 for actual knowledge).

From the rule $(\vdash)$, we may derive the converse rule telling that the speaker is committed to the truth of what he asserts.

$(\vdash')$ If someone asserts $\vdash A$, he knows actually that A is true.

Notice that knowledge in the rule $(\vdash)$ can only be actual knowledge. If you only know potentially that A is true, that is, if A true just happens to follow from what you know actually, you do not follow the rule $(\vdash)$ when you assert $\vdash A$.

6.13   Wh-questions

To formalize questions like

> *What is the square of 27?*
> *Who killed Julius Caesar?*
> *When did Iceland become independent?*

we introduce the form of question

$$(\text{Wh } x : A)B(x)$$

where A : prop and $B(x)$: prop $(x : A)$. The hearer's rule is

(Wh) Answer the question $(\text{Wh } x : A)B(x)$ by asserting $\vdash B(a)$ for some $a : A$.

The speaker's fairness rule is

(Wh$'$) You may ask $(\text{Wh } x : A)B(x)$ if the hearer knows that $(\exists x : A)B(x)$ is true.

If infinite search is to be prevented, the rule is

(Wh$'$) You may ask $(\text{Wh } x : A)B(x)$ if the hearer knows actually that $(\exists x : A)B(x)$ is true.

If the hearer knows actually a proof of $(\exists x : A)B(x)$, he can simply compute an element $a : A$ and a proof $b : B(a)$, so that he is then justified in asserting $\vdash B(a)$.

The form $(\text{Wh } x : A)B(x)$ can be generalized to iterated Wh- questions,

$$(\text{Wh } x_1 : A_1)\ldots(\text{Wh } x_n : A_n(x_1,\ldots,x_{n-1}))A(x_1,\ldots,x_n)$$

like

> *Who read which book?*

The semantic rule concerning the hearer is to

assert $\vdash A(a_1,\ldots,a_n)$
for some $a_1 : A_1$, ..., $a_n : A_n(a_1,\ldots,a_{n-1})$.

There is another way to understand the question sentence *Who read which book?*, requiring a complete list of pairs of persons a and books b

such that a read b. But semantically, the question is then not the same, because the rule for the hearer is different. Unlike the first form, this one does not presuppose that there is any instance a, b given in the context.

6.14 Questions and answers in a dialogue

To relativize the assertion and question rules to a speech situation, consider a dialogue that two persons, Diana and Thomas, enter in a context

$$\Gamma = x_1 : A_1, \ldots, x_n : A_n(x_1, \ldots, x_{n-1})$$

of common knowledge. At an arbitrary stage of the dialogue, Diana has the context

$$\Delta = \Gamma, y_1 : B_1(x_1, \ldots, x_n), \ldots, y_m : B_m(x_1, \ldots, x_n, y_1, \ldots, y_{m-1}),$$

and Thomas has the context

$$\Theta = \Gamma, z_1 : C_1(x_1, \ldots, x_n), \ldots, z_k : C_k(x_1, \ldots, x_n, z_1, \ldots, z_{k-1}).$$

The interlocutors extend their contexts by making assertions, that is, by introducing new proofs in their contexts. In the beginning, both of them may thus meaningfully assert only propositions $A(x_1, \ldots, x_n)$ given in the common context Γ. But as the discussion goes on, their contexts diverge. Diana may assert a proposition $B(x_1, \ldots, x_n, y_1, \ldots, y_m)$ given in Δ but not in Θ, and Thomas may assert a proposition $C(x_1, \ldots, x_n, z_1, \ldots, z_k)$ given in Θ but not in Δ. In this sense, Diana's assertions may be *nonsense* to Thomas (and conversely), but Thomas of course keeps track of Diana's assertions and therefore knows what context she lives in.

The interlocutors are not required to give constant proofs, or proofs relative to the shared context Γ, when making assertions. (If they were, they could never diverge from the initially common context.) But they are *committed* to what they assert; Thomas may treat as *known* by Diana anything that is given in Δ. He may thus pose the questions

$A \mid B$ provided $A \vee B$ is true in Δ,
(Wh $x : A)B(x)$ provided $(\exists x : A)B(x)$ is true in Δ.

Diana is committed to giving answers in accordance with the rules ($\mid$) and (Wh).

Notice that Thomas may ask $A \mid B$ even if it is nonsense to him, that is, even if A and B are not propositions in Θ; it is only required that they be propositions in Δ. He may thus challenge Diana's incredible claim that there is a lion in the garden by asking

Is the lion male or female?

without committing himself to the existence of the lion. In other words, since Diana's context is now

$$\Gamma, \, y \, : \, (\exists x \, : \, lion)(x \; is \; in \; the \; garden),$$

she knows, by the decidability of the sex of lions, that the lion $p(y)$ is either male or female. Thomas is thus entitled to make the question

$$(p(y) \; is \; male) \mid (p(y) \; is \; female)$$

where $p(y) \, : \, lion$ is not given in his context.

Notice, furthermore, that there is a type of dialogue in which fairness clearly does not require actual knowledge. If Diana is a mathematics teacher, and Γ consists of basic analytic geometry, Diana may ask her pupil Thomas

What is the length of the line AB?

on the basis that

$$(\exists r \, : \, R)(the \; length \; of \; the \; line \; AB \; is \; r) \; true \; in \; \Gamma$$

can be derived from Γ, although the length is not mechanically computable from what is actually given in Γ. In this case, Thomas does not actually know the truth of $(\Sigma r \, : \, R)(the \; length \; of \; the \; line \; AB \; is \; r)$. He must find it out by making creative use of his knowledge of Γ.

Note. A recipe in a cookery book functions typically like a pure text, in an initial context providing kitchen utensils and basic raw materials. Take, for instance, the recipe for *moules marinière* (from *Larousse Gastronomique*, Paul Hamlyn, London, 1988, p. 655).

Trim, scrape, and wash 1 kg mussels.
Peel and chop 1 large shallot.
Put the chopped shallot in a buttered pan with 2 tablespoons chopped parsley, a small sprig of thyme, half a bay leaf, 2 dl dry white wine, 1 tablespoon wine vinegar, and 2 tablespoons butter.
Add the mussels, cover the pan, and cook over a high heat, shaking the pan several times, until all the mussels have opened.
Remove the pan from the heat and place the mussels in a large serving dish.
Remove the thyme and the bay leaf from the saucepan and add 2 tablespoons butter to the cooking liquid.
Whisk the sauce until it thickens and pour it over the mussels.
Sprinkle with chopped parsley.

Anaphoric reference is made to portions of materials given in the earlier context. Such portions can be logically treated as individuals, defining, for example, the set of n gram portions of mussels and n centilitre portions of wine,

$(n \ g \ mussels) \ : \ set \ (n \ : \ N)$,
$(n \ cl \ wine) \ : \ set \ (n \ : \ N)$.

The recipe is not a series of assertions but of instructions $!A$, for which the following rules apply.

(!) React to the instruction $!A$ by making A true, that is, by producing an object of type A.

(!′) You may give the instruction $!A$ if the reader is able to produce an object of type A.

In a series of instructions, the progression is based on the assumption that the reader has fulfilled the tasks expressed by earlier instructions. Thus it is possible for the reader to *remove the thyme and the bay leaf from the saucepan* because he has followed the instruction to *put ... in a buttered pan ... a small sprig of thyme, half a bay leaf ....*

7

CONTEXTS AND POSSIBLE WORLDS

The analysis of natural language within classical logic makes heavy use of *possible worlds* (see e.g. Montague 1974, almost any chapter). There is strong principal reason for this in the coarse notion of identity of propositions: every proposition is either True or False, but it is felt that some finer 'intensional distinctions' must be drawn. In type theory, we do not have this reason. Moreover, type theory has the notion of definitional equality as distinct from the equality predicate (see Section 2.25), which in fact comes close to the notion of *intensional isomorphism* of Carnap (1947, p. 56). Hence compared with classical logic we have less need of possible worlds to draw intensional distinctions.

On the other hand, many of the analyses classical logic makes in terms of possible worlds are based on ideas that resemble our intuitions about contexts. It turns out that this resemblance is systematic: the most important notions of the theory of possible worlds can be interpreted in the theory of contexts. Thus we can compare our analyses with those of possible worlds semantics, as well as make use of its results. But like elsewhere in this book, we shall be able to strengthen the classical modes of expression into progressive versions enabling a treatment of anaphoric relations to be conducted.

7.1   The extensions of a context

Let us take a closer look at three ways in which a context is extended when knowledge is acquired. The simplest way, already considered, is the addition of a hypothesis. We extend the context $\Gamma =$

$$x_1 : A_1, \ldots, x_n : A_n(x_1, \ldots, x_{n-1})$$

into the context

$$x_1 : A_1, \ldots, x_n : A_n(x_1, \ldots, x_{n-1}), \ x : A(x_1, \ldots, x_n)$$

by adding a hypothesis $x : A(x_1, \ldots, x_n)$ where $A(x_1, \ldots, x_n)$ is a proposition in Γ. It is obvious that everything that is given in Γ is given in the new context as well, and we can speak of growth of knowledge in the extension of the context. It may now happen that the new proposition $A(x_1, \ldots, x_n)$

is potentially true in Γ, in which case only actual knowledge grows. This is a typical situation in argumentative text. As a limiting case, $A(x_1, \ldots, x_n)$ is even actually true in Γ. But it may also happen that $A(x_1, \ldots, x_n)$ has no proof in Γ. This is the way knowledge usually grows in a narrative text.

The second way of extending a context is by adding to it a definition of one of its variables. That is, we move from Γ to

$$\Gamma, \ x_k = a(x_1, \ldots, x_n) \ : \ A_k(x_1, \ldots, x_{k-1})$$

provided, of course; that the conditions stated in Section 6.8 are satisfied. But the new context is now equivalent to the context

$$\Gamma(a(x_1, \ldots, x_n)/x_k)$$

obtained from Γ by removing the hypothesis $x_k \ : \ A_k(x_1, \ldots, x_{k-1})$ and replacing the occurrences of x_k by $a(x_1, \ldots, x_n)$ (some permutations may be necessary). Thus the new context is shorter than Γ rather than longer. But still, everything that is given in Γ is given in the new context as well. In a series of lectures on choice sequences at the University of Stockholm in 1990–1991, Per Martin-Löf showed how the growth of knowledge in experiments can be understood in this way: an unknown quantity is assigned a value, which may depend on other unknown quantities.

The third way to extend the context Γ is by presenting a new context Δ in which Γ can be interpreted, in the sense of Section 6.10. The new context Δ need not look the same as Γ at all; what is essential is just that there is a *mapping* from Δ to Γ, that is, a sequence of definitions of all variables of Γ in terms of the variables of Δ. For instance, the context

$$x \ : \ A, \ y \ : \ C, \ z \ : \ D(y)$$

is an extension of the context

$$u \ : \ A + B, \ v \ : \ (\Sigma x \ : \ C)D(x)$$

by virtue of the mapping

$$u = i(x) \ : \ A + B, \ v = (y, z) \ : \ (\Sigma x \ : \ C)D(x).$$

In general, a mapping **f** from the context

$$\Delta = y_1 \ : \ B_1, \ \ldots, \ y_m \ : \ B_m(y_1, \ldots, y_{m-1})$$

to the context

$$\Gamma = x_1 \ : \ A_1, \ \ldots, \ x_n \ : \ A_n(x_1, \ldots, x_{n-1})$$

is a sequence of functions

$$f_1(y_1, \ldots, y_m) : A_1 \ (\Delta),$$

$$\ldots$$

$$f_n(y_1, \ldots, y_m) : A_n(f_1(y_1, \ldots, y_m), \ldots, f_{n-1}(y_1, \ldots, y_m)) \ (\Delta).$$

It is obvious that the first two ways of extending a context are special cases of the third way. Thus we take the existence of a mapping to be the definition of what it is for a context to be an extension of another context. We write

$$\mathbf{f} : \Delta \longrightarrow \Gamma$$

or, diagrammatically,

$$\Delta$$
$$\mathbf{f} \downarrow$$
$$\Gamma$$

to say that $\mathbf{f}$ is a mapping from Δ to Γ.

Given a mapping $\mathbf{f}$ from Δ to Γ, everything that is given in the context Γ, in the sense of Section 4.9, is also given in Δ, in the form where $f_i(y_1, \ldots, y_m)$ is substituted for x_i, for $i = 1, \ldots, n$. For instance, any proposition given in Γ,

$$A(x_1, \ldots, x_n) : \text{prop} \ (\Gamma),$$

is given in Δ in the form

$$A(f_1(y_1, \ldots, y_m), \ldots, f_n(y_1, \ldots, y_m)) : \text{prop} \ (\Delta).$$

Any proof of a proposition in Γ,

$$a(x_1, \ldots, x_n) : A(x_1, \ldots, x_n) \ (\Gamma),$$

is given in Δ in the form

$$a(f_1(y_1, \ldots, y_m), \ldots, f_n(y_1, \ldots, y_m))$$
$$: A(f_1(y_1, \ldots, y_m), \ldots, f_n(y_1, \ldots, y_m)) \ (\Delta).$$

In this sense, we know at least as much in Δ as in Γ. The knowledge state that we have reached by moving from Γ to Δ along $\mathbf{f}$ still contains variables, if Δ is not the empty context, with $m = 0$. But the variables of Γ have now been defined in terms of the variables of Δ.

7.2 Some notions of possible worlds semantics

Given a mapping

$$\mathbf{f} : \Delta \longrightarrow \Gamma$$

we may speak of Δ as an *epistemic alternative* of Γ, in the sense of Hintikka (1962), since Γ is compatible with everything that is known in Δ, at most adding some knowledge. Another word for this relation is *accessibility:* Δ is accessible from Γ, in virtue of $\mathbf{f}$. The customary notation for accessibility is

$$\Gamma \preceq \Delta.$$

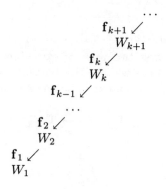

Figure 7.1

To make the mapping explicit, we write

$$\Gamma \preceq_{\mathbf{f}} \Delta.$$

In the general case, there are many contexts accessible from a given one.

$$\Delta \qquad \Theta \ldots \quad \Xi$$
$$\mathbf{f} \searrow \quad \mathbf{g} \downarrow \mathbf{h} \nearrow$$
$$\Gamma$$

This is so because everything is not yet known in Γ, but Γ leaves room for further specifications. The extensions $\Delta, \Theta, \ldots, \Xi$ may be mutually incompatible. They are *alternatives* of each other as extensions of Γ. This is a different sense of alternativeness from the epistemic one, in which they are alternatives of Γ but not necessarily of each other.

Now we can think of a *world* W, a knowledge state in which every question has received an answer, in terms of a sequence (possibly infinite) of contexts W_k and mappings $\mathbf{f}_k : W_{k+1} \longrightarrow W_k$; see Figure 7.1. Each context W_n is an *approximation* of the world W in the sense that what is given in W_n is transmitted to its extensions and to the world itself. What is *given in the world* W is defined precisely as the totality of what is given in the approximating contexts. Moreover, we shall say that the world W is an *extension* of the context Γ, if at least one of the contexts W_n that approximate W is an extension of Γ.

To speak precisely about total worlds we must explain what it is for something to be given in a world W, that is, what a judgement of the form

$$J \text{ in } W$$

means, for each of the four forms of judgement. The judgement

$$A : \text{set in } W$$

means that

$$A(\mathbf{w}_i) : \text{set } (W_i) \text{ for some } i.$$

In other words, a set in any of the contexts W_i is a set in W. We use the vector notation $\mathbf{w}_i$ to abbreviate the sequence of variables introduced in the context W_i. The judgement

$$a : A \text{ in } W,$$

where $A(\mathbf{w}_i) : \text{set in } W_i$, means that

$$a(\mathbf{w}_j) : A(\mathbf{f}_i(\ldots \mathbf{f}_{j-1}(\mathbf{w}_j)\ldots)) \ (W_j) \text{ for some } j \geq i.$$

In other words, any element of a set in some W_i, possibly given at a stage j later than the stage at which the set has been formed, is an element of that set in W. By the propositions as types principle,

$$A \text{ true in } W$$

means that the proposition A, formed at some stage i, has a proof at some stage j that may be later than i. (For equality judgements, see Ranta 1991c. The semantic explanations of judgements in a world are essentially due to Martin-Löf (1990).)

A given context typically has indefinitely many contexts that extend it, and thus, *a fortiori*, indefinitely many such worlds. It does not determine a unique world, but what might be called a *bunch of worlds*. In our account, the notion of context is prior to the notion of world. Some authors, like Stalnaker (1986), argue for the priority of worlds, but this seems constructively unintelligible (cf. Ranta 1991c).

To make comparisons with classical analyses of natural language in terms of possible worlds, it is useful to interpret the locution

in every world that has a certain property

as

in the context that defines this property.

One example of such a property is the property of being compatible with what a text says. The context that defines this property is the formalization of the text. That this form of expression is so central in possible worlds semantics indicates that even there worlds are thought of in terms of finite approximations.

Note. It is easy to see that accessibility, in the sense of existence of a mapping, is reflexive and transitive, and that alternativeness, relative to a given initial context, is an equivalence relation.

Example. In the series of lectures on choice sequences in 1990–1991, Martin-Löf gave the following definition of modalities relative to a context Γ. Given $A(\mathbf{x})$: prop (Γ), we define

$$(\Box\Gamma)A(\mathbf{x}) = (\Pi\Gamma)A(\mathbf{x}) : \text{prop},$$
$$(\Diamond\Gamma)A(\mathbf{x}) = (\Sigma\Gamma)A(\mathbf{x}) : \text{prop}.$$

The following laws of monotonicity can be proved, assuming $\mathbf{f} : \Delta \longrightarrow \Gamma$. Let $\mathbf{x}$ be the sequence of variables introduced by Γ and $\mathbf{y}$ the sequence introduced by Δ.

$$(\Box\Gamma)A(\mathbf{x}) \supset (\Box\Delta)A(\mathbf{f}(\mathbf{y})),$$
$$(\Diamond\Delta)A(\mathbf{f}(\mathbf{y})) \supset (\Diamond\Gamma)A(\mathbf{x}).$$

(See Section 7.6 for the vector notation $\mathbf{x}$, or think of the special case of a context consisting of one hypothesis only.) There is a further notion of possibility of a context, defined

$$\text{Pos}(\Gamma) = (\Sigma\Gamma)\top : \text{prop},$$

where $\top$ is the one-element set with $\dagger : \top$. One can prove the following propositions.

$$(\text{Pos}(\Gamma) \supset (\Box\Gamma)A(\mathbf{x})) \supset (\Box\Gamma)A(\mathbf{x}),$$
$$(\Diamond\Gamma)A(\mathbf{x}) \supset \text{Pos}(\Gamma).$$

7.3   Worlds of fiction

When a text is formalized as a context, *objects given in the text* can be explained as objects given in the context. In the simplest case, they are just variables, like *Nick* in our reading of 'Big Two-Hearted River'. *Nick's father* is a complex expression in which the variable *Nick* occurs. In the same vein, *truth in fiction* is truth in the context.

This result comes very close to what David Lewis (1978, p. 39) introduced as his 'first approximation' of truth in fiction f:

ϕ is true in f if ϕ is true in every possible world in which the plot of f is enacted.

Lewis gives two main reasons to reject this analysis. First, it appeals to the plot of f, as if the plot were something given independently of considerations of what is true in f. Lewis points out that 'this extraction of plot from text is no trivial or automatic task. Perhaps the reader accomplishes it only by finding out what is true in the story—that is, only by exercising his tacit mastery of the very concept of truth in fiction that we are now investigating.' Second, this definition makes it possible to include the actual world in the worlds relevant for truth in f, if there happen to exist homonymous persons that actualize the plot here, although it has not been the author's intention to refer to those persons.

To see that these objections do not concern our definition of truth in fiction, let us restate our definition in terms of worlds.

A is true in f as formalized by Γ if A is true in every world that Γ approximates.

Unlike Lewis, we do not speak of truth in f *tout court*, but of truth in f as formalized by Γ. To proceed from f to Γ is to formalize f in accordance with type-theoretical grammar. It is precisely an activity that Lewis calls extraction of plot from text. It is by no means a trivial or automatic task; to accomplish it, you must figure out what propositions the text asserts and thus what is explicitly true in it. The way we have done this relies compositionally on the formalization of individual sentences in type theory.

Second, no identifications follow from coincidences between names in the story and names in the actual world. For names in the story are treated as variables, and it is only in interpretations that they are anchored in the actual world. *Nick Adams* in Hemingway's stories is a variable even if there happens to be a man named *Nick Adams* in the actual world. In the formalization of fiction, this treatment is even extended to names that are perfectly well known to refer to something in the actual world, such as *Prague* in Kundera's works.

Besides this difference from the situation Lewis discusses, there is a related one. Lewis discusses truth of just any sentence ϕ, where we speak of a proposition A in Γ. Each sentence in a story expresses a proposition in the context of the foregoing story, but not, in general, a proposition in the actual world. It is only when values have been assigned to *Nick* and *the blanket* that *Nick stretched under the blanket comfortably* expresses a proposition.

7.4 Judgement, knowledge, and belief

In order to consider the knowledge of an agent, we can assign to the agent a context consisting of judgements he has made, thereby adopting a sequence of beliefs. As the context may be progressive, later beliefs may depend on earlier ones. What the agent believes are all judgements that are provable in this context. Among the agent's beliefs defined in this way, there is an ordering based on the relative actuality of these judgements, as described in Section 4.10.

In the philosophy underlying intuitionistic type theory, the notions of knowledge and belief are secondary to the notion of judgement (cf. Martin-Löf 1985). Knowledge and belief are dispositions, or states, whereas judgements are acts. Judgements are acts by which knowledge is acquired, so that to say of an agent p,

$$p \text{ makes the judgement } J$$

amounts to the same as saying

$$p \text{ comes to know } J.$$

To know J means, accordingly, to have made the judgement J. (Cf. Section 5.8, where *prove* was introduced as another ingressive for *know*.)

It is customary in analytic philosophy that *believe* is taken as the basic epistemic verb. Knowledge is then defined as belief that has some extra characteristic, for example, of being true and justified.

Martin-Löf uses the verb *know* uniformly for what is usually divided between *know* and *believe* in analytic philosophy. What I know is what I have judged. However, my judgement may turn out to be wrong. I may contradict it by another judgement, or just withdraw it; or someone else may, after my death perhaps. The analytic philosopher would then say that my knowledge was not real knowledge after all. But on the other hand, there is no method of settling the question positively, to remove all doubt concerning my knowledge. Knowledge thus cannot be anything *more* than what is acquired by making a judgement.

In *epistemic logic*, as introduced by Hintikka (1962), to know is something more than to believe. That something is an anchoring of the belief in 'how things really are', in 'the actual world'. This distinction between knowledge and belief can of course be spelt out in type theory. Formalize an agent's belief that a proposition A is true as his having made the judgement

$$A \text{ true,}$$

but without possessing a constant proof. In other words, the agent has the hypothesis

$$x : A$$

in his belief context. For his belief that A is true to count as knowledge, it is required, first, that A be true, that is, that there be a constant proof

$$a : A,$$

and second, that the agent know this constant proof, that is, that he have made the definition

$$x = a : A.$$

This definition of x can be called an *anchoring* of the belief that A is true in the actual world. This terminology also harmonizes with the one in which variables are something *unknown* and constants something *known*. Notice that in the absence of proof objects, it is difficult to define precisely this second condition, that is, what it is for the agent really to know an anchoring of his belief in the actual world.

But this analysis of belief and knowledge is based on the comparison of the agent's judgement $x : A$ with some other judgement $a : A$, and fails to tell how this latter judgement is evaluated. It plays with a relative notion of knowledge: your belief counts as knowledge if you can anchor it in my beliefs, or in some authority's beliefs, to which I solemnly attach the title 'the actual world'. As for the authority itself, there is no positive way to tell knowledge from belief. There is just the positive way to tell mere belief from knowledge: mere belief is knowledge that has turned out to be erroneous.

The formalization of *know* and *believe* in the style of epistemic logic thus shows only a limited aspect of human knowledge. The same concerns the formalization in terms of contexts that we are about to present. But it seems to be quite adequate, at least, for computers understood as knowing agents, since databases can be formalized as contexts in type theory. Moreover, we will be able to generalize from knowledge of truth to knowledge of a judgement of any of the four forms.

7.5 Belief contexts

To discuss questions of epistemic logic, let us follow the standard terminology of epistemic logic and use the word *believe* instead of *know* for the state of having judged. Consider an agent p making judgements one after another, later ones possibly making reference to earlier ones. Consider only judgements of the form $x : A$ where $A :$ prop, and treat the proofs the agent has as variables. In other words, assign to p a *belief context*

$$\Gamma_p = x_1 : A_1, \ldots, x_n : A_n(x_1, \ldots, x_{n-1}).$$

The intended significance of Γ_p is that it consists of judgements p has made, in other words, of beliefs he has adopted. It is natural to think of Γ_p as representing p's beliefs on one occasion, as the background against which p acts on that occasion, rather than as the corpus of his lifetime beliefs. (Cf. Hintikka 1962, p. 7, on the corresponding point in possible worlds semantics.) Thus it will make sense for p to modify his beliefs, to move from context Γ_p to another context Δ_p, but such changes will be ignored now. (Cf. however Section 6.14, where belief contexts are extended by making assertions.)

Given Γ_p, we can study clauses of the form

$$p \text{ believes } J,$$

where J is a judgement of any of the four forms, in which the variables of Γ_p may occur free, as judgements

$$J \text{ in } \Gamma_p.$$

These, in turn, are interpreted as hypothetical judgements, namely

$$J \ (\Gamma_p),$$

as explained in Section 4.9. Thus

$$p \text{ believes } A \text{ is a proposition}$$

means that
$$A(x_1, \ldots, x_n) : \text{prop} \ (\Gamma_p).$$
Given a proposition A,

p *believes that A is true*

means
$$A \text{ true } (\Gamma_p),$$
that is, that there is a proof
$$a(x_1, \ldots, x_n) : A \ (\Gamma_p).$$
This generalizes immediately to
$$a(x_1, \ldots, x_n) : A(x_1, \ldots, x_n) \ (\Gamma_p),$$
that is,

p *believes $A(x_1, \ldots, x_n)$ is true,*

where $A(x_1, \ldots, x_n)$ need not be a proposition categorically, but it is enough that p believes it is a proposition. This happens, for example, when $A(x_1, \ldots, x_n)$ contains an anaphoric reference to an object given in Γ_p only; cf. Section 7.7.

In the same way, we can speak about sets and their elements in p's beliefs. For instance, a man in p's beliefs is
$$a(x_1, \ldots, x_n) : man \ (\Gamma_p).$$
To say that p believes there is a man is thus the same thing as to say that there is a man in p's beliefs.

The distinction between actual and potential belief can be made as in Section 4.10: actual belief is actual givenness in Γ_p. The same ordering of relative actuality applies. Observe that the problem of availability of interpretations of anaphoric expressions discussed in Section 4.10 now appears as exactly the same as the problem of logical omniscience.

7.6   The belief operator

The basic form of expression of epistemic logic is
$$B_p A$$
whose intended meaning is that p believes A. The possible worlds semantics given to it says that

$B_p A$ is true if A is true in every world that is compatible with everything that p believes.

Our interpretation of this principle, stated in Section 7.2, says that $B_p A$ is true if A is true in p's belief context. This is nothing but the meaning we gave to p *believes A is true* in the previous section. To express this in the form of a proposition, instead of a hypothetical judgement, we just bind all variables of Γ_p with Π. Then we can define

$$B_p A = (\Pi x_1 : A_1) \ldots (\Pi x_n : A_n(x_1, \ldots, x_{n-1}))A : \text{prop}$$

for $p : agent$, $A : \text{prop}$. This is a notion of potential belief, not actual. For if we drop out the proof object of A and consider the proposition only, we cannot distinguish between proofs of different forms. All that counts is that A is true in Γ_p; the proof may be of any complexity.

Now we can generalize the belief operator to take as its second argument a proposition in p's beliefs. The generalized belief operator $(B\Gamma_p)$ binds the variables of Γ_p.

$$\frac{p : agent \quad A(x_1, \ldots, x_n) : \text{prop in } \Gamma_p}{\begin{cases} (B\Gamma_p)A(x_1, \ldots, x_n) : \text{prop}, \\ (B\Gamma_p)A(x_1, \ldots, x_n) = \\ \quad (\Pi x_1 : A_1) \ldots (\Pi x_n : A_n(x_1, \ldots, x_{n-1}))A(x_1, \ldots, x_n) : \text{prop} \end{cases}}.$$

The judgement $(B\Gamma_p)A(x_1, \ldots, x_n)$ true is equivalent to the hypothetical judgement

$$A(x_1, \ldots, x_n) \text{ true in } \Gamma_p.$$

If we use vector notation to abbreviate sequences of terms, for example,

$$\mathbf{x} = x_1, \ldots, x_n,$$

we can abbreviate

$$(\Pi\Gamma_p)A(\mathbf{x}) =$$
$$\quad (\Pi x_1 : A_1) \ldots (\Pi x_n : A_n(x_1, \ldots, x_{n-1}))A(x_1, \ldots, x_n) : \text{prop},$$
$$(\lambda\mathbf{x})a(\mathbf{x}) = (\lambda x_1) \ldots (\lambda x_n)a(x_1, \ldots, x_n) : (\Pi\Gamma_p)A(\mathbf{x}),$$
if $a(x_1, \ldots, x_n) : A(x_1, \ldots, x_n)$ in Γ_p,
$$\text{ap}(c, \mathbf{a}) = \text{ap}((\ldots \text{ap}(\text{ap}(c, a_1), a_2), \ldots), a_n) : A(a_1, \ldots, a_n)$$
if $c : (\Pi\Gamma_p)A(\mathbf{x})$,
$$a_1 : A_1, \ldots, a_n : A_n(a_1, \ldots, a_{n-1}),$$
$$\mathbf{a} = a_1, \ldots, a_n.$$

In the previous section, we explained individuals in p's beliefs as what is given in hypothetical judgements of the form

$$a(x_1, \ldots, x_n) : A(x_1, \ldots, x_n) \ (\Gamma_p).$$

In other words, elements of the set A in Γ_p are A-valued functions depending on the variables of Γ_p. To be able to treat this totality as a set, we use Π to bind the variables. Thus the set of men in p's beliefs is the set

$$(\Pi\Gamma_p)man.$$

Note that this set is definitionally equal to the proposition $(B\Gamma_p)man$. To say that p believes there is a man is thus, again, the same thing as to say that there is a man in p's beliefs.

7.7   Anaphoric reference to believed objects

Given Bob's belief context

$$\Gamma_{Bob} = x_1 : A_1, \ldots, x_n : A_n(x_1, \ldots, x_{n-1}),$$

we can formalize the sentence

Bob believes there is a unicorn

as the proposition

$$(B\Gamma_{Bob})unicorn,$$

that is, as

$$(\Pi\Gamma_{Bob})unicorn.$$

Introduce a variable proof of this proposition,

$$z : (B\Gamma_{Bob})unicorn.$$

This hypothesis gives us a unicorn Bob believes there is,

$$\mathrm{ap}(z, \mathbf{x}) : unicorn \text{ in } \Gamma_{Bob}.$$

We apply the pronominalization rule (see Section 4.2) to this unicorn and obtain

$$\mathrm{Pron}(unicorn, \mathrm{ap}(z, \mathbf{x})) : unicorn \text{ in } \Gamma_{Bob}.$$

This pronoun can occupy the argument place of the propositional function

$$(x \text{ is saddled}) : \mathrm{prop} \ (x : unicorn),$$

to form

$$(\mathrm{Pron}(unicorn, \mathrm{ap}(z, \mathbf{x})) \text{ is saddled}) : \mathrm{prop} \text{ in } \Gamma_{Bob}.$$

Hence we have

$$(B\Gamma_{Bob})(\mathrm{Pron}(unicorn, \mathrm{ap}(z, \mathbf{x})) \text{ is saddled}) : \mathrm{prop}$$
$$(z : (B\Gamma_{Bob})unicorn).$$

By Σ formation, we discharge the hypothesis and form the proposition

$$(\Sigma z : (B\Gamma_{Bob})unicorn)(B\Gamma_{Bob})(\mathrm{Pron}(unicorn, \mathrm{ap}(z, \mathbf{x})) \text{ is saddled}),$$

which formalizes the sentence

Bob believes there is a unicorn and he believes it is saddled.

in a compositional way. In classical epistemic logic, there is only an indirect formalization that captures the anaphoric reference made by the pronoun *it*,

$$B_{Bob}(\exists x)((x \text{ is a unicorn})\&(x \text{ is saddled})).$$

This formalization does not treat the sentence *Bob believes there is a unicorn* as a constituent. Moreover, the analogous formalization of the sentence where the second conjunct is negated, *he does not believe it is saddled*, is

$$B_{Bob}(\exists x)((x \ is \ a \ unicorn)\&\sim (x \ is \ saddled)),$$

according to which Bob positively believes the unicorn is not saddled. There is nothing that corresponds to the type-theoretical proposition

$$(\Sigma z \ : \ (B\Gamma_{Bob})unicorn)\sim (B\Gamma_{Bob})(\mathrm{ap}(z,\mathbf{x}) \ is \ saddled),$$

according to which Bob merely does not believe the unicorn is saddled.

In the same way as Σ formation, we could have applied Π formation to form the proposition

$$(\Pi z \ : \ (B\Gamma_{Bob})unicorn)(B\Gamma_{Bob})(\mathrm{Pron}(unicorn,\mathrm{ap}(z,\mathbf{x})) \ is \ saddled),$$

which sugars into

> *if Bob believes there is a unicorn he believes it is saddled.*

Notice that the anaphoric reference by *it* to a unicorn in Bob's beliefs is only possible if we open up Bob's belief context, for example, by means of the operator $(B\Gamma_{Bob})$. There is no anaphoric interpretation of *it* in

> *if Bob believes there is a unicorn it is saddled.*

Besides $(B\Gamma_p)$, there are a number of other operators that open up p's belief context. It makes sense to say things like

> *if Bob believes there is a unicorn he wants to saddle it,*
> *if Bob believes there is a unicorn he tries to saddle it,*
> *if Bob believes there is a unicorn he wonders whether it is saddled.*

But although *know* seems to admit of an explanation in terms of contexts as well, we cannot make sense of the sentence

> *if Bob believes there is a unicorn he knows it is saddled,*

since belief does not guarantee knowledge, in the sense of epistemic logic of the belief context being anchored in the actual world.

7.8 Intentional identity for distinct agents

Under the title of *intentional identity*, Geach (1967) discussed situations where 'a number of people, or one person on different occasions, have attitudes with a common focus, whether or not there actually is something at that focus' (op. cit., p. 627). Nob may thus have attitudes with focus on objects that Hob thinks exist, in Geach's example sentence

> *Hob thinks a witch has blighted Bob's mare, and Nob wonders whether she (the same witch) killed Cob's sow.*

The analysis of this sentence can be modelled after an analysis of a sentence modified by changing both *thinks* and *wonders whether* to *believes*. Two different formalizations are available in classical epistemic logic,

$$(\exists x)((x \text{ is a witch}) \& B_{Hob}(x \text{ has blighted Bob's mare})$$
$$\& B_{Nob}(x \text{ killed Cob's sow})),$$
$$B_{Hob}(\exists x)((x \text{ is a witch}) \& (x \text{ has blighted Bob's mare}))$$
$$\& B_{Nob}(\exists x)((x \text{ is a witch}) \& (x \text{ killed Cob's sow})).$$

The first alternative is not compositional with respect to the conjuncts. What is more, it can only be true if there really are witches. The second alternative does not show any dependence between the conjuncts, any 'common focus'.

Type theory gives two more ways of understanding the sentence. In the first alternative, Hob and Nob have in common an initial belief context, call it $\Gamma_{Hob \ and \ Nob}$. They both have their individual belief contexts that extend this context of common beliefs.

$$\Gamma_{Hob} \qquad\qquad \Gamma_{Nob}$$
$$\mathbf{f} \searrow \qquad\qquad \swarrow \mathbf{g}$$
$$\Gamma_{Hob \ and \ Nob}$$

To formalize the first conjunct, consider an arbitrary witch given in the common context of Hob and Nob,

$$w : (\Pi\Gamma_{Hob \ and \ Nob}) \textit{witch}.$$

Now open up Hob's belief context, that is, assume

$$\Gamma_{Hob},$$

which gives the sequence of variables $\mathbf{x}$. Applying the mapping $\mathbf{f}$ gives

$$\mathbf{f(x)} : \Gamma_{Hob \ and \ Nob},$$

whence by application of w,

$$\text{ap}(w, \mathbf{f(x)}) : \textit{witch in } \Gamma_{Hob}.$$

Now we can form

$$(\text{ap}(w, \mathbf{f(x)}) \text{ has blighted Bob's mare}) : \text{prop in } \Gamma_{Hob}.$$

Bind the variables $\mathbf{x}$ by $(B\Gamma_{Hob})$, and get the proposition

$$(B\Gamma_{Hob})(\text{ap}(w, \mathbf{f(x)}) \text{ has blighted Bob's mare})$$

only depending on $w : (\Pi\Gamma_{Hob \ and \ Nob}) \textit{witch}$. Bind this variable by Σ formation, and obtain, as the formalization of the first conjunct, the proposition

$$(\Sigma w : (\Pi\Gamma_{Hob \ and \ Nob}) \textit{witch})$$
$$(B\Gamma_{Hob})(\text{ap}(w, \mathbf{f(x)}) \text{ has blighted Bob's mare}).$$

In order to form the second conjunct, assume u is a proof of this proposition. Then

$$p(u) : (\Pi\Gamma_{Hob \ and \ Nob}) \textit{witch}.$$

In Nob's belief context, which introduces the sequence of variables **y**,

$$\mathrm{ap}(p(u), \mathbf{g(y)}) : witch.$$

Of this witch, we know by $q(u)$ that Hob believes she has blighted Bob's mare. But Nob need neither know this nor believe the same thing himself.

Now pronominalize the witch, form a proposition in Nob's belief context, apply the belief operator, and obtain the proposition

$$(B\Gamma_{Nob})(\mathrm{Pron}(witch, \mathrm{ap}(p(u), \mathbf{q(y)}))) \; killed \; Cob\text{'}s \; sow)$$

to formalize the second conjunct. Bind the free variable u by Σ formation, and you have a progressive conjunction formalizing the sentence,

$$(\Sigma u \; : \; (\Sigma w \; : \; (\Pi\Gamma_{Hob \; and \; Nob})witch)$$
$$(B\Gamma_{Hob})(\mathrm{ap}(w, \mathbf{f(x)}) \; has \; blighted \; Bob\text{'}s \; mare))$$
$$(B\Gamma_{Nob})(\mathrm{Pron}(witch, \mathrm{ap}(p(u), \mathbf{q(y)}))) \; killed \; Cob\text{'}s \; sow).$$

The second alternative requires that Nob's beliefs extend Hob's beliefs,

$$\begin{array}{c} \Gamma_{Nob} \\ \mathbf{h} \downarrow \\ \Gamma_{Hob} \end{array}$$

It is a special case of the first situation: $\Gamma_{Hob \; and \; Nob}$ is identified with Γ_{Hob}. If there is a witch in Hob's beliefs, she is also available in Nob's beliefs in a form modified by **h**. We can form the proposition

$$(\Sigma w \; : \; (B\Gamma_{Hob})(\Sigma u \; : \; witch)(u \; has \; blighted \; Bob\text{'}s \; mare))$$
$$(B\Gamma_{Nob})(\mathrm{Pron}(witch, p(\mathrm{ap}(w, \mathbf{h(y)})))) \; killed \; Cob\text{'}s \; sow).$$

(Cf. Ranta 1990b for the derivation of this proposition in categorial grammar.) Because of the mapping **h**, the first conjunct implies that Nob also believes that the witch has blighted Bob's mare. Hence we cannot analyse in this way the sentence

Hob believes that a witch has blighted Bob's mare whereas Nob believes she has not blighted Bob's mare,

without assigning contradictory beliefs to Nob. This sentence must thus be understood along the lines of the first, more general alternative. Moreover, only the first formalization satisfies the desideratum of Geach, that Hob has not thought anything about Cob's sow, nor Nob about Bob's mare (Geach 1967, p. 630).

The failure of intentional identity in classical epistemic logic consists in there being, in Geach's words, no notion of *focus* of an attitude that may depend on the agent. In our type-theoretical formalization, the focus may be something given in the agent's belief context. A focus given in a common belief context, like the witch in our analyses of Geach's sentence, is a common focus.

Note. To get a better intuition about the structure we have given to Geach's sentence, recall that belief reports are propositions of Π form, which is also the form of conditionals. To make sense of the sentence

if you press the button a coin will appear,
and if you turn the wheel it (the same coin) will drop out.

we usually presuppose that if you turn the wheel you have pressed the button, that is, a function

$f(x)$: *(you have pressed the button)* $(x : (you\ turn\ the\ wheel))$

which makes a formalization possible along the second alternative. But if you want to say,

if you press the button a coin will appear,
and if you turn the wheel it will not appear,

you clearly presuppose a coin that is there to appear or not, thus giving *a coin* the widest scope, or use the pronoun *it* as a substitute for the phrase *a coin*.

8

HIGHER-LEVEL TYPE THEORY AND CATEGORIAL GRAMMAR

Until now, speaking of types has been speaking of sets. In this chapter, we shall extend the notion of *type* to cover the type of sets, the type of propositions, various types of propositional functions, the type of quantifiers, etc. This notion of type, or *category*, was introduced by Martin-Löf in 1984, pp. 21–23. He soon developed a calculus of types, the *higher-level type theory*. The type theory of Martin-Löf 1982 and 1984, within which we have been working so far, is accordingly called *lower-level type theory*, or *Martin-Löf's set theory*.

Higher-level type theory relates to lower-level type theory in the same way as simple type theory (Church 1940) relates to classical predicate calculus. At the same time, it provides a *logical framework*, in which many different logical calculi and mathematical theories can be presented. This generality has motivated intensive work in computer implementation, exemplified by the ALF system of Gothenburg ('Another Logical Framework'; see Magnusson 1992).

This chapter will focus on the use of higher-level type theory as a *categorial grammar*, which gives in a judgement form the expressions that on the lower level have been introduced by inference rules. These *categorizations* are then easily comparable with the categorizations of classical categorial grammar, which is based on simple type theory.

Martin-Löf has not published his higher-level theory himself, but it can be found in Nordström *et al.* 1990 and in Ranta 1991a. The following sections will give a self-contained description of higher-level type theory.

8.1 Types

The judgement N : set, which we have been reading

$$N \text{ is a set,}$$

can also be read

$$N \text{ is an object of type set.}$$

Moreover, one can speak of functions from a type to another type, for example,

$\sim$ is a function from the type prop to the type prop,
$+$ is a two-place function from the type set to the type set.

This form of speech derives from the rule notation. The premises of the rule tell the types of the arguments of the function, the conclusion tells the type of the value. Thus the functions $\sim$ and $+$ have been given in the $\sim$ and $+$ formation rules,

$$\frac{A \ : \ \text{prop}}{\sim A \ : \ \text{prop}} \sim F, \qquad \frac{A \ : \ \text{set} \quad B \ : \ \text{set}}{A + B \ : \ \text{set}} + F.$$

The type set is not a set itself, since there is no system of introduction rules that generates all sets. Nor is the type of functions from propositions to propositions. Type is a totality of a more general kind. To explain a type, you need not give exhaustive introduction rules. You must only tell *what it is to be an object of it*, as well as *what it is for its objects to be equal*. The explanation of a type α, that is, what it is to be an object of α, is often given in terms of *what can be done with* an object of α. Such an explanation does not determine any canonical forms an object of α should have, but allows the task to be performed in different ways. For instance, one can introduce a never-before-imagined function taking a proposition into another proposition.

8.2   Higher-level formulation of lower-level type theory

Lower-level type theory has formation rules for sets of Σ, Π, and $+$ forms, as well as for enumerated sets, for the set of natural numbers, and for equality propositions (see Sections 2.18–2.25). It is open to the addition of new forms. The theory also has introduction rules for constructors of sets, and elimination rules for selectors (cf. Section 2.17). Higher-level type theory can present all such rules, both previously given and later added ones, as judgements of the form

$$a \ : \ \alpha,$$

read

$$a \text{ is an object of type } \alpha,$$

in a framework consisting of a small number of rules.

Four forms of judgement are needed just like in lower-level type theory; see Table 8.1. There are three rules that define the *type hierarchy* consisting of *basic types* and *product types*. The basic types are the type set of sets, as well as every set itself. The product type is formed from a given type α and a type β that may depend on $x \ : \ \alpha$.

$$\text{set} \ : \ \text{type}, \qquad \frac{A \ : \ \text{set}}{A \ : \ \text{type}}, \qquad \frac{\alpha \ : \ \text{type} \quad \overset{(x \ : \ \alpha)}{\beta \ : \ \text{type}}}{(x \ : \ \alpha)\beta \ : \ \text{type}}.$$

Judgement	where	means
α : type	—	α is a type
$\alpha = \beta$: type	α : type, β : type	α and β are equal types
$a : \alpha$	α : type	a is an object of α
$a = b : \alpha$	α : type, $a : \alpha$, $b : \alpha$	α and β are equal objects of α

Table 8.1

The type prop of propositions is equal to the type of sets,

prop : type,

prop = set : type.

The right-hand-side premise of the product type rule shows a *family of types*, that is, a type β depending on the hypothesis $x : \alpha$. The hypothetical judgement

$$\beta : \text{type} \ (x : \alpha)$$

means that the substitution instance $\beta(a/x)$ is a type whenever $a : \alpha$, as well as that $\beta(a/x) = \beta(b/x)$: type whenever $a = b : \alpha$. As an example of a family of types that is not a family of sets, take

$$(x : X)\text{prop} : \text{type} \ (X : \text{set}),$$

which for any set A yields the set $(x : A)$prop of propositional functions on A.

Objects of the product type $(x : \alpha)\beta$ are *functions* that can be *applied* to objects a of α to yield objects of $\beta(a/x)$. This is expressed by the rule of *application*,

$$\frac{c : (x : \alpha)\beta \quad a : \alpha}{c(a) : \beta(a/x)}.$$

Application to equal objects $a = b : \alpha$ yields equal objects

$$c(a) = c(b) : \beta(a/x).$$

The equality of objects of the function type,

$$c = d : (x : \alpha)\beta$$

means that $c(a) = d(a) : \beta(a/x)$ for any $a : \alpha$.

As the first example of higher-level type theory, consider the negation formation rule. It presents $\sim$ as a function that takes a proposition as its argument and yields a proposition as value. Negation is thus an object of type $(X : \text{prop})$prop,

$$\sim : (X : \text{prop})\text{prop}.$$

Notice that prop : type does not depend on the hypothesis X : prop. It is thus vacuously a family of types over the type prop. We shall assume the notational convention of writing

$(\alpha)\beta$ instead of $(x : \alpha)\beta$ when β : type does not depend on $x : \alpha$.
Accordingly, we can write

$$(\text{prop})\text{prop}$$

instead of $(X : \text{prop})\text{prop}$ for the type of $\sim$.

Consider then the rule $+F$. It gives $+$ as a function of two arguments of type set. By the method known as *currying* in categorial grammar (cf. Curry 1963, p. 62), we can represent it as a one-place function on sets that yields a one-place function on sets that yields a set,

$$+ : (\text{set})(\text{set})\text{set}.$$

Sometimes we shall follow the 'de-currying' convention of writing

$$(x_1 : \alpha_1, \ldots, x_n : \alpha_n)\beta \text{ instead of } (x_1 : \alpha_1)\ldots(x_n : \alpha_n)\beta.$$

This notation shows the type clearly as a type of n-place functions. Thus the $+$ formation rule can be written

$$+ : (\text{set}, \text{set})\text{set},$$

or, if the de-currying convention is followed but the convention of omitting the variables is not, even

$$+ : (A : \text{set}, B : \text{set})\text{set},$$

where the schematic letters of the rule are used as bound variables.

When applied to sets A and B, $+$ yields the set $+(A)(B)$. This can be simplified to $+(A, B)$ in accordance with another de-currying convention of writing

$$f(a, b) \text{ instead of } f(a)(b) \text{ for repeated application.}$$

A further convention introduces the *infix* notation for writing

$$(afb) \text{ instead of } f(a, b) \text{ for two-place functions } f.$$

Thus $+(A, B)$ can be written $(A + B)$. But this convention is not followed with all two-place functions.

The Σ formation rule

$$\frac{A : \text{set} \quad \overset{(x : A)}{B(x) : \text{set}}}{(\Sigma x : A)B(x) : \text{set}}$$

presents Σ as an operator that takes two arguments, a set A and a family of sets over A. A family of sets over A is a function that can be applied to an element of A to yield a set. In other words, it is a function of type $(A)\text{set}$. The lower-level rule of Σ formation is thus expressed by the following judgement of higher-level type theory.

$$\Sigma : (X : \text{set})((X)\text{set})\text{set}.$$

Given A : set and B : (A)set, we can thus apply Σ to form, first, the *quantifier* $\Sigma(A)$: $((A)$set$)$set, and then the set $\Sigma(A, B)$. We shall often follow the convention of writing

$(Qx : A)B(x)$ instead of $Q(A, B)$
for Q : $(X : set)((X)set)$set, A : set, B : (A)set.

The following list gives the higher-level formulations of the formation, introduction, and elimination rules of Σ, Π, and $+$ from Sections 2.18–2.20.

Σ : $(X : set)((X)set)$set,
pair : $(X : set)(Y : (X)set)(x : X)(Y(x))\Sigma(X, Y)$,
E : $(X : set)(Y : (X)set)(Z : (\Sigma(X, Y))set)$
   $(z : \Sigma(X, Y))(u : (x : X)(y : Y(x))Z($pair$(X, Y, x, y)))Z(z)$,
p : $(X : set)(Y : (X)set)(\Sigma(X, Y))X$,
q : $(X : set)(Y : (X)set)(\Sigma(X, Y))Y(p(X, Y, z))$,
Π : $(X : set)((X)set)$set,
λ : $(X : set)(Y : (X)set)((x : X)Y(x))\Pi(X, Y)$,
ap : $(X : set)(Y : (X)set)(\Pi(X, Y))(x : X)Y(x)$,
$+$: $($set$)($set$)$set,
i : $(X : set)(Y : set)(X)(X + Y)$,
j : $(X : set)(Y : set)(Y)(X + Y)$,
D : $(X : set)(Y : set)(Z : (X + Y)set)(z : X + Y)$
   $((x : X)Z(i(X, Y, x)))((y : Y)Z(j(X, Y, y)))Z(z)$.

The equality rules of lower-level type theory are expressed as definitions of selectors, in contexts providing them with arguments of canonical form.

$E(X, Y, Z, $pair$(X, Y, x, y), u) = u(x, y)$: $Z($pair$(X, Y, x, y))$
   $(X : $set, $y : (X)$set, $Z : (\Sigma(X, Y))$set, $x : X$, $y : Y(x)$,
      $u : (x : X)(y : Y(x))Z($pair$(X, Y, x, y)))$,
$p(X, Y, $pair$(X, Y, x, y)) = x$: X
   $(X : $set, $y : (X)$set, $x : X$, $y : Y(x))$,
$q(X, Y, $pair$(X, Y, x, y)) = y$: $Y(x)$
   $(X : $set, $y : (X)$set, $x : X$, $y : Y(x))$,
ap$(X, Y, \lambda(X, Y, z), x) = z(x)$: $Y(x)$
   $(X : $set, $y : (X)$set, $z : (x : X)Y(x)$, $x : X)$,
$D(X, Y, Z, i(X, Y, x), u, v) = u(x)$: $Z(i(X, Y, x))$
   $(X : $set, $Y : $set, $Z : (X + Y)$set, $x : X$,
      $u : (x : X)Z(i(X, Y, x))$, $v : (y : Y)Z(j(X, Y, y)))$,
$D(X, Y, Z, j(X, Y, y), u, v) = v(y)$: $Z(j(X, Y, y))$
   $(X : $set, $Y : $set, $Z : (X + Y)$set, $y : Y$,
      $u : (x : X)Z(i(X, Y, x))$, $v : (y : Y)Z(j(X, Y, y)))$.

Formation and proving of propositions can be performed entirely by using the higher-level rules, so that specific formation, introduction, and elimination rules are not needed. But such rules can be derived, in accordance with the scheme

$$\frac{a \ : \ \alpha \quad \ldots \quad b \ : \ \beta}{F(a, \ldots, b) \ : \ \gamma} \ F, \text{ for } F \ : \ (x \ : \ \alpha) \ldots (y \ : \ \beta)\gamma.$$

Hence we get, from $\Sigma \ : \ (X \ : \ \text{set})((X)\text{set})\text{set}$, the Σ formation rule in the form

$$\frac{A \ : \ \text{set} \quad B \ : \ (A)\text{set}}{\Sigma(A, B) \ : \ \text{set}} \ \Sigma.$$

From pair $: \ (X \ : \ \text{set})(Y \ : \ (X)\text{set})(x \ : \ X)(Y(x))\Sigma(X, Y)$, we get the Σ introduction rule in the form

$$\frac{A \ : \ \text{set} \quad B \ : \ (A)\text{set} \quad a \ : \ A \quad b \ : \ B(a)}{\text{pair}(A, B, a, b) \ : \ (\Sigma x \ : \ A)B(x)} \ \text{pair}.$$

By suppression of the premises $A \ : \ \text{set}$ and $B \ : \ (A)\text{set}$ and of the corresponding arguments of the pair, we get the customary Σ introduction rule.

With the higher-level constructors and selectors, set and propositional function arguments are explicit. This leads to a *monomorphic* lower-level theory, in which every singular term is uniquely typed. The customary lower-level theory is *polymorphic*. For instance, the term $(\lambda x)x$ can be of any type $(\Pi x \ : \ A)A$ where $A \ : \ \text{set}$. The corresponding term in the higher-level theory is $\lambda(A, (x)A, (x)x)$.

8.3   Abstraction and conversions

Objects of type $(x \ : \ \alpha)\beta$ can be formed by *abstraction*, in accordance with the rule

$$\frac{\begin{array}{c}(x \ : \ \alpha)\\ b \ : \ \beta\end{array}}{(x)b \ : \ (x \ : \ \alpha)\beta}.$$

This rule is justified by telling how the objects introduced by it are applied, by the rule of β *conversion*,

$$\frac{\begin{array}{c}(x \ : \ \alpha)\\ b \ : \ \beta \quad a \ : \ \alpha\end{array}}{((x)b)(a) \ = \ b(a/x) \ : \ \beta(a/x)}.$$

We shall often write

$$(x_1, \ldots, x_n)b \text{ instead of } (x_1) \ldots (x_n)b$$

for iterated abstraction.

Abstraction, application, and β conversion are analogous to Π introduction, Π elimination, and Π equality, respectively. But as $(x \ : \ \alpha)\beta$ is a type and $(\Pi x \ : \ A)B(x)$ is a set, the conceptual order of these rules is different. The introduction rules of a set prescribe the canonical forms of all of its elements. For $(\Pi x \ : \ A)B(x)$, there is just one canonical form, $(\lambda x)b(x)$

where $b(x) : B(x)$ $(x : A)$, as prescribed by Π introduction. The operator ap introduced by Π elimination gives rise to non-canonical elements. Π equality justifies Π elimination by telling how ap is computed.

But types are not restricted by canonical forms. The abstract form $(x)b$ is just one of the forms an object of type $(x : \alpha)\beta$ may have. It is not the abstraction rule that tells what it is to be an object of $(x : \alpha)\beta$ but the application rule. The β conversion rule is thus needed to justify the abstraction rule, not the application rule.

The following rule of η *conversion* is also valid.

$$\frac{c : (x : \alpha)\beta}{c = (x)(c(x)) : (x : \alpha)\beta}.$$

The functions c and $(x)(c(x))$, when applied to $a : \alpha$, yield the same value $c(a)$. To yield the same value for any argument is precisely what it is for objects of type $(x : \alpha)\beta$ to be equal. The corresponding lower-level rule stating that

$$c = (\lambda x)\mathrm{ap}(c, x) : (\Pi x : A)B(x)$$

is not valid (cf. Nordström *et al.* 1990, p. 67).

8.4 An example of a proof in higher-level type theory

The higher-level version of the propositional scheme

$$(\Pi z : (\Sigma x : A)B(x))C(p(z)),$$

which is repeatedly used in Chapter 3, and formally derived in Figure 3.1 in Section 3.4, is

$$\Pi(\Sigma(A, B), (z)C(p(A, B, z))).$$

Figure 8.1 shows a higher-level derivation of this set from the assumptions

$$A : \mathrm{set}, \; B : (A)\mathrm{set}, \; C : (A)\mathrm{set}.$$

Observe, in particular, that the binding of the variable z is made by the abstraction rule and not by the application of Π.

8.5 Simple type theory

The rules of type formation and application in simple type theory are the following.

$$e : \mathrm{type}, \qquad t : \mathrm{type}, \qquad \frac{\alpha : \mathrm{type} \quad \beta : \mathrm{type}}{(\alpha)\beta : \mathrm{type}}, \qquad \frac{c : (\alpha)\beta \quad a : \alpha}{c(a) : \beta}.$$

In comparison with constructive higher-level type theory, simple type theory is the special case with function types of form $(\alpha)\beta$ only, that is, without the possibility of β : type depending on $x : \alpha$. The generalization of these function types to $(x : \alpha)\beta$ is, in a way, the paradigm case of the progres-

$$\cfrac{A:\text{set} \quad \cfrac{C:(A)\text{set} \quad \cfrac{\cfrac{A:\text{set} \quad B:(A)\text{set} \quad z:\Sigma(A,B)}{p(A,B,z):A}\ p}{C(p(A,B,z)):\text{set}}\ appl.}{\cfrac{(z)C(p(A,B,z)):(\Sigma(A,B))\text{set}}{}}\ abs.,1.}{\Pi(\Sigma(A,B),(z)C(p(A,B,z))):\text{set}}\ \Pi$$

$$\cfrac{A:\text{set} \quad B:(A)\text{set}}{\Sigma(A,B):\text{set}}\ \Sigma$$

1.

Figure 8.1

sive structures that constructive type theory adds to ordinary predicate calculus. For instance, the ordinary conjunction

$$\& \ : \ (\text{prop})(\text{prop})\text{prop}$$

is generalized into the progressive conjunction

$$\Sigma \ : \ (X \ : \ \text{prop})((X)\text{prop})\text{prop},$$

even the type of which does not belong to simple type theory. But observe that even in classical logic, dependent types are needed as soon as several domains of quantification are taken into account. In simple type theory, a quantifier takes a propositional function into a proposition,

$$\forall \ : \ ((e)t)t.$$

If the quantifier is to take as its arguments a domain and a propositional function on that very domain, the type of the second argument depends on the first argument,

$$\forall \ : \ (X \ : \ \text{set})((X)\text{prop})\text{prop}.$$

8.6   Categorial grammars

Linguistically, simple type theory can be seen as the *categorial grammar* of the language of predicate calculus. Higher-level type theory is, analogously, the categorial grammar of lower-level type theory.

To natural languages, simple type theory has been applied as a categorial grammar since Ajdukiewicz (1935). In this grammar, essentially the forms of predicate calculus are imposed on natural language. In other words, natural language is formalized in predicate calculus. Now that we have shown how to formalize parts of English in lower-level type theory, we can summarize the results by giving *categorizations* of some English expressions, that is, judgements of form $c : \alpha$, where c is an English expression and α is a type. We first give Table 8.2, which shows the types corresponding to certain categories of school grammar. For comparison, we

school grammar	example	classical	constructive
sentence	*Bob runs*	t	prop
proper name	*John*	e	A, where A : set
common noun	*man*	$(e)t$	set
adjective	*old*	$(e)t$	(A)prop
intransitive verb	*run*	$(e)t$	(A)prop
transitive verb	*love*	$(e)(e)t$	$(A)(B)$prop
progressive	*return*		$(x : A)(B(x))$prop
sentential verb	*believe*	$(e)(t)t$	$(x : A)((\Gamma(x))\text{prop})$prop
connective	*or*	$(t)(t)t$	$(\text{prop})(\text{prop})$prop
progressive	*and*		$(A : \text{prop})((A)\text{prop})$prop
quantifier	*someone*	$((e)t)t$	$((A)\text{prop})$prop
with domain	*some*	$((e)t)((e)t)t$	$(A : \text{set})((A)\text{prop})$prop
personal pronoun	*he*	e	$(A : \text{set})(A)A$
definite article	*the*	$((e)t)((e)t)t$	$(A : \text{set})(A)A$
relative pronoun	*that*	$((e)t)((e)t)(e)t$	$(A : \text{set})((A)\text{prop})\text{set}$

Table 8.2

also give the counterparts from classical categorial grammar. The classical categories are gathered from Lambek (1958), Montague (1974), and van Benthem (1990). What is missing is the replacement of expressions of type e by functions of type $((e)t)t$ devised by Montague. In constructive type theory, the corresponding technique would be to replace elements $a : A$ by functions

$$(Y)Y(a) : ((A)\text{prop})\text{prop}.$$

Lewis (1972) recognizes a third basic category, C, of common nouns, which makes it possible to find closer counterparts for common nouns, quantifiers, definite articles, and relative pronouns. He does not, however, relate proper names to common nouns, as he does not interpret common nouns as domains of individuals. To make full use of such an interpretation, one would of course have to introduce dependent types.

The table does not indicate the constructive identification of the categories prop and set. What is more, the categorization of sentences as propositions does not cover sentences that have a mood. The mood component does not belong to the categorial grammar at all, since categorial grammar concerns expressions that *denote* something. In other words, categorial grammar gives a structure only to the descriptive content of the sentence (cf. Section 2.7). It is still often adequate to categorize indicative sentences like *John runs* as propositions, for this is how they function when they occur as constituents of complex sentences.

The analysis we have given of personal pronouns and definite articles would be possible in simple type theory as well, by putting

Pron $= (x)x : (e)e,$
the $= (X)(x)x : ((e)t)(e)e,$

but I have not seen it in the linguistic literature, except implicitly in game-theoretical semantics. It is presumably not very powerful in the absence of the propositions as types principle.

8.7   Progressively typed verbs

In Section 4.12, we discussed some verbs categorized to progressive function types, such as

divorce $: (x : man)(y : woman)(married(x, y))$prop,
stop $: (A : set)(B : (A)$prop$)(x : A)(B(x))$prop.

The verb *start* is simpler than *stop*, as it does not require a proof of the proposition that the individual has the property,

$$start : (A : set)(B : (A)\text{prop})(A)\text{prop}.$$

(It might require a proof of $\sim B(x)$, though.) These categorizations can be made more accurate by introducing a time scale *time* : set,

stop $: (A : set)(B : (A)(time)$prop$)(x : A)(t : time)(B(x, t))$prop,
start $: (A : set)(B : (A)(time)$prop$)(A)(time)$prop.

The verb *want*, as used in the sentence

John wants to ride a horse,

is applied to an agent and a propositional function on agents,

$$want : (agent, (agent)\text{prop})\text{prop}.$$

But in the sentence

John wants to ride the unicorn,

the propositional function is only given in the belief context $\Gamma(x)$ of the agent x,

$$want : (x : agent, (\Gamma(x))(agent)\text{prop})\text{prop}.$$

(We assume $\Gamma(x)$ to be defined as a set, for example, as a Σ set, in accordance with the correspondence of contexts and Σ sets presented in Section 6.1.) In the other want construction,

John wants the unicorn to run to the golden mountain,

the direct object is an element of some set A given in $\Gamma(x)$, and the infinitival phrase is a propositional function over elements of A given in $\Gamma(x)$,

$$want : (x : agent, A : set, y : (\Gamma(x))A, (\Gamma(x))(A)\text{prop})\text{prop}.$$

What is more, even the set A may depend on the context $\Gamma(x)$, like in the sentence

John wants the tooth of the unicorn to be found by the Martian.

Then

$$want : (x : agent, A : (\Gamma(x))set, y : (z : \Gamma(x))A(z),$$
$$(z : \Gamma(x))(A(z))prop)prop.$$

8.8 English logical operators

The following categorizations follow, basically, from the intuitionistic meaning explanations by Heyting, presented in Table 2.1 in Section 2.15 above.

$every = \Pi : (X : set)((X)prop)prop,$
$any = \Pi : (X : set)((X)prop)prop,$
$if = \Pi : (X : prop)((X)prop)prop,$
$some = \Sigma : (X : set)((X)prop)prop,$
$\text{Indef} = \Sigma : (X : set)((X)prop)prop,$
$and = \Sigma : (X : prop)((X)prop)prop,$
$that = \Sigma : (X : set)((X)prop)set,$
$such\_that = \Sigma : (X : set)((X)prop)set,$
$or = + : (prop)(prop)prop,$
$\text{Neg} = \sim : (prop)prop.$

Unlike in Chapter 3, we introduce these variants of the logical operators already in type theory, and not only in sugaring. This treatment prepares the way for deterministic sugaring, to be discussed in the next chapter. The types prop and set are then treated as distinct, as corresponding to sentences and common nouns, respectively. From the point of view of grammatical formalization, this approach has the advantage that the formalization of a sentence only adds some structural information, like parentheses and bound variables, and preserves the meaningful words as they are, without paraphrasing them by, for example, Π and Σ.

Note. By abstraction and application, it is possible to define variants of connectives taking as arguments one-place propositional functions (to form e.g. *walk or run*), two-place propositional functions (*take and give back*), and individuals (*John and Pedro*). But there is a problem of overgeneration here: to block sentences like *John walks and Mary is married to*, restrictions like those to be discussed in Section 9.9 are needed.

8.9 The definitions of anaphoric expressions and tenses

The following categorizations recapitulate the pronominalization rules of Chapter 4.

$$\text{Pron} = (X)(x)x \; : \; (X \; : \; \text{set})(X)X,$$
$$\textit{the} = (X)(x)x \; : \; (X \; : \; \text{set})(X)X,$$
$$\text{ThatMod} = (X)(Y)(x)(y)x$$
$$: (X \; : \; \text{set})(Y \; : \; (X)\text{prop})(x \; : \; X)(Y(x))X,$$
$$\text{SuchThatMod} = (X)(Y)(x)(y)x$$
$$: (X \; : \; \text{set})(Y \; : \; (X)\text{prop})(x \; : \; X)(Y(x))X,$$
$$\text{AdjMod} = (X)(Y)(x)(y)x$$
$$: (X \; : \; \text{set})(Y \; : \; (X)\text{prop})(x \; : \; X)(Y(x))X,$$
$$\text{PartMod} = (X)(Y)(x)(y)x$$
$$: (X \; : \; \text{set})(Y \; : \; (X)\text{prop})(x \; : \; X)(Y(x))X,$$
$$\text{Gen} = (X)(Y)(Z)(x)(y)(z)y$$
$$: (X : \text{set})(Y : \text{set})(Z : (X,Y)\text{prop})(x : X)(y : Y)(Z(x,y))Y,$$
$$\text{Zero} = (X)(x)x \; : \; (X \; : \; \text{set})(X)X.$$

For the purpose of deterministic sugaring in generative grammar, the operator Mod has been replaced by the variants ThatMod, SuchThatMod, AdjMod, PartMod, to produce common nouns modified by relative *that* clauses, *such that* clauses, adjectives, and participles, respectively; cf. Section 5.4. All of these operators are definitionally equal in type theory, but their sugaring rules differ.

For a treatment of reflexive pronouns, there are two main possibilities. In the treatment of Geach (1972, p. 494), the reflexive pronoun REFL(A) of type A is not categorized itself, but arises in the sugaring of the reflexive proposition, obtained by applying a two-place propositional function twice to the same argument.

$$\text{Refl} = (X)(Y)(x)Y(x,x) \; : \; (X \; : \; \text{set})(Y \; : \; (X,X)\text{prop})(X)\text{prop},$$
$$\text{Refl}(A,B,a) \; \triangleright \; B(a,\text{REFL}(A)).$$

For example,

Refl(*man, admire, John*) ▷ *John admires REFL(man)*
  ▷ *John admires himself*,
every(*man*, (*x*)Refl(*man, admire, x*))
  ▷ *every man admires himself*.

An alternative approach would be to categorize the reflexive pronoun as an anaphoric expression itself,

$$\text{REFL} = (X)(x)x \; : \; (X \; : \; \text{set})(X)X,$$

and distinguish it from personal pronouns by rules stating where in the context its interpretation is to be sought. This would be in analogy with Hintikka and Kulas 1985, pp. 119–120.

To categorize temporal reference, we start by assuming that a time scale *time* : set is defined, as in Chapter 5, and then introduce

before : $(N)(time)time,$

after : $(N)(time)time$,
when = $(C)(t)(x)t : (C : (time)\text{prop})(t : time)(C(t))time$,
now = $(t)t : (time)time$.

In Section 5.8, Perfect was introduced as an operator that takes a propositional function on *time* and yields another propositional function on *time*. The tenses Past, Present, and Future make a reference to a given point $now(t) : time$.

Perfect = $(C)(t)\Sigma(N, (n)C(before(s(n), t)))$
  : $((time)\text{prop})(time)\text{prop}$,
Past = $(C)(t)(n)C(before(s(n), now(t)))$
  : $((time)\text{prop})(time)(N)\text{prop}$,
Present = $(C)(t)C(now(t))$
  : $((time)\text{prop})(time)\text{prop}$,
Future = $(C)(t)(n)C(after(s(n), now(t)))$
  : $((time)\text{prop})(time)(N)\text{prop}$.

Compound tenses are defined as compositions of the tenses and Perfect. Their definitions in standard type theory can then be computed stepwise.

Past-Perfect = $(C)(t)(n)\text{Past}((x)\text{Perfect}(C, x), now(t), n)$
  = $(C)(t)(n)\text{Perfect}(C, before(s(n), now(t)))$
  = $(C)(t)(n)\Sigma(N, (m)C(before(s(m), before(s(n), now(t)))))$
  : $((time)\text{prop})(time)(N)\text{prop}$,
Present-Perfect = $(C)(t)\text{Present}((u)\text{Perfect}(C, u), now(t))$
  = $(C)(t)\text{Perfect}(C, now(t))$
  = $(C)(t)\Sigma(N, (n)C(before(s(n), now(t))))$
  : $((time)\text{prop})(time)\text{prop}$,
Future-Perfect = $(C)(t)(n)\text{Future}((x)\text{Perfect}(C, x), now(t), n)$
  = $(C)(t)(n)\text{Perfect}(C, after(s(n), now(t)))$
  = $(C)(t)(n)\Sigma(N, (m)C(after(s(m), before(s(n), now(t)))))$
  : $((time)\text{prop})(time)(N)\text{prop}$.

8.10 Categorial grammar and sugaring

The categorization $c : \alpha$ of an English expression c introduces c as an expression for an object of type α. To justify the categorization, one must tell what object c expresses. Sometimes this is done by an explicit definition, for example,

$$every = \Pi : (X : \text{set})((X)\text{prop})\text{prop}.$$

Sometimes the expression is not defined in terms of other type-theoretical expressions, but must be explained as a new primitive. One must make sense of c as an object of type α. Such is the case with the basic sets

month : set,
man : set,

which are justified by giving introduction rules of the sets *month* and *man*. For the set *month*, such rules are easily given, by introducing twelve constants of type *month*. But the set *man* has been left schematic, freely definable in particular applications of the categorial grammar.

Some expressions are not categorized at all, for example, prepositions, the verb *be*, the third person singular ending. Their occurrences in English expressions are produced by the sugaring procedure, not by the categorial grammar. They are *syncategorematic*, in contrast to categorized expressions. Even formal languages usually include some syncategorematic expressions, such as parentheses and punctuation marks.

An expression can only be categorized if it can be assigned an object of some type as its meaning. This is not possible for all expressions, but, whenever possible, categorization is preferred, as it means that the expression is given an independent meaning.

That a categorial grammar for English must be completed by a sugaring procedure is already clear from the fact that there is ambiguity in English with respect to the functional structure. That is, one and the same string of words may correspond to more than one functional expression.

The division of generative grammar into a semantically motivated categorial grammar and a sugaring procedure is slightly unusual. The same idea can be found in Curry (1963), under the titles *tectogrammatics* and *phenogrammatics*. In Montague's works, the same structure is implicit. A more explicit use of it in Montague grammar has been made by Dowty, who writes,

> the tectogrammatical structure of a sentence is what would be represented by a Montague Grammar analysis tree, minus the specification of what the expressions at the non-terminal nodes look like ... the phenogrammatical structure of the sentence is the way the English operations fill in these non-terminal nodes. (Dowty 1982, p. 88)

In the transformational grammar of Chomsky (1957), the components are still more radically mixed. Phrase structure trees, which are the deepest level of grammatical representation, have not been designed for compositional semantics. Moreover, they already contain the strings of English words in their leaves. Were there no transformations, sugaring would be simple erasure of everything but the leaves.

Even much of the research in categorial grammar has wanted to reduce the task of phenogrammatics to simple erasure of tree structure. Thus Lambek 1958 introduced directional function types, which impose a sequential ordering between the functor and the argument. For Curry, this involved an 'admixture of phenogrammatics' (1963, p. 66): the linear ordering of elements belongs to phenogrammatics, not to the functional structure.

In some developments of categorial grammar based on Lambek's work, the semantic nature of grammatical representations is no more clear. For instance, one and the same expression may belong to several types, which is not possible in type theory (cf. van Benthem 1988). This is accomplished by *type change rules*, like the one van Benthem attributes to Geach (1972),

if $c : (\alpha)\beta$ and γ is a category, $c : ((\gamma)\alpha)(\gamma)\beta$.

In our view, an expression cannot change type, but it may have a variant in another type. In this case there is an abstract,

if $c : (\alpha)\beta$ and γ is a category, $(z)(x)c(z(x)) : ((\gamma)\alpha)(\gamma)\beta$.

Such a variant c' of c may well have the same sugaring as c itself, but to make it equal to c in categorial grammar is, again, an 'admixture of phenogrammatics'.

Later on, bound variables have been introduced on a further level of 'semantics of type change', see van Benthem 1990. This then provides a full tectogrammatic representation, which consists of the categorial representation together with the semantics of type change.

van Benthem (1988) argues in favour of type change rules against the full abstraction rule by saying, for example, that vacuous binding, which takes $c : \beta$ to $(x)c : (\alpha)\beta$, is not adequate for natural language. In our analysis, abstraction is a semantically justified tectogrammatical rule. Restrictions in its use belong to phenogrammatics. Thus in English, a predicate formed by vacuous abstraction may not occur as the second argument of a quantifier sugared by substitution of the quantifier phrase; we cannot sugar

$$every(man, (x)run(Mary)) \; \triangleright \; Mary \; runs.$$

But a vacuous abstract may occur the second argument of a progressive connective,

$$if(man, (x)run(Mary)) \; \triangleright \; if \; there \; is \; a \; man \; Mary \; runs.$$

We shall return to this topic in Section 9.9.

Note. The type change rules formulated for classical categorial grammar often have progressive generalizations, e.g. the progressive Geach rule

if $c : (x : \alpha)\beta$ and γ is a category, $c' : (z : (\gamma)\alpha)(u : \gamma)\beta(z(u)/x)$.

This can be generalized even further by allowing α : type to depend on $u : \gamma$.

8.11 Compositional sugaring

An 'admixture of phenogrammatics' in categorial grammar like the ones presented above does have a certain linguistic motivation. If the principle in sugaring is that anything goes, the distance between the grammatical representation and the string of words may get very long. This is what sometimes happens in Montague grammar. Anything goes means that the sugaring of a complex expression may be just any function of the constituents,

$$\text{SUGAR}(f(a,\ldots,b)) = F(a,\ldots,b).$$

The opposite principle followed in the line of work initiated by Lambek is that sugaring is simple omission of parentheses and commas, which corresponds to the omission of the tree above the leaves:

$$\text{SUGAR}(f(a,\ldots,b)) = f\,a\ldots b.$$

If so little room is left for sugaring, an 'admixture of phenogrammatics', such as type change rules, can hardly be avoided. For if sugaring is so restricted that it cannot delete anything but parentheses, it cannot delete bound variables.

Between these extremities, there is the notion of *compositional sugaring* recently suggested by Per Martin-Löf (private communication). The sugaring of a complex expression is compositional if it is composed from the sugarings of the constituents, which are themselves given independently. The composition consists of concatenation of the sugarings of the components, permitting repetitions and omissions of some of them, as well as insertion of syncategorematic expressions.

$$\text{SUGAR}(f(a,\ldots,b)) = \ldots\text{SUGAR}(a)\ldots\text{SUGAR}(b)\ldots$$

Looking at the PTQ grammar (Montague 1974, chapter 8), we find, for example, that sugaring in the rule S2 is compositional, but in S3 it is not.

S2. $F_0(\zeta)$ is sugared into **every** ζ.

S3. $F_{3,n}(\zeta,\phi)$ is sugared into ζ **such that** ϕ', where ϕ' comes from ϕ by replacing each occurrence of $\mathbf{he}_n$ or $\mathbf{him}_n$ by $\left\{\begin{array}{l}\textbf{he}\\\textbf{she}\\\textbf{it}\end{array}\right\}$ or $\left\{\begin{array}{l}\textbf{him}\\\textbf{her}\\\textbf{it}\end{array}\right\}$ respectively, according as the first basic common noun in ζ is of $\left\{\begin{array}{l}\text{masc.}\\\text{fem.}\\\text{neuter}\end{array}\right\}$ gender.

(Cf. Montague 1974, p. 251.)

In Ranta 1991a, sugaring was not formulated as a function, but as a method leading to multiple sugarings of type-theoretical expressions (cf. Section 3.5 above, where this was not understood procedurally, but as a statement of the different sugaring alternatives). The choice of alternatives was restricted by conditions about the constituents of the expressions to be sugared. The procedure was thus not compositional. To make sugaring more articulate and, in particular, to follow the principle of compositionality, we shall here assume a different approach. Different sugarings of a proposition are obtained from different type-theoretical expressions for that proposition. For instance, the multiple-valued sugaring

$$\Sigma(man, walk) \,\triangleright\, \begin{cases} \textit{there is a man and he walks,} \\ \textit{there is a man and the man walks,} \\ \textit{a man walks,} \\ \textit{some man walks,} \\ \textit{there is a man who walks,} \end{cases}$$

is now obtained as a sequence of single-valued sugarings from definitionally equal variants of $\Sigma(man, walk)$,

$and(\mathit{There}(man), (x)walk(\mathrm{Pron}(man, x)))$,
$and(\mathit{There}(man), (x)walk(\mathit{the}(man, x)))$,
$\mathrm{Indef}(man, (x)walk(x))$,
$some(man, (x)walk(x))$,
$\mathit{There}(\mathrm{Rel}(man, (x)walk(x)))$.

There is no sugaring rule for $\Sigma(man, walk)$ itself, but only for the definitional variants. To sugar a proposition, one must first find a variant to which some sugaring rule applies. Taking all the variants together, the same net outcome is obtained as in Ranta 1991a, but now in two stages.

Yielding different results for definitionally equal expressions, sugaring can no longer be defined as a function of type-theoretical objects, but of their expressions, since by the definition of the function type,

if $f : (\alpha)\beta$ and $a = b : \alpha$, then $f(a) = f(b) : \beta$.

Thus if we had

$$\mathrm{SUGAR} : (\mathrm{prop})E,$$

where E is the set of strings of words, $A = B : \mathrm{prop}$ would entail

$$\mathrm{SUGAR}(A) = \mathrm{SUGAR}(B) : E.$$

Hence we have to let SUGAR operate not on propositions but on propositional expressions.

9

SUGARING AND PARSING

In this book, we have been mainly discussing themes familiar from logical semantics. The previous chapter discussed generative grammar in the special form consisting of a categorial grammar together with a sugaring procedure. A categorial grammar for a fragment of English was described. This chapter will provide a sugaring procedure for a somewhat smaller fragment. We shall also briefly discuss the parsing problem, that is, the task of translating English sentences back to type theory.

The sugaring procedure can be seen as a version of generative semantics: English sentences are obtained from type-theoretical formulae, which are their semantic representations. It is in this direction that semantics is primarily given, and not in the direction of interpreting English sentences or some semantically indifferent grammatical representations of them. We have already noticed that this format is the same as in Montague grammar, where English sentences are derived from semantically interpreted analysis trees.

The sugaring procedure we are going to present here is different from the one in Ranta 1991a. We have now made the procedure compositional, so that each type-theoretical expression has a sugaring rule of its own. This makes sugaring more articulate and surveyable, as well as easier to extend by lexical entries. But it will generate some unintended sugarings, and even some non-grammatical strings, which must be excluded by introducing conditions of sugarability. Such conditions were not needed in Ranta 1991a, but it seems very difficult to avoid them without violating the compositionality of sugaring. Precisely at this point, the design of the formal grammar will appear as incomplete and open to alternative developments; see Section 9.9.

The old procedure was implemented by using Prolog (see Mäenpää and Ranta 1990). The new procedure has been implemented by using ALF, the system of type theory from Gothenburg (see Magnusson 1992). It has proved very natural to program the grammar in type theory itself, as this gives support to the type-theoretical way of thinking on all levels of linguistic description. This will, admittedly, create problems that do not arise in untyped programming languages, such as the impossibility of substitut-

ing a quantifier phrase for a variable in a type-theoretical expression; see
Section 9.4. But such problems only force us to clarify our general views of
these operations.

The full sugaring program is presented in the appendix. It is a self-
contained fragment of a somewhat larger program, including the minimum
needed to illustrate our main points. Programming in type theory is an
important research topic currently, in virtue of the unified view of programming, mathematics, and logic that it provides. (See Martin-Löf 1982,
Nordström *et al.* 1990, Thompson 1991.) The sugaring program is written
entirely in pure type theory: all clauses in it are type-theoretical judgements. No external control features are employed, but all control is taken
care of by the way in which the operators are typed and defined.

The main text shows an alternative way of looking at sugaring, via
translation into phrase structure trees. With these trees, it is also easy to
show how parsing proceeds. The implementation of parsing in ALF is yet
unfinished. But parsing algorithms in Prolog have been written by Davila-
Perez (1993) and Mäenpää (1994).

The sugaring method presented in this chapter shows directly how type-
theoretical expressions can be transformed into strings of English words.
This is an interesting problem in the design of mathematical proof editors, but for linguistic description, it may be better to define sugaring for
a special combinatory notation, briefly described in the note at the end of
Section 9.9. This notation avoids variable bindings. It looks quite different
from standard type theory, but it is interpretable in type theory. When
sugaring is defined for the combinatory notation, it becomes more complicated to find English expressions for given mathematical propositions, but
linguistic description becomes more accurate. Moreover, the typing problem
of quantifier substitution, discussed in Section 9.4, is solved since quantifier
phrases are no longer substituted for bound variables in sugaring.

9.1   The notation of ALF

The sugaring program, to be fully presented in the appendix, is written in
the notation of ALF, which differs slightly from the higher-level notation
used in the previous chapter. The following categorial grammar generates
the fragment for which the sugaring algorithm of this chapter is defined.

```
(* Basic type theory *)

Sigma:(X:Set;(X)Set)Set [] C
 pair:(X:Set;Y:(X)Set;x:X;Y(x))Sigma(X,Y) [] C
p:(X:Set;Y:(X)Set;Sigma(X,Y))X [] I
 p(_,_,pair(A,B,a,b))=a
q:(X:Set;Y:(X)Set;z:Sigma(X,Y))Y(p(X,Y,z)) [] I
```

```
  q(_,_,pair(A,B,a,b))=b
Pi:(X:Set;(X)Set)Set [] C
  lambda:(X:Set;Y:(X)Set;(x:X)Y(x))Pi(X,Y) [] C
ap:(X:Set;Y:(X)Set;Pi(X,Y);x:X)Y(x) [] I
  ap(_,_,lambda(A,B,b),a)=b(a)
Falsum:Set [] C
  Not=[X]Pi(X,[x]Falsum):(Set)Set []
There=[X]X:(Set)Set []

(* Categorial grammar *)

Donkey:Set   [] C
Man:Set [] C
Woman:Set [] C
Rel=Sigma:(X:Set;(X)Set)Set []
John:Man [] C
Mary:Woman [] C
Pron=[X,x]x:(X:Set;X)X []
The=[X,x]x:(X:Set;X)X []
Mod=[X,Y,x,y]x:(X:Set;Y:(X)Set;x:X;Y(x))X []
Every=Pi:(X:Set;(X)Set)Set []
Indef=Sigma:(X:Set;(X)Set)Set   []
Some=Sigma:(X:Set;(X)Set)Set []
Old:(Donkey)Set [] C
Married:(Man;Woman)Set   [] C
Run:(Man)Set   [] C
Own:(Man;Donkey)Set   [] C
Beat:(Man;Donkey)Set   [] C
Love:(Man;Woman)Set [] C
Gamma:(Man)Set [] C    (* belief context *)
Believe=[x,Z]Pi(Gamma(x),Z):(x:Man;(Gamma(x))Set)Set []
If=Pi:(X:Set;(X)Set)Set   []
And=Sigma:(X:Set;(X)Set)Set []
```

The argument types of the function type are separated by a semicolon instead of a comma. All judgements are made in a context, which is written in square brackets. All judgements of the above grammar are made in the empty context []. Constants not defined in terms of other ones, such as constructors of sets, are marked by the letter C. Constants like selectors, which are defined implicitly by series of pattern equations, are marked by the letter I. For instance, the left projection p is defined implicitly by one equation. Underscores _ may replace variables that the system can infer.

Explicitly defined constants are introduced directly with their definitions, and they are not marked by C or I. Finally, abstracted variables are written in square brackets.

(* Comments are written in starred parentheses. *)

To preserve uniqueness of typing, as required by ALF, we shall use
small initials in English words, for example, every,
capital initials in type-theoretical expressions, for example, Every,
capital initials and primes in ambiguated versions of type-theoretical expressions, for example, Every' (see Section 9.4 below).

9.2   Two stages of sugaring

Sugaring is performed in two stages. First, the type-theoretical expression is translated into a simpler formalism we call $\mathcal{F}$, or *functional phrase structure language*. This translation destroys information. Thus we shall call it *ambiguation*. For instance, the type-theoretical expression

If(There(Man),[x]Indef(Woman,[y](Love(Pron(Man,x),y))))

is ambiguated into the functional phrase structure

If'(There(Man),Love(He,Indef'(Woman)))

which shows neither the interpretation of the pronoun He nor the scope of the quantifier Indef'(Woman). The functional phrase structure is then translated into a string of English words,

if there is a man he loves a woman

To the two stages of sugaring correspond two stages of parsing (see Figure 9.1). A string of words is first parsed into functional phrase structure

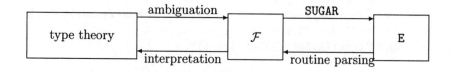

Figure 9.1

form. Up to this stage, parsing requires only standard phrase structure techniques. With the exception of the scopes of the connectives And' and If', sugaring from $\mathcal{F}$ to English does not destroy information, but only rearranges the functors and arguments and adds syncategorematic expressions. Every string of words has a finite number of parses in $\mathcal{F}$, the number depending on the number of connective words in the string.

The difficult part of parsing is from $\mathcal{F}$ to type theory. Here one must restore the scopes of the quantifiers and the interpretations of the pronouns. This task can be compared with the task of translating phrase structure trees into Montague's intensional logic, in the parsing procedure by Friedman and Warren (1978). But the situation is more complex here, because the interpretation of a pronoun is not a binding by a quantifier or a proper name, but an object of appropriate type given in context. This object may be composed from one or more variables introduced in the context. If we restrict the search for an interpretation to the selectors p, q, and ap, as suggested in Section 4.10, even this stage of parsing will always terminate.

Besides the articulation it gives to sugaring and parsing, the division into two stages has an informal motivation. When reading a text, we often grasp the interpretations of pronouns only later (cf. Section 6.4 above). The same may even concern scopes of quantifiers. The sentence

    every man loves a woman

has the functional phrase structure

    Love(Every'(Man),Indef'(Woman))

which disambiguates to

    Every(Man,[x]Indef(Woman,[y]Love(x,y)))

if the next sentence is

    john loves mary and peter loves susan

but to

    Indef(Woman,[y]Every(Man,[y]Love(x,y)))

if the next sentence is

    she is mary

To postpone the decision until there is a ground for it, we need something like functional phrase structure. But to make sense of the different anaphoric references in the next sentence, we of course need more than functional phrase structure.

9.3   Functional phrase structure

The functional phrase structure language $\mathcal{F}$ is a kind of a simple type theory. It has three basic types, S (sentence), CN (common noun), and NP (noun phrase), which are inductively defined sets. Only function types without dependencies are employed.

    S:Set [] C
    NP:Set [] C

```
CN:Set [] C
```

The categorizations that English expressions receive in $\mathcal{F}$ are very similar to their categorizations in simple type theory, with the exception of quantifiers, which do not form sentences but noun phrases. Alternatively, the expressions of $\mathcal{F}$ can be viewed as phrase structure trees (see Section 9.5).

```
John:NP [] C
O:NP [] C
OO:NP [] C
He:NP [] C
She:NP [] C
It:NP [] C
The':(CN)NP [] C
Mod:(CN;(NP)S)NP [] C
Every':(CN)NP [] C
Indef':(CN)NP [] C
Some':(CN)NP [] C
Donkey:CN  [] C
Man:CN [] C
Woman:CN   [] C
Rel:(CN;(NP)S)CN [] C
Old:(NP)S [] C
Married:(NP;NP)S   [] C
Run:(NP)S   [] C
Own:(NP;NP)S   [] C
Beat:(NP;NP)S   [] C
Love:(NP;NP)S   [] C
Believe':(NP;S)S [] C
And':(S;S)S [] C
If':(S;S)S [] C
Not:(S)S [] C
There:(CN)S [] C
```

9.4   Ambiguation

The first step in sugaring is *ambiguation*, which transforms type-theoretical expressions into expressions of $\mathcal{F}$. It is at this stage that type-theoretical information is destroyed, including

substitution of quantifier phrases for variables, for example,
Every(A,B) becomes B(Every'(A));
production of polymorphic expressions by dropping out type information, for example, Equal(A,a,b) becomes Equal'(a,b);

deletion of the interpretations of anaphoric expressions, for example, Pron(Man,a) becomes He, and The(A,a) becomes The'(A).

The first of the above procedures, substitution of quantifier phrases for variables, is the central sugaring principle in Montague grammar. In PTQ, it is stated in the rule S14 (p. 252 in Montague 1974; see also Section 9.9 below). Substitutions produce scope ambiguities of quantifiers. Even pronominal reference is explained in terms of this procedure. We find this explanation too narrow, of course, and formulate separate rules for pronouns. Moreover, we extend the ambiguation by substitution to the progressive connectives And and If.

There is a type-theoretical problem in the ambiguation procedure. Suppose we try to perform ambiguation inside type theory, using three operators,

```
ss:(Set)S   [] I
sc:(Set)CN   [] I
sn:(X:Set; X)NP [] I
```

To formulate the idea of ambiguation of quantified propositions by substitution, we would like to define

```
ss(Every(A,B))  =  ss(B(Every'(sc(A))))
```

But this cannot be done, because of a type mismatch in the definiens: B:(A)Set but Every'(sc(A)):NP. Another possibility would be to mimick the quantifier phrase Every'(A) in type theory itself, writing

```
Every*:(X:Set)X [] C
sn(A,Every*(A)) = Every'(sc(A))
ss(Every(A,B)) = ss(B(Every*(A)))
```

No type mismatch occurs, but type theory becomes inconsistent, since every set A has the element Every*(A). A remedy would be to make Every* depend on a variable of type A, for example, to be the identity mapping

```
Every*=[X,x]x:(X:Set;x:X)X []
```

To sugar Every(A,B) we would then assume that B is in the abstract form [x]C, and define

```
ss(Every(A,[x]C))  =  ss(([x]C)(Every*(A,x)))
```

But this definition is wrong as well, because the variable x occurs free in the definiens but not in the definiendum.

In the current implementation of sugaring, the problem of quantifier phrase substitution is solved by categorizing quantifiers as non-canonical expression forms of $\mathcal{F}$,

```
Every:(CN;(NP)S)S [] I
  Every(A,B)=B(Every'(A))
Some:(CN;(NP)S)S  [] I
```

```
Some(A,B)=B(Some'(A))
Indef:(CN;(NP)S)S   [] I
  Indef(A,B)=B(Indef'(A))
And:(S;(NP)S)S [] I
  And(A,B)=And'(A,B(0))
If:(S;(NP)S)S [] I
  If(A,B)=If'(A,B(0))
```

Ambiguation is thus computation into $\mathcal{F}$ normal form.

Our sugaring procedure can now transform expressions that look exactly like type theory into English strings, but it is not really translation of type theory into English. The first step in sugaring a proposition, an object of type Set, is to switch into treating it as an element of the set S, and this switching is not formally defined. It is trivial for the human eye, since the expression is not changed but only the type, but for a typed programming language, it involves the typing problem discussed above.

At the end of Section 8.11, we noticed, for other reasons, that sugaring is not a function of the type-theoretical proposition but of the type-theoretical expression. When we want to sugar a proposition, or some other type-theoretical object, we must thus first switch into seeing it as an expression, and not as a type-theoretical object.

There are many ways of looking at type-theoretical expressions. The strictest way is the following: the rules defining type-theoretical expressions are precisely the rules defining type-theoretical objects, except that expressions for equal objects are not treated as equal expressions. No garbage is produced, no propositional expressions that cannot be understood as propositions. This way of defining type-theoretical expressions demands the use of dependent types.

The loosest way of looking at type-theoretical expressions is as strings of characters of the alphabet including (,), :, Σ, Π, etc. This way is typical of untyped programming languages like Prolog. The set of expressions viewed in this way includes a lot of garbage, that is, meaningless strings, but its structure is very simple.

Our use of $\mathcal{F}$ lies between these extremes. It produces some garbage, but it does not recognize all strings of characters. Moreover, most of the garbage has a linguistic interpretation: a functional phrase structure is a parsing of an English sentence that cannot (yet, or in the context at hand) be interpreted type-theoretically. The structure of $\mathcal{F}$ is, unlike bare string structure, rich enough for controlling the sugaring procedure.

The very idea of defining a function on a formal language by defining a similar function on a larger language with a simpler structure is often used in metamathematics. (See e.g. the proof of the Church-Rosser theorem in Martin-Löf 1972, which is written for a set of functional terms formed without type restrictions.)

The ambiguation of anaphoric expressions follows the sugaring principles stated in Chapter 4.

```
PRO:(CN)NP [] I
(* PRO(A) is assigned to each common noun A in the
 lexical entry for it, e.g. PRO(Man)=He *)
Pron:(CN;NP)NP [] I
  Pron(A,x)=PRO(A)
The:(CN;NP)NP [] I
  The(A,a)=The'(A)
Mod:(CN;(NP)S;NP;NP)NP [] I
  Mod(A,B,a,b)=Mod'(A,B)
```

It remains to show how singular terms formed by p, q, ap, etc., are ambiguated, for these operators do not occur in functional phrase structure. The most important rule is

```
p:(NP)NP   [] I
  p(c)=c
```

This follows from the treatment of separated subsets as Σ sets; cf. Section 3.3. The rest of the operators should only occur in the argument places of anaphoric expressions, so that they are dropped out in ambiguation. For instance,

```
Pron(Donkey,p(q(ap(z,u)))) = PRO(Donkey) = It
```

To recognize these terms as non-canonical $\mathcal{F}$, we simply define them as identity mappings.

```
q:(NP)NP   [] I
  q(c)=c
ap:(NP;NP)NP [] I
  ap(c,a)=a
```

Monomorphic selectors are also recognized, but we shall not use them in our examples.

9.5   Tree notation for functional phrase structure

Figures 9.2–9.4 provide an alternative way of looking at functional phrase structure, which shows directly how functional phrase structures are sugared into strings of words. It is also useful in the discussion of parsing.

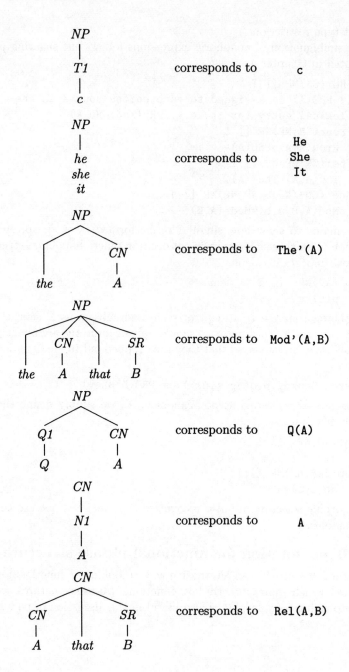

Figure 9.2

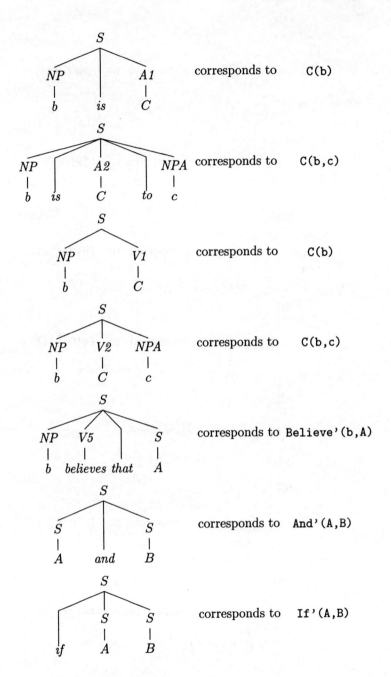

Figure 9.3

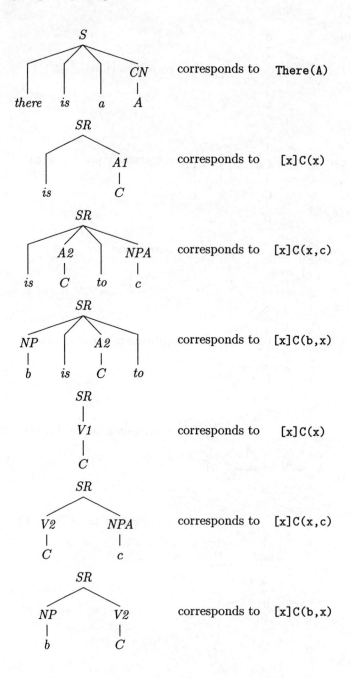

Figure 9.4

In these functional phrase structure trees, *S*, *NP*, and *CN* occur as non-terminal nodes and words as terminal nodes. In addition, there is a special class of non-terminal nodes occurring immediately above terminal nodes. They could be called *lexical categories*, and they include

N1, which dominates common nouns like *man*,
T1, which dominates proper names like *John*,
A1, which dominates one-place adjectives like *old*,
A2, which dominates two-place adjectives like *married*,
V1, which dominates intransitive verbs like *run*,
V2, which dominates transitive verbs like *love*,
V5, which dominates sentential verbs like *believe*,
C2, which dominates infix connectives like *and*,
C3, which dominates prefix connectives like *if*,
Q1, which dominates quantifier words like *every*.

In the appendix, the symbols N1 – Q1 function as sugaring patterns shared by classes of lexical entries. We have simplified the grammar of the appendix by leaving the number of nouns and the inflectional categories of sentences out of consideration.

The treatment of case is made context-free by separating the categories *NP* and *NPA*, which are exact copies of each other except for the pronouns *he* and *she*. The treatment of the indefinite article is simplified by excluding *an*. Relative clauses are restricted to a special category *SR*. Reading the table from right to left tells how sugaring proceeds. Reading left to right tells how parsing proceeds.

9.6 Examples of sugaring

Here are some examples of expressions recognizable both as type-theoretical propositions and as elements of S.

$$
\begin{aligned}
&\text{Ex1} = \text{Every(Man,[x]Some(Woman,[y]Love(x,y)))} : \text{S} \quad [] \\
&\text{Ex2} = \text{Some(Woman,[y]Every(Man,[x]Love(x,y)))} : \text{S} \quad [] \\
&\text{Ex3} = \text{Indef(Man,[x]Indef(Donkey,[y]Own(x,y)))} : \text{S} \quad [] \\
&\text{Ex4} = \text{If(Indef(Man,[x]Indef(Donkey,[y]Own(x,y))),} \\
&\qquad \text{[z]Beat(Pron(Man,p(z)),Pron(Donkey,p(q(z)))))} : \text{S} \; [] \\
&\text{Ex5} = \text{Believe(John,[x]Indef(Donkey,} \\
&\qquad\qquad\qquad \text{[y]Own(Pron(Man,John),y)))} : \text{S} \; [] \\
&\text{Ex6} = \text{If(Believe(John,[x]Indef(Donkey,} \\
&\qquad\quad \text{[y]Own(Pron(Man,John),y))),} \\
&\qquad\qquad \text{[z]Believe(Pron(Man,John),} \\
&\qquad\qquad\qquad \text{[x]Old(Pron(Donkey,p(ap(z,x)))))))} : \text{S} \; [] \\
&\text{Ex9} = \text{Every(Rel(Man,[x]Indef(Donkey,[y]Own(x,y))),} \\
&\qquad\qquad \text{[z]Beat(p(z),Pron(Donkey,p(q(z)))))} : \text{S} \; [] \\
&\text{Ex10} = \text{There(Rel(Woman,[y]Not(Married(John,y))))} : \text{S} \; []
\end{aligned}
$$

```
Ex11 = Not(Every(Rel(Woman,[y]Not(Married(
          Pron(Man,John),y))),[z]Love(John,p(z)))) : S []
Ex12 = Every(Man,[x]Indef(Donkey,[y]Own(x,y))) : S    []
Ex13 = If(Every(Man,[x]Indef(Donkey,[y]Own(x,y))),
     [z]Some(Man,[u]Beat(u,Pron(Donkey,p(ap(z,u))))))):S []
Ex14 = If(Every(Man,[x]Indef(Donkey,[y]Own(x,y))),
     [z]Some(Man,[u]Beat(u,Mod(Donkey,[v]Own(Pron(Man,u),v),
                      p(ap(z,u)),q(ap(z,u)))))):S []
```

Loaded in ALF together with the program of the appendix, we can execute the sugaring of each example A:S by computing SUGAR(A) into the normal form, for example,

```
-> nf SUGAR(Ex1);;
normal form :
 -(every,-(man,-(#(love,s),-(some,-(woman,e)))))
```

The current version of ALF only recognizes the general functional notation -(a,b) for list construction, and cannot convert the list into a string of words, but we shall in the following assume this is done. In this case, the string is

```
every man loves some woman.
```

The sugarings of the remaining examples are

```
(Ex2)  every man loves some woman
(Ex3)  a man owns a donkey
(Ex4)  if a man owns a donkey he beats it
(Ex5)  john believes that he owns a donkey
(Ex6)  if john believes that he owns a donkey
         he believes that it is old
(Ex9)  every man that owns a donkey beats it
(Ex10) there is a woman that john is not married to
(Ex11) john does not love every woman that he is
         not married to
(Ex12) every man owns a donkey
(Ex13) if every man owns a donkey some man beats it
(Ex14) if every man owns a donkey some man beats
         the donkey that he owns
```

The command of computing an example itself into normal form produces a canonical element of S, and thus ambiguates the type-theoretical expression. For instance,

```
-> nf Ex1;;
normal form : Love(Every'(Man),Some'(Woman))
```

9.7   Parsing

Parsing in type theory can be organized in the same way as parsing in Montague grammar (see Friedman and Warren 1978). Given a string of English words, a functional phrase structure is found by routine techniques. (In Friedman and Warren, the technique is transition networks.) The parse tree is then interpreted in type theory to yield a type-theoretical parse of the string (or a failure).

As seen in Section 9.2, functional phrase structure leaves the scopes of quantifiers unspecified. It also leaves pronouns uninterpreted. Some functional phrase structures cannot be interpreted as propositions at all, for example, the structures

```
If'(Own(John,Every'(Donkey)),Beat(He,It))
If'(Own(John,Indef'(Donkey)),Beat(She,Her))
```

which sugar into the sentences

```
if john owns every donkey he beats it
if john owns a donkey she beats her
```

respectively. But even if a sentence cannot be interpreted alone, it may be interpretable in the context of some other sentences.

Friedman and Warren interpret context-free parse trees in intensional logic by assigning a set of free variables and a set of bindings to each node. We must assign contexts instead, since the interpretation of a pronoun is not a binding by a quantifier or a proper name, like in Montague grammar, but an object given in context. This object can be composed from more than one variable introduced in the context.

To assign a context to each node is to tell what variables of what types are free in them. A fresh variable x is introduced by each quantifier phrase, that is, by each expression of $\mathcal{F}$ having the sugaring pattern Q1, like Every'. In the tree notation, a quantifier phrase is a subtree of the form

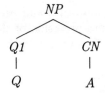

The type of the variable introduced by the quantifier phrase is the interpretation of the common noun A. This variable gets bound at some sentence node above A. The variable belongs to the context of every node below that S node, except in the quantifier phrase itself (i.e. in the nodes dominated by the NP node in question). That is, x is not free in its own type; we cannot form $(\Pi x : A(x))$. Moreover, a variable y is not free in the type of

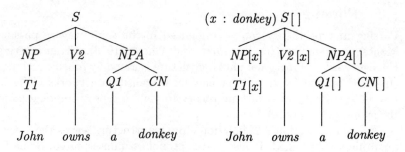

Figure 9.5

a variable x bound above y; we can have

$$(\Pi x : A)(\Sigma y : B(x)),$$

but not

$$(\Sigma y : B(x))(\Pi x : A).$$

Contexts having been assigned in this way, functional phrase structures containing quantifier phrases can be effectively interpreted as quantified propositions in type theory. For example, the tree on the right in Figure 9.5 shows the way in which variables are assigned to the tree on the left. The typed variable in parentheses, $(x : A)$, marks the node at which the variable gets bound; x can only belong to the contexts of the nodes below that node. Of two bindings at the same node, the one on the left is 'above', that is, has the wider scope. Contexts are written in square brackets [ ]. To save space, we indicate the type of the variable only at the binding. The tree in Figure 9.5 corresponds to the type-theoretical expression

    Indef(Donkey,[x]Own(John,x))

An S node dominating the word *if* and two S nodes introduces a fresh variable whose type is the interpretation of the sentence below the left S node, and which belongs to the context of the right S node and all nodes it dominates. An S node dominating two S nodes and *and* between them is treated in an analogous way.

Thus our second example

    If'(Own(John,Indef'(Donkey)),Beat(He,It))

is interpreted

    If(Indef(Donkey,[x]Own(John,x)),[z]Beat(He,It)).

Figure 9.6 shows this in tree form. The next section will tell how to interpret the pronouns.

$(z \,:\, \mathrm{Indef}(donkey,(x)own(John,x)))$

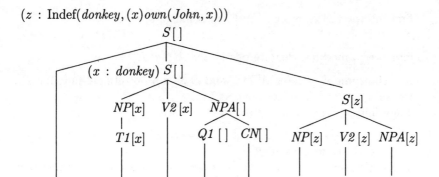

Figure 9.6

The interpretation of a common noun modified by a relative clause is already indicated in Figure 9.4, showing correspondences between trees and functional phrase structures. The set term $\mathrm{Rel}(A,B)$ is not ambiguated, but the function B remains as a function with occurrences of variables. Such an occurrence corresponds to the 'hole' there is in an SR clause as compared with an S clause. The variable x belongs to the context of the SR node and the nodes below it.

When an interpreted tree is translated into a type-theoretical expression, a variable z of type $\mathrm{Rel}(A,B)$ is usually translated as the left projection $p(z) \,:\, A$. (Recall that $p(z)$ produces z in sugaring.)

9.8 The interpretation of anaphoric expressions

To interpret a pronoun c in the context Γ is to

find an element $a \,:\, A$ given in Γ such that
$\mathrm{Pron}(A,a) \,\rhd\, c$.

If there is none, a failure results (or, alternatively, a background hypothesis is added to the context). If there are several, a failure results (or, alternatively, all of the different interpretations are stored.)

Parsing to functional phrase structure does not check the type matching of verbs and their arguments. This can be done by type-theoretical type checking as soon as the phrase structure is intepreted as a type-theoretical expression. This may lead to the rejection of some interpretations of pronouns; cf. Section 4.8.

The interpretation of definite noun phrases *the A* is analogous to the interpretation of pronouns,

first interpret A as a set A' in Γ, then find
$a : A'$ in Γ.

To interpret a modified definite phrase *the A that B*,

first interpret A as a set A' in Γ and B as a propositional function B',
where $B'(x)$: prop in the context Γ, $x : A'$.
Then find $a : A'$ and $b : B'(a)$ in Γ.

For the uniqueness of interpretation, it is enough that $a : A'$ is unique; elements of $B'(a)$ do not count.

The conclusion of the discussion of actuality in Section 4.10 was that we need not consider everything given in context. It is enough to consider

the variables themselves,
proper names (i.e. expressions of category *T1*) used in the sentence,
what is obtained from these objects by selectors.

For instance, the pronouns in the right-hand-side S clause in Figure 9.6 must find their interpretations among the objects

$z :$ Indef($donkey, (x)own(John, x)$),
$John : man$,
$p(z) : donkey$,
$q(z) : own(John, p(z))$.

It is obvious how the method of parsing just described generalizes to texts. Each whole sentence brings in a new variable, whose type is the interpretation of the sentence. Each S node dominating a whole sentence is interpreted in the context created by the foregoing sentences. We obtain a sequence of trees

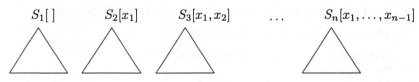

$$S_1[\ ] \qquad S_2[x_1] \qquad S_3[x_1, x_2] \qquad \ldots \qquad S_n[x_1, \ldots, x_{n-1}]$$

To give an example, the text

Every man is married to a woman.
Some man loves the woman that he is married to.

produces two phrase structure trees. The former tree introduces a variable z, which belongs to the context of every node of the latter tree. The pronoun *he* gets its interpretation inside the second sentence, the variable u. But the modified definite phrase *the woman that he is married to* is interpreted as the woman $p(\text{ap}(z, u))$. (See Figure 9.7.)

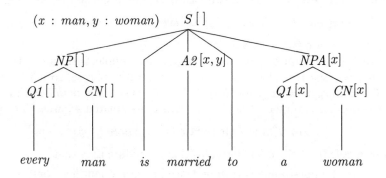

$(z : every(man, (x)\text{Indef}(woman, (y)married(x, y))))$

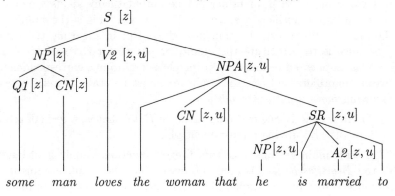

Figure 9.7

9.9   Conditions of sugarability

If the input of sugaring is a well-formed propositional expression type-theoretically, the resulting English sentence has a type-theoretical semantics. Thus the grammar does not overgenerate in the sense of producing meaningless sentences. But it does produce some strange results, like

$$every(man, (x)run(Mary)) \;\triangleright\; Mary \; runs,$$

where there is no variable to substitute the quantifier phrase for, and

$$every(man, (x)admire(x, x)) \;\triangleright\; every \; man \; admires \; every \; man,$$

where there are two such variables.

In the direction of parsing, corresponding problems do not arise. The sentence *Mary runs* does not contain a quantifier phrase, so it is not formalized $every(man, (x)run(Mary))$. The sentence *every man admires every man* contains two quantifier phrases, which are treated separately, to yield

$$every(man, (x)every(man, (y)admire(x, y))).$$

A principle implicit in the formalization procedure says that

> there is a one-to-one correspondence between quantifier phrases in English and quantifiers in type theory.

In formalization, each quantifier phrase automatically yields a new quantifier, and no quantifiers are produced otherwise. This is the simplest and the most intuitive formalization procedure. But in sugaring, the simplest procedure is to substitute the quantifier phrase for the variable—and it may get duplicated or lost. The principle of one-to-one correspondence between quantifiers and quantifier phrases must be stated explicitly, as the following *main argument condition*.

> There is exactly one main argument in $B(x)$, that is, a term of the form x or $p(x)$ occupying an argument place.

(The term main argument is from Frege's functional analysis of language in the *Begriffsschrift*, §9. Frege observes that the 'main argument' of a sentence is usually the subject, but that any constituent can be made into the main argument.) The reason for including $p(x)$ in addition to x is the treatment of separated subsets as Σ sets; cf. Section 3.3.

In PTQ, Montague (1974, chapter 8) implements a similar condition in the rule S14 for forming quantified sentences. The rule S14 reads

> If $\alpha \in P_T$ and $\phi \in P_t$, then $F_{10,n}(\alpha, \phi) \in P_t$, where either (i) α does not have the form he_k, and $F_{10,n}(\alpha, \phi) \in P_t$ comes from ϕ by replacing the first occurrence of he_n or him_n by α and all other occurrences of he_n or him_n by $\left\{ \begin{array}{c} he \\ she \\ it \end{array} \right\}$ or $\left\{ \begin{array}{c} him \\ her \\ it \end{array} \right\}$ respectively, according as the

gender of the first $\mathrm{B_{CN}}$ or $\mathrm{B_T}$ in α is $\left\{\begin{array}{l}\text{masc.}\\ \text{fem.}\\ \text{neuter}\end{array}\right\}$, or (ii) $\alpha = \mathbf{he}_k$, and $F_{10,n}(\alpha, \phi) \in \mathrm{P_t}$ comes from ϕ by replacing all occurrences of $\mathbf{he}_n$ or $\mathbf{him}_n$ by $\mathbf{he}_k$, or $\mathbf{him}_k$ respectively.

(Montague 1974, p. 252.) Multiple substitution of a quantifier phrase is blocked by the substitution of pronouns for all occurrences of the variable but the leftmost one. Nothing prevents vacuous substitutions.

We followed the model of S14 in Ranta 1991a, and prevented multiple substitutions of quantifier phrases by introducing pronouns in sugaring. Moreover, we took care of vacuous substitutions by choosing connectives instead of quantifiers in cases with no main arguments. Definite noun phrases were used instead of pronouns if unique reference was in danger. What we have now are compositional rules for quantifiers on the one hand, and for anaphoric expressions on the other. The main argument condition is stated separately.

What makes the main argument condition problematic is that it does not belong to categorial grammar, nor to the compositional sugaring procedure. All rules of categorial grammar are of the form

$$\frac{J_1, \ldots, J_n}{J}$$

saying that, given the judgements $J_1, \ldots, J_n$, you may make the judgement J. They are may-rules, positive rules. There are no may-not-rules, nor any must-rules. If there are any such rules in natural language, they do not belong to the categorial grammar. They are rules that exclude expressions generated by the positive rules from the fragment proper.

Informally, it is often natural to describe language by negative rules. Thus there is a positive rule saying

he can be used for referring to any man,

and a negative rule saying

if there is a risk of confusion, do not use *he* but some more specific expression.

(Cf. Section 4.3.)

Negative conditions occur, in some form or other, in formal grammars as well. In transformational grammar, the positive rules include phrase structure rules and optional transformations. But in addition, there are some obligatory transformations (Chomsky 1957, p. 47). In the government and binding theory, there is the positive transformational rule move α, 'move anything anywhere', which has much of the same effect as the abstraction rule in categorial grammar. A considerable part of the principles of the grammar are then restrictions to move α (van Riemsdijk and

Williams, 1986, p. 127). In generalized phrase structure grammar, there are both 'permissive' and 'restrictive' rules, the latter motivated by the claim that some generalizations about language are negative rather than positive (Gazdar *et al.* 1985, pp. 76–77). One expects to get a set of simple positive rules and of simple negative rules, instead of a set of complicated positive rules—complicated because negative insights are artificially forced inside them.

The main argument condition is a *condition of sugarability*, which tells what expressions yield correct results in sugaring. We have already indicated some more principles that formally amount to conditions of sugarability, for example,

> the ordering principles (see Section 3.2),
> the conditions of uniqueness and actuality of anaphoric expressions (see Chapter 4),
> the restriction of relative clauses to sentences of limited complexity (see Section 9.5).

When formulated separately from the sugaring rules proper, such conditions appear as much more simple and evident than their joint consequences for individual sugaring rules. Our generative grammar thus consists of three components,

> categorial grammar,
> compositional sugaring rules,
> conditions of sugarability.

(In Ranta 1991a, the conditions of sugarability are scattered around in the sugaring rules proper. In the ALF implementation of sugaring, they are not yet included.)

Apart from the task of giving a generative grammar for a fragment of English, there is the task of finding a sugaring algorithm for the whole of type theory. To sugar an arbitrary proposition A, one must start by finding a proposition A' definitionally equal to A in the sugarable fragment. Sugaring thus involves a unification of sugarability and definitional equality to A. Whether this can always be done—that is, whether all type-theoretical propositions can be expressed in English—is an open question. The most difficult theoretical problem seems to be to find enough anaphoric expressions to guarantee uniqueness.

To sugar the example propositions from the beginning of this section, declared unsugarable by the one-to-one principle, we find the following variants of them.

> $if(There(man), (x)run(Mary))$
> ▷ *if there is a man Mary runs,*

$every(man, (x)\text{Refl}(man, admire, x))$
$\qquad \triangleright$ *every man admires himself.*

Note. The burden of the conditions of sugarability can be reduced by avoiding the abstraction rule and using *combinators* instead, in the way shown by Steedman (1988). For instance, the two-quantifier proposition

$$every(man, (x)\text{Indef}(donkey, (y)own(x, y)))$$

can be expressed without variable bindings as

$\text{SUBJQ}(man, every(man), \text{OBJQ}(man, donkey, own, \text{Indef}(donkey)))$

by using the combinators

$\text{SUBJQ} = (A, Q, C)Q(C)$
$\quad : (A : \text{set}, Q : ((A)\text{prop})\text{prop}, C : (A)\text{prop})\text{prop},$
$\text{OBJQ} = (A, B, C, Q)(x)Q((y)C(x, y))$
$\quad : (A : \text{set}, B : \text{set}, C : (A, B)\text{prop}, Q : ((B)\text{prop})\text{prop})(A)\text{prop}.$

(These two combinators, in effect, already appear in the PTQ rules S4 and S5, respectively; see Montague 1974, p. 251.) The structure of the combinator expression is easier to see if type information is hidden,

$$\text{SUBJQ}(every(man), \text{OBJQ}(own, \text{Indef}(donkey))).$$

To extend this treatment to

$every(\text{Rel}(man, (x)\text{Indef}(donkey, (y)own(x, y))),$
$\qquad\qquad\qquad (z)Beat(p(z), \text{Pron}(donkey, p(q(z)))))),$

we need a generalization of the composition of functions to dependent types,

$\text{GFC} = (A, B, C, f, g)(x)g(x, f(x))$
$\quad : (A : \text{set}, B : (A)\text{set}, C : (x : A, B(x))\text{set},$
$\qquad f : (x : A)B(x), g : (x : A, y : B(x))C(x, y))(x : A)C(x, f(x))$

as well as a combinator giving the arguments of a transitive verb as mappings of one given element,

$\text{DUO} = (A, B, C, F, f, g)(z)F(f(z), g(z))$
$\quad : (A : \text{set}, B : \text{set}, C : \text{set}, F : (A, B)\text{prop}, f : (C)A, g : (C)B)(C)\text{prop}.$

At its simplest, the condition of sugarability for quantifiers could be that the second argument must be a one-place propositional function built by means of a combinator. Abstraction could only be used to form arguments of connectives.

9.10 Applications of sugaring and parsing

I have been presenting sugaring first as a point of view in grammatical thinking, and then as an element in a certain arrangement of generative grammar. In addition to these theoretical roles, one can also think of some practical applications of the sugaring procedure. Connected to an interactive proof system like ALF, it provides a method of expressing mathematical theorems in natural language. As type theory (like predicate calculus) is originally a language of mathematics, this is a task for which type-theoretical grammar should be adequate, at least. The mathematical use provides a strict condition of adequacy for sugaring and parsing:

> a correct formal derivation results, when sugared, in a correct informal proof, and conversely.

Moreover, we want not just to give a generative grammar for a fragment of informal mathematical language, but to

> find a method for expressing every mathematical proposition by an unambiguous English sentence.

Much remains to be done in this direction, and it is not obvious that the problem can be solved by the modes of expression provided by standard English. That is, it may well be the case that the use of formalisms in mathematics is essential. In particular, it may be necessary to use explicit variables instead of anaphoric expressions to guarantee uniqueness in a context in which many objects of one and the same type are given.

More generally, as it is relatively easy to define sugaring procedures for new languages, the task of translating a text into a collection of languages reduces to the task of formalizing it in type theory. Fully automatic translation would, in addition, require a formalization procedure, and there seems to be little hope for an absolutely reliable one. There is a general reason for this, namely that we cannot anticipate everything there is in a natural language text. And there is a more precise theoretical reason, discussed above in Section 4.8: a correct translation may demand the interpretation of a pronoun, but this can be arbitrarily difficult. Some kind of interactive formalization should be more easily realizable.

APPENDIX: SUGARING IN ALF

```
(* Sugaring program presented in the TTG book by A.R. 1993
            using ALF version 3/12 1992 *)

(* 1. Structural framework *)

    (* basic categories *)
    S:Set [] C
    NP:Set [] C
    CN:Set [] C

    (* Word is the set of English words*)
    Word:Set  [] C
      a':Word [] C
      an:Word [] C
      are:Word [] C
      be:Word [] C
      case':Word [] C
      does:Word [] C
      do:Word [] C
      is':Word  [] C
      it:Word [] C
      not:Word [] C
      that:Word [] C
      the:Word [] C

   Suffix:Set [] C
     s:Suffix [] C
     ed:Suffix [] C
     #:(Word;Suffix)Word [] C
(* Complex words are formed by adding suffixes, like s,
by using the constructor #. This gives e.g. the plural noun
form #(donkey,s) and the third person verb form #(run,s).
More words and suffixes are introduced in lexical
entries at need *)
```

```
(* E is the set of lists of English words. e is the empty
list, conventionally NIL. - is the list constructor
conventionally CONS. APP appends two lists *)
E:Set [] C
  e:E  [] C
  -:(c:Word;b:E)E [] C
APP:(E;E)E [] I
  APP(e,y)=y
  APP(-(c,b),y)=-(c,APP(b,y))

CASE:Set [] C
  NOM:CASE [] C  (* the nominative *)
  ACC:CASE [] C  (* the accusative *)
NUMBER:Set [] C
  SG:NUMBER [] C   (* the singular *)
  PL:NUMBER [] C   (* the plural *)
INFL:Set [] C
  POS:INFL [] C   (* unnegated *)
  NEG:INFL [] C   (* negated *)
(* tenses would belong to INFL as well,
   but they are not treated here *)

NUM:(NP)NUMBER [] I
  (* every noun phrase has a number *)

SUGCN:(NUMBER;CN)E [] I
  (* every common noun can be sugared into
     singular and plural *)

SUGNP:(CASE;NP)E [] I
  (* every noun phrase can be sugared into
     nominative and accusative *)

SUGS:(INFL;S)E [] I
  (* every sentence has an
     unnegated and a negated sugaring *)

SUGAR=[A]SUGS(POS,A):(S)E []
  (* to produce unnegated sentences *)

PRO:(CN)NP [] I  (* "gender" of common noun *)

INDART:(CN)Word [] I (* a or an *)
```

```
VF:(INFL;NUMBER;Word)E [] I   (* verb forms *)


VF(POS,SG,be)=-(is',e)
VF(NEG,SG,be)=-(is',-(not,e))
VF(POS,PL,be)=-(are,e)
VF(NEG,PL,be)=-(are,-(not,e))


REGVERB:(INFL;NUMBER;Word)E [] I (* regular verb forms *)
  REGVERB(POS,SG,C)=-(#(C,s),e)
  REGVERB(NEG,SG,C)=-(does,-(not,-(C,e)))
  REGVERB(POS,PL,C)=-(C,e)
  REGVERB(NEG,PL,C)=-(do,-(not,-(C,e)))
```

(* 2. Sugaring patterns s. lexical categories *)

```
  N1:(NUMBER;Word)E [] I   (* common nouns like donkey *)
    N1(SG,C)=-(C,e)
    N1(PL,C)=-(#(C,s),e)


  T1:(Word)E [] I     (* proper names like John *)
    T1(C)=-(C,e)


  A1:(INFL;NP;Word)E [] I    (* adjectives like old *)
    A1(m,a,C)=APP(SUGNP(NOM,a),APP(VF(m,NUM(a),be),-(C,e)))


  (* observe the subject-verb agreement *)


  A2:(INFL;NP;Word;Word;NP)E [] I
        (* adjectives like married to someone *)
    A2(m,a,C,P,b)=
        APP(SUGNP(NOM,a),
          APP(VF(m,NUM(a),be),-(C,-(P,SUGNP(ACC,b)))))


  V1:(INFL;NP;Word)E [] I   (* verbs like run *)
    V1(m,a,C)=APP(SUGNP(NOM,a),APP(VF(m,NUM(a),C),e))


  V2:(INFL;NP;Word;NP)E [] I (* verbs like love someone *)
    V2(m,a,C,b)=
      APP(SUGNP(NOM,a),APP(VF(m,NUM(a),C),SUGNP(ACC,b)))


  V5:(INFL;NP;Word;S)E [] I     (* verbs like believe *)
```

```
      V5(m,a,C,A)
        =APP(SUGNP(NOM,a),
           APP(VF(m,NUM(a),C),-(that,SUGS(POS,A))))

   C2:(INFL;S;Word;S)E [] I    (* connectives like and *)
     C2(POS,A,C,B)=APP(SUGS(POS,A),-(C,SUGS(POS,B)))
     C2(NEG,A,C,B)=-(it,-(is',-(not,-(the,-(case',-(that,
        C2(POS,A,C,B)))))))

   C3:(INFL;Word;S;S)E [] I    (* connectives like if *)
     C3(POS,C,A,B)=-(C,APP(SUGS(POS,A),SUGS(POS,B)))
     C3(NEG,C,A,B)=-(it,-(is',-(not,-(the,-(case',-(that,
        C3(POS,C,A,B)))))))

   Q1:(Word;CN)E [] I     (* quantifiers like every *)
     Q1(C,A)=-(C,SUGCN(SG,A))
```

(* 3. Lexicon *)

(* proper names *)

```
   John:NP [] C              (* the proper name itself *)
    john:Word [] C           (* new English word *)
    NUM(John)=SG             (* number *)
    SUGNP(C,John)=T1(john)   (* no case distinction *)

   Mary:NP [] C
    mary:Word [] C
    NUM(Mary)=SG
    SUGNP(C,Mary)=T1(mary)
```

(* zero signs *)

```
   0:NP [] C      (* singular zero *)
    NUM(0)=SG
    SUGNP(C,0)=e
   00:NP [] C      (* plural zero *)
    NUM(00)=PL
    SUGNP(C,00)=e
```

(* anaphoric expressions *)

```
   Pron:(CN;NP)NP [] I
```

```
  Pron(A,a)=PRO(A)      (* ambiguation *)
He:NP [] C
 he:Word [] C
 him:Word [] C
 NUM(He)=SG
 SUGNP(NOM,He)=-(he,e)
 SUGNP(ACC,He)=-(him,e)
She:NP [] C
 she:Word [] C
 her:Word [] C
 NUM(She)=SG
 SUGNP(NOM,She)=-(she,e)
 SUGNP(ACC,She)=-(her,e)
It:NP [] C
 NUM(It)=SG
 SUGNP(C,It)=-(it,e)

The:(CN;NP)NP [] I
 The':(CN)NP [] C
 The(A,a)=The'(A)
 NUM(The'(A))=SG
 SUGNP(C,The'(A))=-(the,SUGCN(SG,A))

Mod:(CN;(NP)S;NP;NP)NP [] I
 Mod':(CN;(NP)S)NP [] C
 Mod(A,B,a,b)=Mod'(A,B)
 NUM(Mod'(A,B))=SG
 SUGNP(C,Mod'(A,B))=
   -(the,APP(SUGCN(SG,A),-(that,SUGAR(B(O)))))

(* quantifiers *)

Every:(CN;(NP)S)S [] I (* the type-theoretical form *)
 Every':(CN)NP [] C    (* the scope-ambiguous form *)
 Every(A,B)=B(Every'(A))  (* ambiguation *)
 every:Word [] C
 NUM(Every'(A))=SG
 SUGNP(C,Every'(A))=Q1(every,A)

Indef:(CN;(NP)S)S [] I
 Indef':(CN)NP [] C
 Indef(A,B)=B(Indef'(A))
 NUM(Indef'(A))=SG
```

```
    SUGNP(C,Indef'(A))=Q1(INDART(A),A)

Some:(CN;(NP)S)S [] I
 Some':(CN)NP [] C
 Some(A,B)=B(Some'(A))
 some:Word [] C
 NUM(Some'(A))=SG
 SUGNP(C,Some'(A))=Q1(some,A)

(* selectors *)
p:(NP)NP [] I
  p(c)=c
fst_prop:(S;(NP)S;NP)NP   [] I
  fst_prop(A,B,c)=p(c)
fst_set:(CN;(NP)S;NP)NP   [] I
  fst_set(A,B,c)=p(c)

q:(NP)NP [] I
  q(c)=c
snd_prop:(S;(NP)S;NP)NP   [] I
  snd_prop(A,B,c)=q(c)
snd_set:(CN;(NP)S;NP)NP   [] I
  snd_set(A,B,c)=q(c)

ap:(NP;NP)NP [] I
  ap(c,a)=a
apply:(CN;(NP)S;NP;NP)NP [] I
  apply(A,B,c,a)=ap(c,a)

(* common nouns *)

Donkey:CN   [] C    (* the common noun itself *)
 donkey:Word [] C   (* the new English words needed *)
 SUGCN(n,Donkey)=N1(n,donkey) (* regular SG and PL *)
 INDART(Donkey)=a'  (* the indefinite article *)
 PRO(Donkey)=It     (* "gender", the personal pronoun *)

Man:CN   [] C
 man:Word [] C
 men:Word [] C
 SUGCN(SG,Man)=-(man,e)   (* irregular SG and PL *)
 SUGCN(PL,Man)=-(men,e)
 INDART(Man)=a'
```

```
   PRO(Man)=He

Woman:CN   [] C
 woman:Word [] C
 women:Word [] C
 SUGCN(SG,Woman)=-(woman,e)
 SUGCN(PL,Woman)=-(women,e)
 INDART(Woman)=a'
 PRO(Woman)=She

Rel:(CN;(NP)S)CN [] C (* the relative pronoun that *)
 SUGCN(SG,Rel(A,B))=APP(SUGCN(SG,A),-(that,SUGAR(B(O))))
 SUGCN(PL,Rel(A,B))=APP(SUGCN(PL,A),-(that,SUGAR(B(OO))))
 INDART(Rel(A,B))=INDART(A)
 PRO(Rel(A,B))=PRO(A)

(* adjectives *)

Old:(NP)S [] C
 old:Word [] C
 SUGS(m,Old(a))=A1(m,a,old)

Married:(NP;NP)S  [] C
 married:Word [] C
 to:Word [] C
 SUGS(m,Married(a,b))=A2(m,a,married,to,b)

(* verbs *)

Run:(NP)S   [] C
 run:Word [] C
 VF(m,n,run)=REGVERB(m,n,run)
 SUGS(m,Run(a))=V1(m,a,run)

Walk:(NP)S [] C
 walk:Word [] C
 VF(m,n,walk)=REGVERB(m,n,walk)
 SUGS(m,Walk(a))=V1(m,a,walk)

Own:(NP;NP)S  [] C
 own:Word [] C
 VF(m,n,own)=REGVERB(m,n,own)
 SUGS(m,Own(a,b))=V2(m,a,own,b)
```

```
Beat:(NP;NP)S   [] C
 beat:Word [] C
 VF(m,n,beat)=REGVERB(m,n,beat)
 SUGS(m,Beat(a,b))=V2(m,a,beat,b)

Love:(NP;NP)S   [] C
 love:Word [] C
 VF(m,n,love)=REGVERB(m,n,love)
 SUGS(m,Love(a,b))=V2(m,a,love,b)

Believe:(NP;(NP)S)S [] I
 Believe':(NP;S)S [] C
 Believe(a,A)=Believe'(a,A(0))
 believe:Word [] C
 VF(m,n,believe)=REGVERB(m,n,believe)
 SUGS(m,Believe'(a,A))=V5(m,a,believe,A)

(* connectives *)

And:(S;(NP)S)S [] I
 And':(S;S)S [] C
 And(A,B)=And'(A,B(0))
 and:Word [] C
 SUGS(m,And'(A,B))=C2(m,A,and,B)

If:(S;(NP)S)S [] I
 If':(S;S)S [] C
 If(A,B)=If'(A,B(0))
 if:Word [] C
 SUGS(m,If'(A,B))=C3(m,if,A,B)

Not:(S)S [] C
 SUGS(POS,Not(A))=SUGS(NEG,A)
 SUGS(NEG,Not(A))=
   -(it,-(is',-(not,-(the,-(case',-(that,
                      SUGS(NEG,A)))))))

There:(CN)S [] C
 there:Word [] C
 SUGS(m,There(A))=
  -(there,APP(VF(m,SG,be),-(INDART(A),SUGCN(SG,A))))
```

BIBLIOGRAPHY

René Ahn and Hans-Peter Kolb. Discourse representation meets constructive mathematics. In L. Pólos and L. Kálmán, editor, *Papers from the Second Symposium on Logic and Language*, pages 105–124, Budapest, 1990. Akadémiai Kiadó.

Kazimierz Ajdukiewicz. Die syntaktische Konnexität. *Studia Philosophica*, 1:1–27, 1935.

Elizabeth Anscombe and Peter Geach. *Three Philosophers*. Basil Blackwell, Oxford, 1961.

Apollonius Dyscolus. *Syntaxis*. John Benjamin's, Amsterdam, 1981. Transl. by Fred Householder.

Aristotle. *The Categories, On Interpretation, Prior Analytics*. The Loeb Classical Library. William Heinemann Ltd, London, 1953. Edited by Harold Cooke and Hugh Tredennick.

John Austin. *How to Do Things with Words*. Harvard University Press, Cambridge, Ma., 1962.

Charles Bally. *Linguistique générale et linguistique française*. A. Francke S.A., Berne, 2nd edition, 1944.

Jon Barwise. Scenes and other situations. *The Journal of Philosophy*, 78:369–397, 1981.

Jon Barwise and Robin Cooper. Generalized quantifiers and natural language. *Linguistics and Philosophy*, 4:159–219, 1981.

Jon Barwise and John Perry. Situations and attitudes. *The Journal of Philosophy*, 78:668–691, 1981.

Johan van Benthem. The Lambek calculus. In R. Oehrle, E. Bach, and D. Wheeler, editors, *Categorial Grammars and Natural Language Structures*, pages 35–68. D. Reidel, Dordrecht, 1988.

Johan van Benthem. Categorial grammar and type theory. *The Journal of Philosophical Logic*, 19:115–168, 1990.

L. E. J. Brouwer. Over de grondslagen der wiskunde. In A. Heyting, editor, *Collected Works, Vol. 1.*, pages 11–101. North-Holland, Amsterdam and Oxford, 1975. Thesis, Amsterdam, 1907.

N. G. de Bruijn. The mathematical language AUTOMATH, its usage and some of its extensions. *Lecture Notes in Mathematics*, 125:29–61, 1970.

Rudolf Carnap. *Meaning and Necessity*. The University of Chicago Press, Chicago, 1947.

Noam Chomsky. *Syntactic Structures*. Mouton, The Hague, 1957.

Noam Chomsky. Remarks on nominalization. In Roderick A. Jacobs and Peter S. Rosenbaum, editors, *Readings in English Transformational Grammar*, pages 184–221. Ginn and Company, Waltham, Ma., 1970.

Alonzo Church. A formulation of the simple theory of types. *Journal of Symbolic Logic*, 5:56–68, 1940.

Bernard Comrie. *Tense*. Cambridge University Press, Cambridge, 1985.

Thierry Coquand and Gerard Huet. The calculus of constructions. *Information and Computation*, 76:95–120, 1988.

Haskell B. Curry. Some logical aspects of grammatical structure. In Roman Jakobson, editor, *Structure of Language and its Mathematical Aspects: Proceedings of the Twelfth Symposium in Applied Mathematics*, pages 56–68. American Mathematical Society, 1963.

Haskell B. Curry and Rudolf Feys. *Combinatory Logic, Vol. 1*. North-Holland, Amsterdam, 1958.

Donald Davidson. *Essays on Actions and Events*. Clarendon Press, New York, 1980.

Rogelio Davila-Perez. A system of rules and an algorithm for translating English into Martin-Löf's type theory. Paper read at the Workshop on Applications of Type Theory held in Helsinki in September 1993.

David Dowty. *Word Meaning and Montague Grammar*. D. Reidel, Dordrecht, 1979.

David Dowty. Grammatical relations and Montague grammar. In P. Jakobson and G.K. Pullum, editors, *The Nature of Syntactic Representation*, pages 79–130. D. Reidel, Dordrecht, 1982.

Michael Dummett. *Frege: Philosophy of Language*. Duckworth, London, 1973.

Michael Dummett. The philosophical basis of intuitionistic logic. In H. E. Rose and J. C. Shepherdson, editors, *Logic Colloquium '73*, pages 5–40. North-Holland, Amsterdam, 1975.

Gottlob Frege. *Begriffsschrift*. Louis Nebert, Halle A/S, 1879. In English, van Heijenoort 1967.

Gottlob Frege. *Grundgesetze der Arithmetik, I. Band.* Verlag von H. Pohle, Jena, 1893.

Joyce Friedman and David Warren. A parsing method for Montague grammar. *Linguistics and Philosophy*, 2:347–372, 1978.

Gerald Gazdar, Ewan Klein, Geoffrey Pullum, and Ivan Sag. *Generalized Phrase Structure Grammar.* Basil Blackwell, Oxford, 1985.

Peter Geach. *Reference and Generality.* Cornell University Press, Ithaca, New York, 1962.

Peter Geach. Intentional identity. *Journal of Philosophy*, 64:627–632, 1967.

Peter Geach. A program for syntax. In D. Davidson and G. Harman, editors, *Semantics of Natural Language*, pages 483–497. D. Reidel, Dordrecht, 1972.

Gerhard Gentzen. Untersuchungen ueber das logische Schliessen. *Mathematische Zeitschrift*, 39:176–210 and 405–431, 1934.

Kurt Gödel. Zur intuitionistischen Arithmetik und Zahlentheorie. In *Ergebnisse eines Mathematischen Kolloquiums, vol. 4*, 1932. Gödel 1932a.

Kurt Gödel. Eine Interpretation des intuitionistischen Aussagenkalküls. In *Ergebnisse eines Mathematischen Kolloquiums, vol. 4*, 1932. Gödel 1932b.

Jeroen Groenendijk and Martin Stokhof. Dynamic predicate logic. *Linguistics and Philosophy*, 14:39–100, 1991.

Martin Heidegger. *Sein und Zeit.* Max Niemeyer Verlag, Tuebingen, 1927.

Jean van Heijenoort, editor. *From Frege to Gödel.* Harvard University Press, Cambridge, Ma., 1967.

Irene Heim. File change semantics and the familiarity theory of definiteness. In R. Baeuerle, C. Schwarze, and A. von Stechow, editors, *Meaning, Use and Interpretation of Language*, pages 164–189. de Gruyter, Berlin, 1983.

Carl Hempel. Studies in the logic of confirmation (I). *Mind*, 54:1–26, 1945.

Arend Heyting. Die formalen Regeln der intuitionistischen Logik. In *Sitzungsberichte der Preussischen Akademie der Wissenschaften, Physikalisch-mathematische Klasse*, pages 42–56, 1930.

Arend Heyting. Die intuitionistische Grundlegung der Mathematik. *Erkenntnis*, 2:106–115, 1931.

Arend Heyting. *Intuitionism.* North-Holland, Amsterdam, 1956.

David Hilbert and Paul Bernays. *Grundlagen der Mathematik II.* Springer Verlag, Berlin, 1939.

Jaakko Hintikka. *Knowledge and Belief.* Cornell University Press, Ithaca, New York, 1962.

Jaakko Hintikka. *The Semantics of Questions and the Questions of Semantics*, volume 28 of *Acta Philosophica Fennica.* North-Holland, Amsterdam, 1976.

Jaakko Hintikka. Quantifiers in natural languages: some logical problems. In E. Saarinen, editor, *Game-Theoretical Semantics*, pages 81–117. D. Reidel, Dordrecht, 1979.

Jaakko Hintikka and Lauri Carlson. Conditionals, generic quantifiers, and other applications of subgames. In A. Margalit, editor, *Meaning and Use*, pages 179–214. D. Reidel, Dordrecht, 1979.

Jaakko Hintikka and Jack Kulas. *Anaphora and Definite Descriptions.* D. Reidel, Dordrecht, 1985.

William Howard. The formulae-as-types notion of construction. In R. Hindley and J. P. Seldin, editors, *To H.B. Curry: Essays on Combinatory Logic, Lambda Calculus and Formalism*, pages 479–490. Academic Press, London, 1980.

Hans Kamp. A theory of truth and semantic representation. In J. Groenendijk, T. Janssen, and M. Stokhof, editors, *Formal Methods in the Study of Language, Part 1*, pages 277–322. Mathematisch Centrum, Amsterdam, 1981.

Stephen Kleene. *Introduction to Metamathematics.* North-Holland, Amsterdam, 1952.

Andrej Kolmogorov. On the principle of the excluded middle. *Mat. Sb.*, 32:414–437, 1925. In Russian; in English, van Heijenoort 1967.

Andrej Kolmogorov. Zur Deutung der intuitionistischen Logik. *Mathematische Zeitschrift*, 35:58–65, 1932.

Steven Kuhn. Tense and time. In D. Gabbay and F. Guenthner, editors, *Handbook of Philosophical Logic, Vol. IV*, pages 513–552. D. Reidel, Dordrecht, 1989.

Milan Kundera. *L'art du roman.* Gallimard, Mesnil-sur-l'Estrée, 1986.

Joachim Lambek. The mathematics of sentence structure. *American Mathematical Monthly*, 65:154–170, 1958.

David Lewis. General semantics. In D. Davidson and G. Harman, editors, *Semantics of Natural Language*, pages 169–218. D. Reidel, Dordrecht, 1972.

David Lewis. Truth in fiction. *American Philosophical Quarterly*, XV:37–46, 1978.

John Lyons. *Semantics*. Cambridge University Press, Cambridge, 1977.

Petri Mäenpää. The Art of Analysis. Logic and History of Problem Solving. PhD thesis, University of Helsinki, 1993.

Petri Mäenpää. Parsing English into lower level type theory. University of Helsinki, January 1994.

Petri Mäenpää and Aarne Ranta. An implementation of intuitionistic categorial grammar. In L. Pólos and L. Kálmán, editors, *Papers from the Second Symposium on Logic and Language*, pages 299–318, Budapest, 1990. Akadémiai Kiadó.

Lena Magnusson. The new implementation of ALF. To appear in the Proceedings of the Workshop on Logical Frameworks held at Baastad in 1992.

Per Martin-Löf. An intuitionistic theory of types. Technical report, University of Stockholm, 1972.

Per Martin-Löf. An intuitionistic theory of types: predicative part. In H. E. Rose and J. C. Shepherdson, editors, *Logic Colloquium '73*, pages 73–118. North-Holland, Amsterdam, 1975.

Per Martin-Löf. Constructive mathematics and computer programming. In Cohen, Los, Pfeiffer, and Podewski, editors, *Logic, Methodology and Philosophy of Science VI*, pages 153–175. North-Holland, Amsterdam, 1982.

Per Martin-Löf. *Intuitionistic Type Theory*. Bibliopolis, Naples, 1984.

Per Martin-Löf. On the meanings of the logical constants and the justifications of the logical laws. In *Atti degli incontri di logica matematica, Vol. 2*, pages 203–281, Siena, 1985. Scuola di Specializzazione in Logica Matematica, Università di Siena.

Per Martin-Löf. Truth of a proposition, evidence of a judgement, validity of a proof. *Synthese*, 73:407–420, 1987.

Per Martin-Löf. Mathematics of infinity. In P. Martin-Löf and G.Mints, editors, *Colog 88, International Conference on Computer Logic, Tallinn, December 1988, Lecture Notes in Computer Science 417*, pages 146–197, Berlin and Heidelberg, 1990. Springer.

Per Martin-Löf. A path from logic to metaphysics. In *Atti del congresso Nuovi problemi della logica e della filosofia della scienza, Viareggio, 8-13 gennaio 1990, Vol. II*, pages 141–149, Bologna, 1991. CLUEB.

Uwe Mönnich. Untersuchungen zu einer Konstruktiven Semantik für ein Fragment des Englischen. Habilitationsschrift, Tuebingen, 1985.

Richard Montague. *Formal Philosophy*. Yale University Press, New Haven, 1974. Collected papers edited by Richmond Thomason.

Kevin Mulligan, Peter Simons, and Barry Smith. Truthmakers. *Philosophy and Phenomenological Research*, 44:287–321, 1984.

Paul Needham. Temporal Perspective. PhD thesis, University of Uppsala, 1975.

Bengt Nordström, Kent Petersson, and Jan Smith. *Programming in Martin-Löf's Type Theory. An Introduction*. Clarendon Press, Oxford, 1990.

Barbara Partee. Some structural analogies between tenses and pronouns in English. *The Journal of Philosophy*, 70:601–609, 1973.

Dag Prawitz. *Natural Deduction*. Almqvist & Wiksell, Stockholm, 1965.

Dag Prawitz. Meaning and proofs: on the conflict between classical and intuitionistic logic. *Theoria*, 43:2–40, 1977.

Arthur Prior. *Time and Modality*. Clarendon Press, Oxford, 1957.

Aarne Ranta. Propositions as games as types. *Synthese*, 76:377–395, 1988.

Aarne Ranta. Anaphora in game theoretical semantics and in intuitionistic type theory. In Leila Haaparanta, Martin Kusch, and Ilkka Niiniluoto, editors, *Language, Knowledge, and Intentionality: Perspectives on the Philosophy of Jaakko Hintikka*, pages 265–274, Helsinki, 1990a. Acta Philosophica Fennica.

Aarne Ranta. Propositional attitude operators in intuitionistic categorial grammar. To appear in the proceedings of a meeting on Categorial grammar, linear logic, and related topics held in Munich in July 1990. Ranta 1990b.

Aarne Ranta. Intuitionistic categorial grammar. *Linguistics and Philosophy*, 14:203–239, 1991a.

Aarne Ranta. Understanding and interpretation of text. To appear in C. Schwarze (ed.), Interface Aspects of Syntax, Semantics, and the Lexicon, John Benjamin's, Amsterdam and Philadelphia. Ranta 1991b.

Aarne Ranta. Constructing possible worlds. *Theoria*, 57:77–100, 1991. Ranta 1991c.

Hans Reichenbach. *Elements of Symbolic Logic*. The Macmillan Company, New York, 1948.

Nicholas Rescher. Plurality quantification (abstract). *The Journal of Symbolic Logic*, 27:373–374, 1962.

Henk van Riemsdijk and Edwin Williams. *Introduction to the Theory of Grammar*. The MIT Press, Cambridge, Ma., 1986.

Bertrand Russell and A.N. Whitehead. *Principia Mathematica*. Cambridge University Press, Cambridge, 1913.

Ferdinand de Saussure. *Cours de linguistique générale*. Payot, Paris, 1983. Édition critique préparée par Tullio de Mauro.

Peter Schroeder-Heister. A natural extension of natural deduction. *The Journal of Symbolic Logic*, 49:1284–1300, 1984.

Scott Soames. Presupposition. In D. Gabbay and F. Guenthner, editors, *Handbook of Philosophical Logic, Vol. IV*, pages 553–616. D. Reidel, Dordrecht, 1989.

Robert Stalnaker. Possible worlds and situations. *The Journal of Philosophical Logic*, 15:109–123, 1986.

Mark Steedman. Combinators and grammars. In R. Oehrle, E. Bach, and D. Wheeler, editors, *Categorial Grammars and Natural Language Structures*, pages 417–442. D. Reidel, Dordrecht, 1988.

Erik Stenius. Mood and language-game. *Synthese*, 17:254–274, 1967.

Erik Stenius. Syntax of symbolic logic and transformational grammar. *Synthese*, 26:57–80, 1973.

Peter Strawson. *Introduction to Logical Theory*. Methuen & Co., London, 1952.

Göran Sundholm. Proof theory and meaning. In D. Gabbay and F. Guenthner, editors, *Handbook of Philosophical Logic, Vol. III*, pages 471–506. D. Reidel, Dordrecht, 1986.

Göran Sundholm. Constructive generalized quantifiers. *Synthese*, 79:1–12, 1989.

Alfred Tarski. Der Wahrheitsbegriff in den formalisierten Sprachen. *Studia Philosophica*, 1:261–405, 1935.

Simon Thompson. *Type Theory and Functional Programming*. Addison-Wesley, Reading (Ma.), 1991.

Friedrich Waismann. Logische Analyse des Wahrscheinlichkeitsbegriffs. *Erkenntnis*, 1:228–248, 1931.

John R. Wallace. Sortal predicates and quantification. *The Journal of Philosophy*, 62:8–13, 1965.

Åke Wikström. *Functional Programming Using Standard ML*. Prentice-Hall, London, 1987.

Ludwig Wittgenstein. *Philosophical Investigations*. Basil Blackwell, Oxford, 1953.

INDEX OF NOTATION

INDEX